DOCKS
AND
DESTINATIONS
WITH GPS WAYPOINTS

D1562488

Peter Vassilopoulos

· MARINAS ·
· FUEL DOCKS ·
· SUPPLY STORES ·
· GOLF COURSES ·

Books by the same author
Anchorages and Marine Parks
North of Desolation Sound
Gulf Islands Cruising Guide
Cruising to Desolation Sound
Mariner Artist–John M. Horton
Antiques Afloat
from the Golden Age of Boating in British Columbia

www.marineguides.com

Pacific Marine Publishing • Vancouver Canada

Photographs, text, drawings and diagrams copyright 1994/1998/2000/2003/2005/2007/2010 Peter Vassilopoulos.
Pacific Marine Publishing. 4805 A Aveue Delta BC V4M 1R3 Canada.
In the USA: PO Box 984, Point Roberts, WA. 98281-0984
Prepress graphics and typesetting by Pacific Marine Publishing.
Printed in Canada.
Photographs by author unless otherwise indicated.

The information in this book is accurate and correct as far as can be determined. All cautions, GPS coordinates and docking information are provided without guarantee and it is up to the boat operator to ensure the proper use of navigational charts and other aids to navigation. Depths are approximate where recorded and should be verified by use of NOAA and CHS charts, depth sounders, BC Sailing Directions, Small Craft Guide and other sources. Maps and diagrams are approximate and not to scale and should not be used for navigation purposes. Hydrographic Charts should be used at all times when navigating waterways, bays, coves, harbours and marinas. GPS readings are not guaranteed to be precise. They are taken at or near facilities or at entrances to inlets, bays, coves or harbours–in the case of the location of multiple marinas. While every care has been taken to ensure accuracy of information this cannot be guaranteed due to the possibility of error in transposing. The publisher and author is not liable for marine operations leading to accident, damage or injury in any way connected with reference to this guide. It is intended purely as a reference to available facilities at marinas on the coast.

© Peter Vassilopoulos 2010 by Pacific Marine Publishing. All rights reserved. No part of this book may be reproduced or transmitted in any form by any means without the permission of the publisher, except by a reviewer, who may quote brief passages or show any one diagram in a review unless otherwise arranged with the publisher.

First Printing–August 1994. Second Printing–March 1995. Third Printing–March 1996 (Revised–2nd edition).
Fourth Printing–October 1998 (Revised–3rd edition). Fifth Printing–Dec 2000 (Revised–4th edition).
Sixth Printing–January 2003 (Revised–5th edition, with GPS Waypoints).
Seventh Printing–January 2005 (Revised–6th edition). Eighth Printing–January 2007 (Revised–7th edition).
Ninth Printing–2010 (Revised–8th edition–29,000 copies to date).

Library and Archives Canada Cataloguing in Publication

Vassilopoulos, Peter, 1940-
      Docks and destinations / Peter Vassilopoulos. -- 8th edition.

Includes bibliographical references and index.
ISBN 978-0-919317-43-7

1. Marinas--British Columbia--Pacific Coast--Guidebooks.
2. Marinas--Washington (State)--San Juan Islands--Guidebooks.
3. Marinas--Washington (State)--Puget Sound--Guidebooks.
4. Pacific Coast (B.C.)--Guidebooks. 5. San Juan Islands (Wash.)--
Guidebooks. 6. Puget Sound (Wash.)--Guidebooks. I. Title.

FC3845.P2A3 2010   387.1'5097111   C2010-902086-3

Eighth edition. Ninth printing, with new,
expanded, revised and updated information

Copies available from marine stores, marinas and book stores. Distribution enquiries to Pacific Marine Publishing Ph: 604-943-4618. email: *boating@dccnet.com*

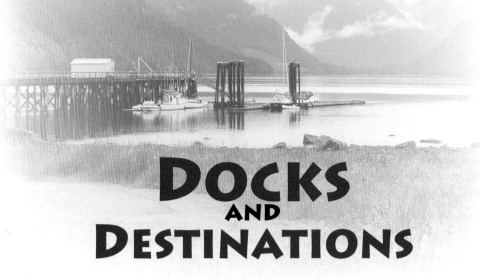

DOCKS AND DESTINATIONS

Peter Vassilopoulos

A coastal guide to marinas, fuel and moorage
facilities in the Pacific Northwest

Featuring Puget Sound and Hood Canal,
the San Juan Islands, the Gulf Islands, Desolation Sound,
Haida Gwaii, North of
Cape Caution to Ketchikan, Alaska,
plus the west coast of Vancouver Island

WITH GPS WAYPOINTS

Includes the San Juan Islands, the Strait of Georgia,
the Lower Mainland, Howe Sound, the Sunshine Coast,
Desolation Sound, Johnstone Strait, the Broughton Islands, Alert Bay
area, Rivers Inlet to Prince Rupert, Haida Gwaii,
Vancouver Island–Quatsino Sound to Sooke, Juan de Fuca Strait,
Admiralty Inlet, Hood Canal,
Puget Sound.

Cover: Nanaimo Boat Basin, a busy place in summer with lots of appeal and many attractions.

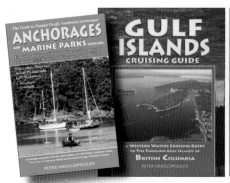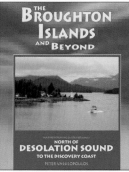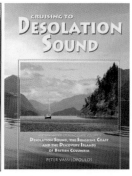

The author's detailed guides to the coast's more popular areas include lots of information about route planning, waterways, marinas and anchorages. They are packed with aerial photographs and diagrams. The Broughtons and Beyond replaces North of Desolation Sound, available 2011.

Preface

This guide covers marinas and docks with and without services. Use it whenever approaching any of the ports in order to know what dock layout and services are available. Mariners have found it particularly useful for planning and telephoning or emailing ahead for reservations. Please refer to **Anchorages and Marine Parks** for comprehensive coverage of the anchorages and marine parks on the BC coast and in the San Juan Islands. For more detailed information on popular areas covered by this guide refer to the author's **Gulf Islands Cruising Guide, The Broughtons and Beyond** (formerly **North of Desolation Sound,** pictured above) and **Cruising to Desolation Sound**.

Boat owners are kindly asked to observe proper etiquette on the water and at the various marinas and other facilities. At some places there are severe water shortages and mariners are requested to use available water with discretion. Garbage cannot be disposed of easily at most island locations and mariners are asked to not leave their garbage at the docks. Expectations by mariners of the marina operators can sometimes be unreasonable. Please consider the difficulties under which people on the coast have to function. Their season is extremely short—about two and a half months to possibly three months of the summer holidays. They have to make a living and cover their annual costs in those short months. They have to bring in supplies, groceries and building materials from varying and often long distances.

There are many competent people working at marinas but staff who assist in summer are not always experienced and it is difficult for them to know the specific preferences of individual arriving boat operators. The facilities found along the more remote parts of the coast are usually very small businesses and mariners arriving in need of moorage and supplies are more than welcome, giving the operators an opportunity also to meet people and communicate on a friendly, personal level.

Boating friends and acquaintances have yet again offered advice on what to include and change in this new edition. I thank them for their input and have used some of their suggestions. Note that reference to water availability at marinas has been included mostly in areas where water is likely to be scarce. GPS readings have been taken with great care while visiting the various reference points. Others were referenced by using state of the art GPS equipment. Please use discretion when referencing the coordinates provided. Great care has been taken in publishing them but we cannot accept responsibility for typographic or other errors made in the process of transposing them.

I thank the following for their help: My wife Carla, Robin Battley, Chris Fraser, Robert Hale and those fellow boat owners who have told me or reminded me about places I may otherwise have missed. Thanks also to Pacific Yachting Magazine, Waggoner, Boat Journal, Nor'Westing, Northwest Yachting, 48° North, Latitudes and Attitudes, local newspapers and others which have had kind reviews on the previous editions. Thanks to the many readers of the previous editions who reported back to me with information on changes and variations at coastal facilities.

GPS References

Kevin Monahan of Shipwrite Productions and author of the book,
GPS–Instant Navigation, *has kindly written the following about the use of the GPS coordinates in this guide:*

Latitude and Longitude—It's not quite that simple

Boaters using a modern GPS receiver can probably determine their position more accurately than was possible even for map-makers until just a few years ago. An unassisted GPS can now resolve a position to within 10 to 15 meters, 95% of the time. As a result, your GPS may be more accurate than your chart. As if this wasn't enough, the chart may also be drawn to a different horizontal datum than is used in your GPS, resulting in errors of up to 200 meters in Northern BC.

A datum is simply a reference point from which latitude and longitude are measured.

In 1927, map-makers in North America established the first truly continental datum at Meade's Ranch in Kansas. This datum was known as North American Datum 1927 (NAD27).

By 1983, using satellite telemetry data scientists had learned enough about the shape of the earth, that they were able to accurately model the surface of the earth. This allowed a new horizontal datum to be developed in North America—(NAD1983)—a datum that did not depend on any physical reference point.

When charts were drawn to the new datum, cartographers discovered that the positions of geographic features on older charts could not be reconciled with their positions on new charts—the lines of latitude and longitude on the older charts were in the wrong places. In many areas of the continent, these differences are minimal—just a few meters—but in northern B.C. and Alaska, the difference between NAD27 and NAD83 is over 200 meters.

Now that world-wide satellite positioning is available, GPS uses a truly universal chart datum—World Geodetic Survey 1984 (WGS84). In North America, WGS84 is equivalent to NAD83.

So much for the idea that latitude and longitude are absolute. Any one location can be represented by different lat/long co-ordinates, depending on the datum that is used. So in order to accurately identify a position, you must know not only the latitude and longitude, but the horizontal datum used as well.

The positions of the various docks etc. in this book have been taken directly from a Garmin GPS set to the WGS84 Horizontal Datum.

In general, it is best to match the datum your GPS reads out to the datum of the chart you are using. Thus if you are working with a chart drawn to NAD27, you should set your GPS to the same datum. Every chart should incorporate a Horizontal Datum note describing the datum used in that particular chart and the corrections to be applied to convert to NAD83 (or NAD27 as the case may be).

Boaters using electronic navigation systems with electronic charts will find that all their electronic charts have been compensated to read out in NAD83, and should simply ensure that their GPS is set to NAD83 at all times.

However, if you are using paper charts drawn to NAD27 and have set your GPS to the same datum, the latitudes and longitudes in this book will not match the positions on the chart, nor will they match the readings on your GPS. The only way to resolve this is to convert the latitudes and longitudes using the conversion factors in the Horizontal Datum note. *–Kevin Monahan*

For more information on GPS and Horizontal Datums, visit www.shipwrite.bc.ca

---

In producing this latest edition of **Docks and Destinations** it is my sincerest hope that you will use it to expand your boating horizons in finding new and interesting destinations and convenient and safe overnight moorage. Like its companion guide, **Anchorages and Marine Parks**, it is designed to provide guidance but not to remove the joy of exploring for yourself. It is intended to encourage you to moor at a marina and go exploring ashore where walking the local roads and trails provides a good exercise break. Thanks to my wife Carla for assisting me in contacting marinas by boat, phone, email and fax for verification of the new information gathered for this edition. Thanks also to the marinas themselves for checking, verifying and providing information. A special thanks to David Hoar and Noreen Rudd, Norman Elliot, Robin Battley, Duncan Taylor, Sharon Allman and Iz Goto and others who supplied photographs and details for diagrams. And to Heinz Bold, Peter Schlieck of Canadian Flight Centre, Bruce Jackman of Port McNeill and Grizzly Helicopters, Justin Taylor, Ray Roussy, Peter Barratt of West Coast Helicopters, Amelia Kerr and others who assisted me with aerial vantages. Thanks to John and Sheryl Mass for their generous assistance at Bamfield, and thanks also to Pacific Coastal Airlines for providing access to Haida Gwaii.

BC is abundantly blessed with magnificent landscapes, waterfalls, mountain peaks and deep waterways. The use of photographs and other illustrations helps reveal the charm of the islands and inside passages of the area known as the Pacific Northwest. The best descriptions have been coined in the names of some coastal places such as Pleasant Harbor, God's Pocket, Minstrel Island, Bones Bay, Telegraph Cove, Kingcome, Ocean Falls and many others. *–Peter Vassilopoulos*

Justin Taylor photo

Above: Downtown Vancouver has marinas which cater to visiting yachts. The harbour is protected from severe weather throughout most of summer and the marinas are just a short walk into the city centre. Several restaurants located on the waterfront will cater to you right at your boat. Venture on

through the harbour to the waters of Indian Arm, as remote as any you will find farther up the coast towards Alaska. Or pull into False Creek where marinas and anchorage are

available and where you can easily go ashore and visit the renown tourist attractions at Granville Island (three hour stopping is permitted at the docks pictured above).

MARINAS–GUEST MOORAGE

NOTE: GOLF COURSES are listed on
marina pages by name and phone number.
Take your golfing equipment with you.

Guest Docks and Marinas

From Olympia to Ketchikan

The format of this book takes the reader in a south to north progression from one dock to the next, beginning in the San Juan Islands and terminating at Ketchikan, southeast Alaska. Vancouver Island west coast information is arranged from north to south. It concludes by continuing south from Juan de Fuca Strait to Olympia. The intention is to provide a logical sequence of references to fuel stops and overnight moorage en route to a final destination.

Information accompanying the graphics and photographs is up to date but constant changes are being made at various marinas. From season to season mostly small changes occur at marinas, however this book is revised and updated periodically depending on the frequency and extent to which coastal facilities are altered or improved.

Helpful Information

Many Pacific Northwest marinas are exclusively operated for privately owned pleasure boats. Here boats are stored and maintained throughout the year. As the dawn breaks each year on a new spring and the chill of winter is diminished, owners and yacht club members take to scrubbing and polishing their boats in preparation for a colourful sailpast followed by as many boating weekends and prolonged periods away as possible. Cruising to general destinations such as the the San Juans, the Gulf Islands or Desolation Sound is the trend. Frequently there are no specific plans for overnight moorage other than a vague intention to stop if there is suitable anchorage or moorage at one of several possible overnight shelters. With ever increasing numbers of boats converging on popular destinations, it is becoming essential that reservations for moorage be made in advance.

This guide is intended to help mariners decide where to stop in safe, sheltered moorage overnight and where services, needed by the boat owners or their crews, can be readily acquired. To this end it provides phone numbers, details of marina facilities, fuel stops and other pertinent information.

Heading Out

Yachts bound for the northwest inside passage from southern Pacific coastal routes each summer appreciate the relative comfort once inside Juan de Fuca Strait. They, and Puget Sound and Lake Washington boat owners, however, may still be faced with current and tide rips off Whidbey Island. Some face the challenge of locking through the Hiram M. Chittenden locks, while La Conner mariners contend with strong tidal currents through the Swinomish Canal. Victoria and vicinity mariners require a passage around an often rough and tide-ripped Trial Islands and up through a sometimes testy Haro Strait before they reach the more placid waters off Sidney. Fortunately most Victoria residents can take one look out to sea and determine the ease of passage. Checking with the tide and current tables is always sound logic to ensure a comfortable beginning of a cruise.

Sidney and Saanich Inlet mariners are in much the same position, but they have the advantage of being where they are going without even leaving the dock (that is–practically in the heart of the Gulf Islands). And the same applies to Maple Bay, Ladysmith and Nanaimo. Mariners in these areas have enviably easy access for extended seasonal periods to the anchorages and marinas of the Gulf Islands but often look farther afield for their major trips. Their favoured distant destinations include Desolation Sound and beyond. At Nanaimo, locals and visiting mariners alike, may await the slack at Dodd Narrows before venturing south into the islands, or may stay at the docks while seas off Entrance Island settle after a storm before crossing the Strait to Vancouver, the Sunshine Coast or en route north.

Vessels at marinas on the Sunshine Coast or at places north of Nanaimo are already part way to cruising in Desolation Sound and beyond. Check your marine charts for area WG and call to ensure that no military exercises are in progress before crossing this part of the Strait of Georgia.

Mariners on the Vancouver side of the Strait of Georgia may spend days monitoring weather forecasts prior to a major trip, and certainly will listen to the reports on VHF prior to any other departure. Wind and wave height are of utmost interest, tidal changes and currents can be critical and even openings of fishing to the commercial industry can affect one's plans to set off on a voyage. Vessels leaving Vancouver and Port Moody are subject to the currents under Lions Gate bridge and Second Narrows.

Leaving False Creek is quite straight forward and bumpy conditions off Stanley Park are the quick

Hot Springs Cove on the west coast of Vancouver Island. This is a Parks Board operated dock. Mariners are encouraged to anchor out and go ashore by dinghy. There is a fuel dock at the First Nations village beyond.

indicator that worse stuff lies ahead, usually beginning at Point Atkinson. Boats departing Richmond and running down the North Arm of the Fraser may reach open water before determining that it was not such a good idea to leave the dock.

Most vessels from Vancouver and Richmond areas have Howe Sound as their playground. The facilities in Howe Sound are among the best on the coast and yachtsmen find satisfaction in spending time at places on Bowen Island or at Gibsons. Out of Surrey or Delta the Gulf Islands are closer than Howe Sound, and mariners mooring their boats at Ladner, Crescent Beach or Point Roberts can be in the midst of the Gulf Islands in less than an hour (a little longer in a sail boat or displacement trawler).

Leaving the Fraser River is one of the biggest challenges on the west coast. (Returning is another.) A receding tide near low water, especially against a west or northwesterly moderate breeze (don't even think about a strong wind or worse) can be dangerous in the extreme. Refer to the government publication on Weather, and Thompson's **Oceanology** for interesting information about current, wind and wave patterns at the river mouth. Bear in mind that while the weather report covers Sand Heads windspeeds it does not always provide wave height at the river mouth, a sadly lacking service, especially considering the dangerous nature of the seas at that point. You can always turn back and wait at Steveston for improved conditions, or return to your marina.

Leaving Crescent Beach is straight forward enough except that it is a long run across an open bay before entering the Strait. Point Roberts is well located for quick, visual assessment of conditions in the Strait and close enough to the San Juan and Gulf islands that a crossing of the Strait is quick enough even for slower travelling vessels. But it is very exposed to bad weather conditions for a return trip and mariners should carefully determine what they can expect off Point Roberts before leaving the safety of a comfortable mooring on the other side.

Boats cruising to Canada out of other Washington ports have some extra distance to travel through US waters to reach their Canadian destinations. Many simply stay in the San Juan Islands, which have numerous well run marinas and boating facilities. Vessels passing through en route to Canada have to be mindful of wind and tidal conditions at several passages, but with careful weather monitoring the trip can be most pleasant.

Canadians travelling to the San Juans and Puget Sound should know where they are headed and check the route before leaving. Watch for obvious current-swept waterways and consult the tide and current tables. When cruising any unknown waters check what other boats are doing. If there are no other boats about be particularly cautious and double check the current predictions and weather reports.

Vessels travelling across the border, unless they have a US cruising pass and/or subscribe to *Canpass* or *Nexus* must stop at a customs dock for clearance and should carry their clearance reporting number for checking back into their home country. It is mandatory for vessels crossing the border either way to clear customs. Vessels may be stopped by the RCMP in Canadian waters and fined for not having a customs clearance number, even if just passing through with 'Right of Passage.'

Marina Etiquette

Some homes at marinas are more than just your average bungalow. There is bound to be a helipad on the yacht as well.

Marinas are a home away from home. When you tie up to a dock at a private marina you are in effect stopping in to visit other boat owners and the owners and operators of the marina. What you do and how you operate your vessel says a lot about you and a lot about your experience as a mariner. Your reception from marina managers and fellow boat owners will be determined by the impression you create from the moment you nudge your boat up to the dock.

Some boat owners, and often this applies to novices, don't really care how they are perceived by others. Those same people also tend to not learn from their errors. For mariners who wish to fit in, be they newcomers or old hands, here are some basic tips, but first, take the mandatory boating course and obtain your operator's proficiency certificate.

During the peak months of summer telephone or email ahead for reservations. Remember changes are being made constantly and you can expect to find new additions at some docks, name and phone number changes, different regulations, revised services and other variances from the information contained in this guide. Please note the changes for your own convenience. Check websites.

Before you arrive at a marina ensure you are not passing other installations at speed. Slow down well before you reach the dock. Sitting at a dock in West Sound in the San Juans once I saw a large boat come by at full speed leaving a wash in excess of two feet that caused some damage at the dock. He was heading for a club at the head of the bay and had totally ignored the existence of the marina tucked in behind the island to his starboard. That same week I saw a similar sized vessel do the same thing entering Bedwell Bay.

Before you enter the marina establish exactly where your assigned slip is. In many marinas you can call on VHF for slip assignment. The dock photographs and diagrams in this book should help you easily locate the slip or general area of the slip to which you have been assigned. As you approach your slip note effects of current and wind and plan your docking manoeuvres accordingly. It's always easiest to angle in towards the dock against the flow of water or direction of the wind. If you are backing your boat into a tight slip it is even more essential that you are aware of these conditions. Have your crew at the ready and prepared for landing.

Play it the way the pros do. They attach a line to a centre cleat and hold the end coiled in one hand as they step ashore. Snubbing the line to a cleat on the dock when the boat is close to that cleat will keep it there and prevent the bow or stern from breaking away and swinging out, as often occurs when only a line at the bow or the stern is used. Have fenders down at a height compatible with the height of the docks and positioned one ahead of the centre cleat and one near the stern. Once the boat is stopped the skipper can casually step ashore, secure the bow and stern lines and adjust fenders at leisure.

Crew: Other people may offer assistance. Usually they expect to be handed a line and all too often when they take it they totally destroy your docking plan. This is usually done by yarding on the bow line, bringing the bow in too close to the dock and disabling you from handling the stern. You don't have to pass them a line. Do so if absolutely necessary or when the skipper has the boat docked. No harm saying to a person "Here is the line, please just hold it" or have two docksiders haul in bow and stern simultaneously. Don't try to look as though you are proficient if you cannot pull it off. You are better off to say to anyone watching as you are approaching your slip that you are new at this and would appreciate some experienced help in docking. You'll be surprised how readily people will come

Most boating accidents occur when guests are aboard. Do not be distracted while operating your boat.

Right, top to bottom: Summer is a busy time at Salt Spring Island. Marylou and Courtenay at the old Salty Shop in Ganges have a wide selection of books, cards and souvenirs for visitors. At Bedwell Bay, tending the fuel dock is just part of running a marina. There is always something new and interesting happening at Otter Bay Marina. A well-known family on the coast, the Richters, see the coming and going of a regular flow of mariners at their Blind Channel marina just north of Desolation Sound.

to your aid and how pleasant they will be when you are up front about your docking abilities.

Docking is just the beginning. You will not enamour yourself or your crew to anyone at the dock if you yell, either at them or at your crew. At many marinas there are full-time personnel employed to assist boaters docking. They are not always the most experienced but as long as you follow some of the above advice their assistance will enable you to perform a good landing.

If you are docking parallel to a long open dock, tie up your boat in such a way that you allow maximum room for the next boat coming in. If you have a dinghy in the water tuck it in under the bow of your boat while you are not using it in order that you leave room for the next boat.

Anchoring off and going ashore to visit a marina and its facilities, perhaps to have a meal, a snack or browse for some souvenir is a common practise during summer. Also common is the individual who goes ashore only to drop off a huge bag of garbage. On most islands this is a major problem. If you are a mooring guest you may do well to assess how convenient it is to leave garbage behind, even though some places have disposal bins. If you know you are continuing to a mainland facility soon, save the garbage for that stop. The same applies to water. If you are travelling to an area with limited water resources fill up before going there and use water sparingly. Do not use scarce, island water to wash your boat.

Some boat owners have been known to tie up at a marina for long periods during the day, fill up with water, perhaps use the facilities such as shower and laundry and then take off and anchor across the bay for the night. There are times when such use of moorage has denied a prospective paying overnight moorage customer space to tie up. Marinas have a very limited season in which to prosper and mariners who cause lost overnight moorage will not be appreciated.

Most marina operators will be happy to have you stop for a short period if you don't plan to spend the night. Some have a charge per hour. Others, like most public docks, allow two hours free and then an overnight charge is levied. If you make use of marinas and their services as a paying guest you will help ensure their survival for the future.

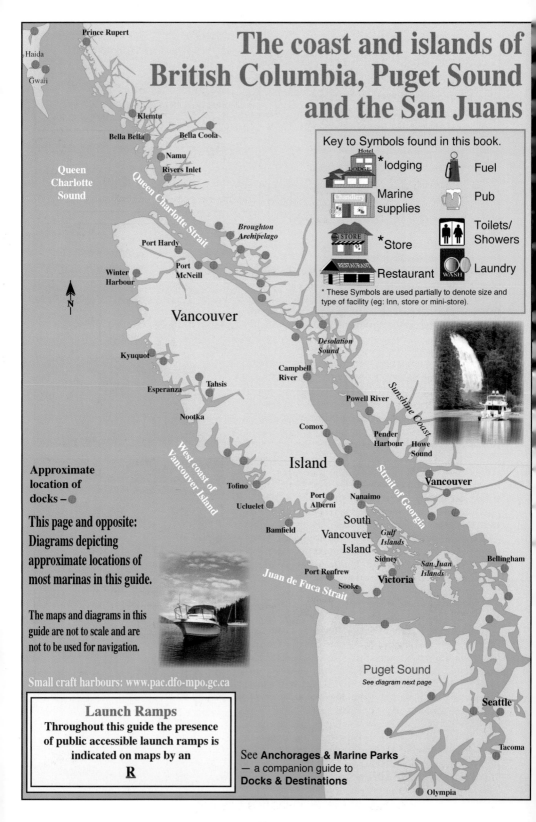

The coast and islands of British Columbia, Puget Sound and the San Juans

Prince Rupert

Haida

Gwaii

Klemtu

Bella Bella

Bella Coola

Namu

Rivers Inlet

Queen Charlotte Sound

Queen Charlotte Strait

Broughton Archipelago

Port Hardy

Port McNeill

Winter Harbour

N

Vancouver

Kyuquot

Esperanza

Tahsis

Nootka

Desolation Sound

Campbell River

Powell River

Comox

Pender Harbour

Howe Sound

Sunshine Coast

Island

West coast of Vancouver Island

Tofino

Ucluelet

Port Alberni

Nanaimo

Bamfield

South Vancouver Island

Gulf Islands

Sidney

Strait of Georgia

Vancouver

San Juan Islands

Bellingham

Approximate location of docks –

This page and opposite: Diagrams depicting approximate locations of most marinas in this guide.

The maps and diagrams in this guide are not to scale and are not to be used for navigation.

Port Renfrew

Sooke

Victoria

Juan de Fuca Strait

Puget Sound
See diagram next page

Seattle

Tacoma

Small craft harbours: www.pac.dfo-mpo.gc.ca

Launch Ramps
Throughout this guide the presence of public accessible launch ramps is indicated on maps by an

R

See **Anchorages & Marine Parks** — a companion guide to **Docks & Destinations**

Olympia

Key to Symbols found in this book.

Hotel

LODGE

*lodging

Chandlery

Marine supplies

STORE

*Store

RESTAURANT

Restaurant

Fuel

Pub

Toilets/ Showers

WASH

Laundry

* These Symbols are used partially to denote size and type of facility (eg: Inn, store or mini-store).

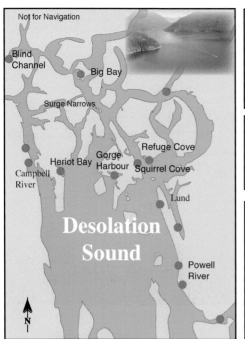

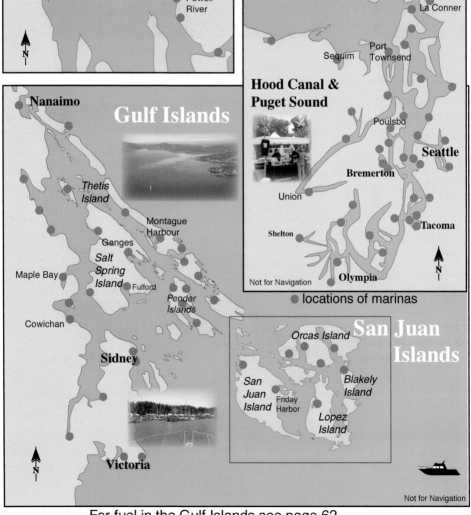

Not for Navigation

Blind Channel
Big Bay
Surge Narrows
Refuge Cove
Gorge Harbour
Heriot Bay
Squirrel Cove
Campbell River
Lund

Desolation Sound

Powell River

N

For more indepth information on the Gulf Islands, the Sunshine Coast, Desolation Sound and the Broughtons see the author's guides:

Gulf Islands Cruising Guide, Cruising to Desolation Sound and *The Broughtons and Beyond (North of Desolation Sound).*

Popular Destinations

The areas shown on these pages depict where most cruising activity takes place during the summer boating season.

Bellingham
Anacortes
La Conner
Port Townsend
Sequim

Hood Canal & Puget Sound

Poulsbo
Seattle
Bremerton
Union
Tacoma
Shelton
N
Not for Navigation
Olympia

● locations of marinas

Nanaimo
Gulf Islands
Thetis Island
Montague Harbour
Ganges
Salt Spring Island
Maple Bay
Fulford
Pender Islands
Cowichan
Sidney

San Juan Islands
Orcas Island
San Juan Island
Friday Harbor
Blakely Island
Lopez Island

N
Victoria

Not for Navigation

For fuel in the Gulf Islands see page 62.

Above: The marina at Roche Harbor. Left: Whale sighting are common nearby– the farther north the bigger the whales, it seems. This was sighted off the southern tip of Alaska. Photo taken by Carla Vassilo- poulos aboard a small inflatable boat. Below: The classic Orcas Hotel overlooks the local San Juan Islands ferry terminal.

San Juan Islands

San Juan Islands

Section 1

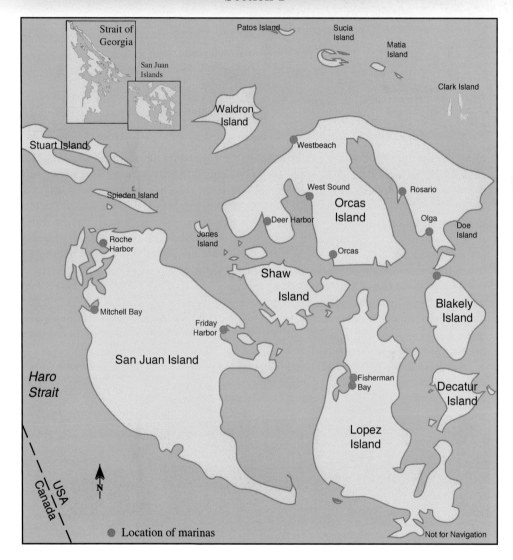

Journeying into the San Juans mariners have the pick of some outstanding marinas, fine restaurants, well-stocked marine, grocery and hardware stores as well as art and gifts centres. There are fast food places, ice cream vendors, pubs, hotels, good accommodations and rustic bed and breakfast places. There are walking and hiking trails and roads as well as car, bicycle and motor scooter rentals. Some stops include dining at a number of fine restaurants or delicatessens for a good bowl of soup, a sandwich, salad or dessert. At Friday Harbour there is such a wide choice of

restaurants and stores it would take an entire vacation to enjoy the place to its fullest. The annual Jazz Festival on the last weekend in July is a busy time so get in early, or keep away if you want to avoid crowds. A more tranquil place may be Fisherman Bay with its good anchorage and marinas, nearby Lopez Village and pleasant dining facilities. Roche Harbor is a busy customs port and attracts some of the larger cruising yachts to its busy marina. It's a place to visit if you like to look longingly at some of those mega vessels that frequent and even monopolize it. The Hotel de Haro usually has fine dining and it's entertaining to watch the evening color ceremony at sundown. Fascinating history of the islands include the early explorations of the Spanish, the presence of the English and the famous Pig War which nearly led to an international confrontation between the British and the Americans. One of the more charming remnants of recent history of the islands is Rosario Resort on Orcas Island. A stop at this facility will provide sheltered moorage as well as a chance to acquaint yourself with its splendid history.

A short or long stay in the San Juans can provide a complete vacation, and many Canadians make the trip once in a while just as their American counterparts are steaming through the San Juans en route to the Canadian Gulf Islands and points beyond.

Left: Rosario Resort on Orcas Island.
Above and opposite right: Friday Harbor.
Opposite page:
The dock at Sucia Island. It is busy in summertime but during fair weather there is also lots of good anchorage in the bay.

The San Juans include a number of smaller islands. The moorage in these islands is associated with marine parks and not included in this book. But there are some facilities such as the two docks at Sucia Island. They are located in Fossil Bay. The one shown below is the dock of choice due to its greater protection from prevailing winds. The other is set deeper into the bay, to the south west. They fill up fast, as do all popular destinations in summer. Please refer to the author's companion book Anchorages and Marine Parks.

For facilities at marine parks see the companion guide to this one:
Anchorages and Marine Parks

Customs
summer
office

Roche Harbor

48° 36.550' N
123° 09.228' W

San Juan Islands

Roche Harbor Resort & Marina

Kevin Carlton
248 Reuben Memorial Dr
PO Box 4001, Roche Harbor WA 98250
Ph: 360-378-2155 Fax: 360-378-9800
Toll Free: 1-800-451-8910
marina@rocheharbor.com
www.rocheharbor.com
Chart 18421, 18433   VHF 78A
Marina services:
Moorage. 377 permanent and transient
slips to about 180 feet. **Pumpout** facilities.
Power at docks: 30, 50, 100 amps.
Fuel: Gas, diesel. Propane. Oil.
Cafe, bar and grill, restaurant.
**Customer services: Showers, laundry,
washrooms.** Public phones ashore. Phone
hook up. Walking: Road access, cycling.
Adjacent and nearby: Store–groceries,
a wide range of provisions. Hotel, fine
dining, accommodations. Gifts. Clothing,
apparel, gifts, ice, fishing tackle, licences,
marine supplies. Moped rentals. Hiking
trails. Boat rentals, kayaks. Good fishing

nearby. Pool and tennis courts. Nature
sculpture park. Jazz festival late July–call
for information. Fourth of July celebra-
tions and fireworks. Color ceremony each
sunset. Coffee wagon.
All facilities open March through October.
Moorage and basic facilities open year
round–partial during winter. Launch ramp
nearby. Taxi or bus service to island centres and ferry to Anacortes. Airfield.
Major Customs Port of Entry.

San Juan Golf and Country Club 360-378-2254

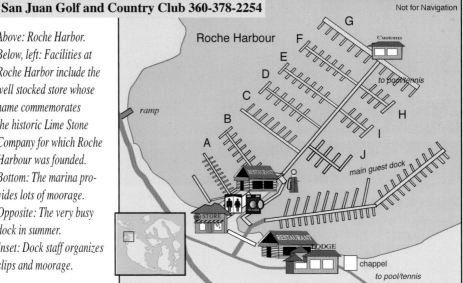

Not for Navigation

Roche Harbour

G
F
E
Customs
D
C
to pool/tennis
B
H
A
I
ramp
J
RESTAURANT
main guest dock
STORE
WASH
RESTAURANT
LODGE
chappel
to pool/tennis

Above: Roche Harbor.
Below, left: Facilities at
Roche Harbor include the
well stocked store whose
name commemorates
the historic Lime Stone
Company for which Roche
Harbour was founded.
Bottom: The marina pro-
vides lots of moorage.
Opposite: The very busy
dock in summer.
Inset: Dock staff organizes
slips and moorage.

Hotel de Haro is the historic landmark at this famous harbor. It is a magnificent building exemplifying the type of construction and opulence of its day. There is a lot to see and do at Roche Harbor. Attend the sundown striking of the colors ceremony.

The resort is a museum in its own right, its buildings dating back to 1886. It was founded in conjunction with the adjacent lime kiln and barrel manufacturing company.

A beautifully landscaped harbor village is being developed adjacent to the marina.

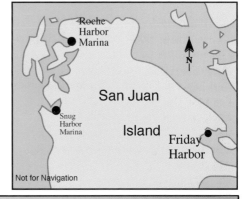

Roche Harbor Marina

Snug Harbor Marina

San Juan

Island

Friday Harbor

N

Not for Navigation

Friday Harbor

San Juan Islands

Port of Friday Harbor

Tami Hayes (Harbormaster)
204 Front St
PO Box 889
Friday Harbour WA 98250-0889
Ph: 360-378-2688 Fax: 360-378-6114
tamih@portfridayharbor.org
www.portfridayharbor.org
Charts 18434, 18421, Waterproof #43
VHF 66A
Marina services:
Moorage. Guest and permanent moorage with over 110 slips.
Power at docks: 30, 50, 100 amp.
Launch ramp. Internet access.
Fuel dock adjacent: Gas, diesel, propane.
Customer services:
Pumpout boat. Garbage disposal. Recycling.
Laundry, showers, ice, bait.
Pharmacies and other necessities.
Scuba diving arrangements and charters–ask at nearby dive store or marina for details.

Walking: Road access walking, cycling, car and scooter rentals.
Entertainment:
Live music Friday night & Sunday afternoons in July & August. County fair in August.
Nearby facilities:
Nearby churches: multi-denominational. Public phones ashore. Ferry to Anacortes. Marine stores–charts, marine hardware, supplies, books, fishing licences, tackle, etc. Post office, liquor, restaurants, banks, accommodations, pubs and grocery and specialty stores. The Doctor's Office–coffee shop, Golf, cinema, airport.
Note:
When arriving at Friday Harbor from Canadian waters first check in at the customs dock on the breakwater.
Call by phone on dock or check in at office on shore. Then proceed to Dock A for slip assignment or call on VHF 66A.

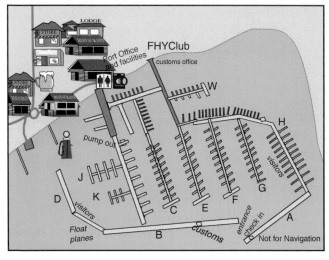

Friday Harbor — major US Customs Port of Entry.
Toll Free: 1-800-562-5943 For PIN number holders only.

Friday Harbor

This large marina is one of the busiest in the Pacific Northwest. It is a major customs stop entering United States waters for Canadian boat operators and one of the major centres for returning American mariners. Located on the east side of San Juan Island it competes with Roche Harbor as a customs stop but the two are vastly different. Friday Harbor has a large town comprising everything from city hall to cinema, supermarkets to specialty shops, hardware store, marine chandleries and a wide variety of restaurants, pubs and bistros. As a major ferry landing, Friday Harbor sees the coming and going of a vast number of people: islanders, cyclists coming to visit, campers, boaters and fly-in sightseers. During summer crowds of boaters flock to the town for the major

event of the year: the county fair in August. A Pig War barbecue is held in June.

For the boat owner there is fuel, moorage, water, showers, laundry, 30 amp electrical service and all the amenities one could imagine necessary for a major stopover. There are two anchorages in the immediate proximity of the huge marina, one adjacent to the north west marina entrance and the other south of the Washington state ferry landing.

Photo Jim Desermeaux Snug Harbor Marina

48° 34.298' N
123° 10.006' W

Snug Harbor

Snug Harbor Marina Resort

Jim Desermeaux
1997 Mitchell Bay Rd
San Juan Island WA 98250-8507
Ph: 360-378-4762 Fax: 360-378-8859
Chart: Waterproof #43. 18421, 18433
sneakaway@snugresort.com
www.snugresort.com

Marina services:
Moorage. Guest moorage 80'.
Reservations suggested.
Power: 30 amp.
Customer services: Garbage bins.
Shower, washrooms. Wifi.
General store, groceries, provisions, charts, books, clothing, gifts, hardware, marine, fishing equipment. Gazebo–seasonal grill.
Public phones ashore.
Road access walking. Accommodations.
Ten self-contained, fully equipped cabins. campground. Launch ramp, whale watching charters, kayak tours. Nearby shuttle service in summer.
Note: Rocks in entrance. Channel to left. Depth 3' at zero tides.
Use large scale chart or Waterproof #43 for navigating inside Henry Island.
Nearest customs at Roche Harbor.
Gas, repairs, marine supplies can be made available.

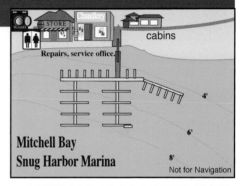

Mitchell Bay
Snug Harbor Marina
Not for Navigation

Top: Snug Harbor Marina in Mitchell Bay is protected from the open waters of Haro Strait by a shallow entrance and drying reef.

Above: The channel into Snug Harbor drops to three feet at zero tides. The bay lies south of Roche Harbor.

Orcas Island

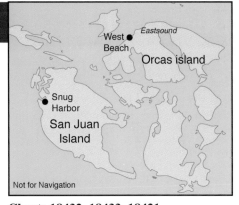

West • Eastsound
Beach
Orcas island
• Snug Harbor
San Juan Island
Not for Navigation

West Beach Resort

Jamey Hance
190 Waterfront Way
Eastsound WA 98245

| 48° 41.268' N |
| 122° 57.783' W |

Ph: 360-376-2240 Fax: 360-376-4746
Toll free: 1-877-937-8224
vacation@westbeachresort.com
www.westbeachresort.com

Marina services:

Moorage. Transient boats to 30'. Larger boats on buoys. About 700' dock space. 10 mooring buoys–seasonal. **Fuel:** Gas. Propane, ice.
Customer services: Internet access. Fish cleaning facility. **Showers, laundry, washrooms.** Resort. Store, coffee shop. Espresso, charts, books, gifts, fishing tackle, bait. Kayak tours. Walking–road access. Playground. Good scuba diving, whale watching in the nearby waters.
Adjacent Facilities: Accommodations. 21 self-contained, fully equipped bungalows. RV/camping. Scuba airfills. Five tent cabins. Launch ramp–guests only (fee includes parking for trailers). Shopping at Eastsound.

Charts 18432, 18433, 18421

Deer Harbor

Deer Harbor Marina

Marc Broman
5164 Deer Harbor Rd
PO Box 344, Deer Harbor WA 98243
Ph: 360-376-3037 Fax: 360-376-6091
info@bellportgroup.com
www.deerharbormarina.com
Chart 18434   VHF 78A
Marina services:
Moorage. Transient and permanent.
110 slips. **Power** at docks: 30 amp.
Pumpout service.
Fuel: Gas, diesel. Garbage disposal.
Customer services: Store–groceries, deli
and provisions. Barbecue area. Accommodations. **Showers, laundry, washrooms**. Ice.
Public phones ashore. ATM. Internet access.
Road access walking, cycling.
Entertainment:
Heated swimming pool and spa. Small boat
rentals, whale watching tours, kayaking,
sunset cruises and fishing charters.
Adjacent facilities: Store–gifts, postcards,
clothing. Haulout nearby.

Deer Harbor Restaurant–elegant dining.
Shuttle to Eastsound, golf course, ferries.
Taxi service to island centres and ferry to
Anacortes. Seaplane service to Seatac.
There is a small beach alongside the
marina.
Note:
• Passage through Pole Pass requires careful
navigation in sometimes strong tidal currents.
Be cautious of the rocky shoreline.
• Clear customs for USA destinations at
Roche Harbor or Friday Harbor.

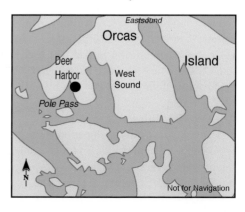

private marina

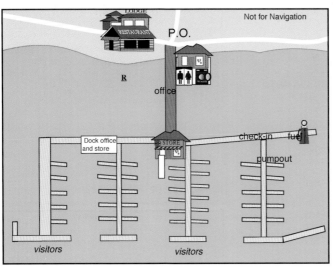

LODGE

RESTAURANT

P.O.

Not for Navigation

R

office

Dock office and store

check-in   fuel

pumpout

visitors   visitors

Above: This is a busy marina in summer. It is designed and operated for visitors and has amenities for boaters on the move. Opposite page: Overnight moorage check-in and fuel dock at Deer Harbor.

Not for Navigation

Deer Harbor

This cosy corner of Orcas Island is a pleasant stopover at docks that face a semi-protected open bay. Most wind conditions do not bother boats at the marina but a southerly or south westerly wind may cause a bit of movement, especially off season. In season many boats visit the docks to stay overnight and enjoy excellent cuisine at nearby restaurants. The marina offers fuel, water, showers, ice, snacks and groceries. A resort located just across the road offers accommodations and spa amentities.

48° 37.765' N 123° 57.631' W

West Sound

West Sound Marina

Betsy Wareham
525 Deer Harbor Rd,
PO Box 119
Orcas Island WA 98280-0119
Ph: 360-376-2314 Fax: 360-376-4634
Chart 18421, 18434
VHF 16

Hazard: Island reef off Picnic Island near
the guest dock. See photo above.

Marina services:
Moorage. Some 300' of guest moorage.
Power at docks: 30 amp. Pumpout. Garbage
disposal. **Showers, washrooms.**
Fuel: Gas, diesel, oils, propane.
Customer services:
Major repair yard. Marine ways. 30 ton
hoist. Complete marine chandlery. Fishing
supplies. Ice. Public phone. Road access
walking, cycling.
Nearby: West Sound Cafe-dinners only.
Bed and Breakfast establishments. Summer
taxi service to island centers and ferry
to Anacortes. Orcas Island Yacht Club.
Small public dock at the head of the bay.

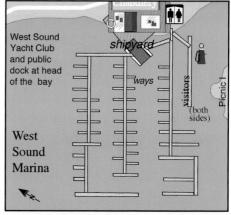

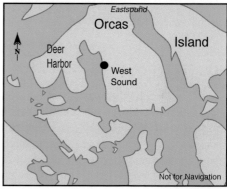

West Sound

This protected moorage is largely for long term resident boats. However, it has an excellent marine service facility with 30 ton travel lift and comprehensive repair services. It has a well stocked marine store and the buildings ashore include a large, modern, heated bay where refinishing and mechanical work can be done in any weather conditions. The

facility caters to all of the San Juan Islands with a 24 hour emergency service. Transient moorage accommodates a number of boats on a 250 foot finger that is an extension of the fuel dock. Gas and diesel are available and are generally priced competitively with fuel at places such as Friday Harbor. It has a pump- out station. The facility is owned and operated by Betsy Wareham. The chandlery offers brand name outboard products, fishing gear, propane, ice and a wide variety of marine supplies. On one visit, a short walk up the road took us to a deli which served light meals at lunchtime.

An island shuttle service every two hours is available for transportation to other parts of Orcas Island such as Orcas ferry landing or the town of Eastsound.

Note: Clear Customs for USA destinations at Roche Harbor or Friday Harbor.

Above: Island riding. Carla rides past madrona trees lining the road near the entrance to West Sound Marina on Orcas Island. Below: Note the docks at the head of the bay. One is the yacht club and the other a public dock.

San Juan Islands

Not for Navigation

48° 35.782' 122° 56.610' W

Orcas Landing
8368 Orcas Rd
PO Box 96, Orcas WA 98280-0200
Ph: 360-376-4389
Chart 18430, 18434, 18421
Time limit: 30 minutes.   **VHF 66A**

There are stores and facilities ashore. Road access walking and sightseeing by bicycle. Stores include liquor, groceries, gifts, clothing, art, souvenirs and refreshments. Orcas Hotel is located nearby. There is a shuttle service to island centers. The ferry to Anacortes is immediately alongside the landing. Be mindful of the wash created by ferries and passing vessels when tying up. No fuel, water or power.

Orcas Island landing
A quaint village at the ferry landing serves the community on Orcas Island. It has an historic hotel (photo page 14) as a focal point. The Orcas Island Hotel has

Above: The small craft dock at Orcas Landing.
Centre: Car show at Eastsound.

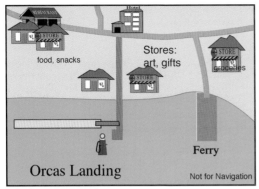

Orcas Landing

Not for Navigation

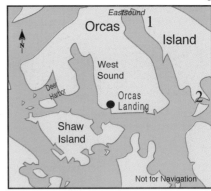

Not for Navigation

rooms and pub and restaurant, the latter of which is reputed to serve excellent meals. Through the week food is served at the pub or at the pub's outdoor terrace area. The dock at Orcas is for transient mariners only. It is long and accessible both sides although the shoreward side has a narrow entrance and if a boat is tied up at the end, entry for anything but a small boat would be tight. There is a 30-minute limit to stays at the dock. On shore there is are gift and craft stores and a grocery store which has a wide selection of wares.

The settlement is popular among transient mariners and land based visitors alike. Summer sees thousands of cyclists, campers and motorists arriving on the island in a constant stream off the ferries. At Orcas it is a common sight for crowds of vacationers to be lining up for their trip home mingling with those just arriving as they flood into the hotel, souvenir stores, grocery store, fast food restaurant, ice cream store or other facilities.

There is a small marina and store across Harney Channel on Shaw Island. It is located alongside the ferry terminal.

Above diagram:

1 Eastsound Float
San Juan Public Works
Moorage: 1 float 12'x35'
Maximum stay: 6 hours

2 Obstruction Pass Float
San Juan Public Works
Moorage: 1 float 12'x35'
Maximum stay: 6 hours

Below: At Orcas Landing, store and the grocery store building beyond.
Opposite: The ferry at Orcas Island. The dock for small craft can be seen to port of the vessel.

East Sound

San Juan Islands

Rosario Resort and Marina

1400 Rosario Rd (Orcas Island)
Eastsound WA 98245-8570
Ph: 360-376-2222
Fax: 360-376-2289
Chart 18421, 18430, 18434
harbormaster@rosarioresort.com
www.rosarioresort.com

Marina services: Fuel: Gas and diesel.
Moorage. Summer April 1 to September 30. In winter the marina remains open and managed by part time staff.
Power at docks: 30 amps.
Customer services: Laundry, showers, ice. The marina is part of a large resort complex. Hotel, pub, spa, pool (indoor and outdoor), retaurants–fine dining or casual. Gift shop. Accommodations and all hotel services. Nearby church. Public phones ashore. Garbage bins. Recycling. Grocery store. Road and trail access walking. Car rentals.
Entertainment: Regular live music, organ recitals in the historic mansion. Slides and Rosario history narration–year round, call for times. Golf nearby. Kayak tours. Air

VHF 78A

tours. Whale watching. Fishing charters.
Hazard: Water depth–shoals towards the end of the south channel in the marina.
Note: Reservations recommended for marina or resort. **Mooring buoys** and anchoring landing fee includes passes to spa and pools.
Nearby: Visitors by boat to **Eastsound** may tie up at the small dock near the town.

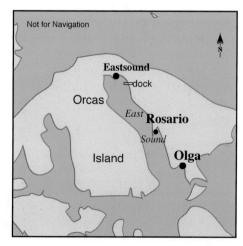

Rosario Resort

There is sheltered moorage at the docks behind the breakwater. The nearby mooring buoys are not necessarily sheltered from the wind and waves that blow up from the southeast in East Sound some afternoons. The hotel is a feature of the San Juan Islands with a colourful history and a delightful ambience. Its facilities include a swimming pool and hot tubs.

Robert Moran, who built Rosario Resort after retiring in 1904, was a former shipbuilder in Seattle. He used shipbuilding methods and materials in the construction of the mansion. The building's walls are made of 12 inch concrete and the roof is sheathed in copper. Windows are 7/8 inch plate glass and many sections of the interior are panelled in mahogany.

One of the resort's major features is the Aeolian pipe organ, said to be the largest installed in a private residence in the United States. The mansion was listed in the National Register of Historic Places in 1979. The estate was sold in 1938 and the new owners created the resort in 1960.

Rosario is the closest sheltered marina for accessing Eastsound, a bustling village that attracts many visitors annually, mostly by ferry via Orcas. There are restaurants, stores, banks, post office, medical clinic, movie theater, pharmacy, churches, galleries and many other facilities. Eastsound airport provides tours for visitors wanting a lofty look at the islands.

The town of **Olga** has a quaint village store and community docks (removed in winter). Stop and dine at the local cafe and art gallery restaurant. A sign on the dock reads: "Dock maintained with community labor and moorage fees collected after 6 pm." Six hours limit.

Olga is exposed to southeast or southwest winds. and not recommended for overnight unless you are certain of favourable weather. It has water and a washroom.

Opposite: Rosario docks are protected behind a breakwater with a fuel dock at the entrance. The mansion overlooks the sweep of East Sound. Right: The landing at Olga. Top: Olga docks are removed in winter. The historic Olga store.

48° 37.067' N
122° 50.050' W

Blakely Island

San Juan Islands

Blakely Island
Store and Marina

Glen Thompkins
1 Marine View Drive
Blakely Island WA 98222
Ph/Fax: 360-375-6121

blakelymarina@comcast.net

Chart 18430   **VHF 66A**

Marina services:

Moorage. Guest moorage–25 slips, year round. **Fuel:** Gas, diesel. 2 cycle oil. **Power** at docks: 30 amp.

Customer services:

Showers, laundry, washroom—seasonal. Wi-fi Internet access. Store. Provisions. Groceries. Beer and wine, gifts. Ice, fresh donuts. Groceries, old-time soda fountain, espresso. Store open June to September 15. Garbage disposal for marina guests. Reservations required.

Nearby facilities: Post office, restaurant, liquor store at Orcas Ferry Landing.

Note:

Fuel dock accessible either side.
Covered docks at entrance are private.
Clear customs for USA destinations at Roche Harbor or Friday Harbor.

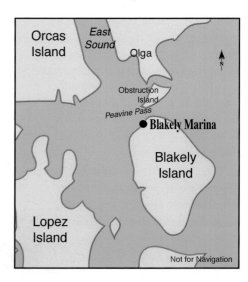

When approaching the harbor from the west, pass the small breakwater to your starboard. This entrance is narrow and shallow at low tide. The level of the water drops to 8 feet but it is an easy passage to the marina.

Not for Navigation

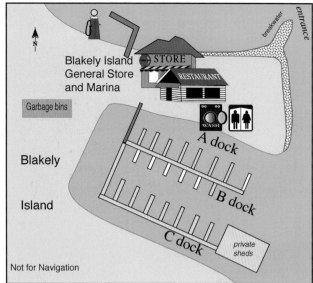

Not for Navigation

Opposite and right: Blakely Island Marina showing the store and fuel dock. There is a patio out front. It faces the open passage and overlooks the entrance. Bottom: The fuel dock is accessible from either side.

Blakely Marina

There is no access to the rest of the island, which is privately owned. The marina has facilities for guest boats and a sheltered bay where a number of boats can moor. Access is limited to higher tides for deep draft vessels. The depth through the channel is 8' at zero tides. A current runs past the entrance. This is a beautifully landscaped island and although most of it is private the scenery is enjoyable from the marina or the patio ashore.

48° 30.848' N
122° 54.936' W

IMC

Entrance
48° 31.580' N
122° 55.267' W

Fisherman Bay

Chart 18434

Islands Marine Center Inc.

Ron Meng **VHF 69**
2793 Fisherman Bay Rd
PO Box 88, Lopez Island WA 98261-0088
Ph: 360-468-3377 Fax: 360-468-2283
imc@rockisland.com
www.islandsmarinecenter.com

Marina services:
Moorage. Guest moorage on the south side of marina. About 1000'. Wireless internet access (fee). **Power:** 20, 30 amp.
Customer services:
Showers, washrooms.
Yacht sales and service. Various makes of marine engines and boating equipment. Marine chandlery, hardware, charts, clothing, gifts, electronics, fishing tackle and information. Ice. Road access walking, cycling. Rental apartments available.
Entertainment: Golf nearby. Picnic and barbecue area. Bicycle rentals. Wine tasting at nearby vineyards.
Adjacent facilities: Lopez Islander Resort and restaurant next door. Boatyard. Repairs and service. Haulouts. 15 ton travel lift and launch ramp.

Lopez Village is less than one mile away. Stores–groceries, provisions, inn, meals, accommodations. Farmers market on Saturdays in summer. Skateboard park. Community center.
Fuel: at nearby Lopez Islander Resort.
Note: Customs Port of Entry at Friday Harbor or Roche Harbor.

Below: The marinas and anchorage in Fisherman Bay. The bay opens off San Juan Channel.

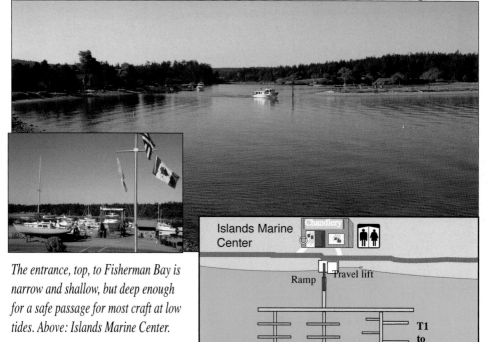

The entrance, top, to Fisherman Bay is narrow and shallow, but deep enough for a safe passage for most craft at low tides. Above: Islands Marine Center.

A sign on marker number five reminds mariners to round marker eight inside the bay leaving it to starboard. It is located not far from the outer floats of Islands Marine Center shown at lower left and inset in the aerial photographs on the opposite page.
Hazard: Be cautious, the shallowest water at the entrance has only five feet of depth at zero tide. Follow all the markers carefully.

Islands Marine Center

Ramp   Travel lift

T1 to T 10

T 10

Not for Navigation   *Guest moorage on T dock (south)*

Pass east of outer marker, #4, keep #5 and #7 to your port and #8 to your starboard when entering the Bay. Use local chart.

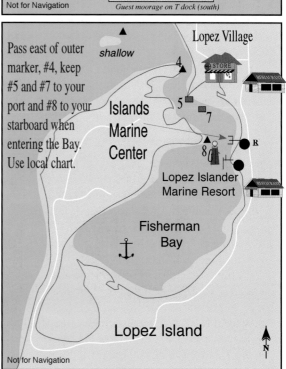

Lopez Village

shallow

Islands Marine Center

Lopez Islander Marine Resort

Fisherman Bay

Lopez Island

Not for Navigation

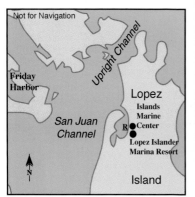

Not for Navigation

Friday Harbor

Upright Channel

San Juan Channel

Lopez
Islands Marine Center
Lopez Islander Marina Resort

Island

Lopez Islander Resort

San Juan Islands

Lopez Islander Bay & Marina

Bill & Earle Diller. Kathy Casey.
2864 Fisherman Bay Rd
PO Box 459, Lopez Island WA 98261-0088
Ph: 360-468-2233 Fax: 360-468-3382
desk@lopezfun.com
www.lopezfun.com
Charts 18421, 18430, 18434 VHF 78A
Marina services:
Moorage. Guest mooring–about 64 slips. Reservations suggested.
Power: 30, 50 amp.
Fuel: Gas, diesel. Sea plane float for planes that call at the marina. Propane nearby.
Customer services:
Showers, laundry, washrooms.

Internet access. Store on dock, groceries, provisions, charts, clothing, gifts, books, bread, fishing tackle. Ice. Playground. Courtesy phone on dock.
Hotel accommodation–28 rooms. Swimming pool. Hot tub. Conference and banquet facilities. Salmon fishing and scuba diving charters. Wildlife & whale watching. Restaurant lounge. Patio service. Live music in summer. Banquet room.
Walking: Road access walking, cycling.
Entertainment: Golf nearby. tennis, winery. Bicycle and kayak rentals and guides.
Adjacent facilities: Lopez Village less than one mile. Groceries, bakery, pharmacy, galleries and liquor stores. Five miles to ferry.

48° 30.781' N
122° 54.992' W

Lopez Islander
Marina Resort

Above: Church at Lopez Village.
Top: Fuel dock at Lopez Islander Resort and
Marina. The marina is the facility on the left of the
two in the top photo on the opposite page.

Not for Navigation ▲
4
shallow

Lopez Village
▲
5
7
▲ ⊟ IMC
8
⬤
**Fisherman
Bay**
Anchoring

Lopez Islander
Resort & Marina

N

Lopez Island Winery 360-468-3644,
is open to the public and wine tasting is available April to mid Decem-
ber, Fridays and Saturdays from 12
noon to 5pm. The vineyards are a
short distance beyond the Lopez Island village and a reasonable walk
or a quick drive away. Lopez wines
are made from local Madeleine An-
gevine, Siegerrebe and from Yakima
Valley Chardonnay and Cabernet
Sauvignon/Merlot.
Lopez Island is one of the easiest
islands in the San Juans for cycling.
Bicycle rentals are available adjacent to Lopez Islander Resort and
Islands Marine Center. An extensive
road system allows wide exploration
of the many interesting things to see and do on the island.

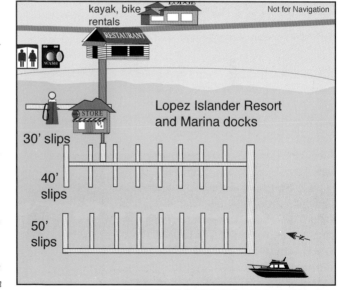

kayak, bike
rentals
LODGE
Not for Navigation

RESTAURANT

WASH

STORE

Lopez Islander Resort
and Marina docks

30' slips

40'
slips

50'
slips

N

Right: The museum at Lopez Island village.

Traveling South?
See Section 8 for marinas
from Blaine to Olympia.

Point Roberts

48° 58.333' N
123° 03.817' W

Point Roberts Marina

Jacquelyne Everett
713 Simundson Dr
Point Roberts WA 98281
Phone: 360-945-2255 Fax: 360-945-0927
prmarina@pointrobertsmarina.com
www.pointrobertsmarina.com
Charts Cdn: 3492, 3463. US: 18421
Customer Services:
Moorage 24' to 125' 220' guest dock.
Fuel: Gas, diesel, propane. **Power:** 20, 30,
50 amp, **Showers, laundry, washrooms.**
Public phones. Restaurant. Chandlery, bait,
tackle, fishing licences, repairs, service. Two
pumpouts at Customs and fuel docks. Workyard. Haulouts–35 ton travel lift, monorail
sling hoist–small boats to 3,500 lbs . The marina is mostly for permanent moorage. Space
for visiting vessels is available. Reservations
are encouraged. **US Port of Entry**–the dock
at the entrance is the Customs dock.
Nearby: Championship golf course. Air park.
Cinnamon buns at the Shell station, snacks,
groceries at the Market Place–Tyee Road.

VHF 16 switch to 66A

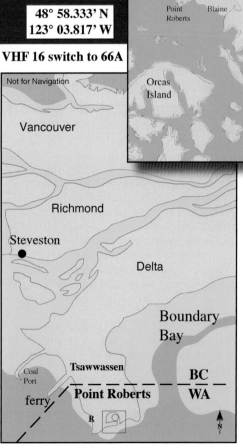

Not for Navigation

Point Roberts   Blaine

Orcas Island

Vancouver

Richmond

Steveston

Delta

Boundary Bay

Coal Port

Tsawwassen

ferry

Point Roberts

BC

WA

N

38

Point Roberts Golf and Country Club 360-945-4653

Although this marina is not in the San Juan Islands, it is very near. Access to it from the islands is closest from Sucia Island. It is a large centre for repairs and provides a good stop for access to the British Columbia mainland. In the photo, opposite, beyond the marina can be seen the island ferry landing and the coal port. Customs requires reporting when landing from Canadian ports. Point Roberts is on the tip of a peninsula which is attached to the BC mainland. A nearby border crossing by land takes you into Greater Vancouver.

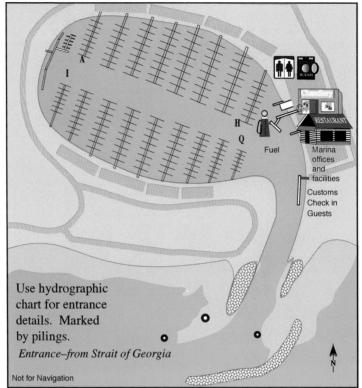

Use hydrographic chart for entrance details. Marked by pilings.

Entrance–from Strait of Georgia

Not for Navigation

Coastal Marine Parks   see also *Anchorages and Marine Parks*

Marine Parks in the San Juan Islands and British Columbia offer tranquil and delightful moorage. They have been established for use by the general public and attract hikers, backpackers, cyclists, RV campers and mariners. Many parks have picnic and overnight camp sites with trails and beaches. Some have docks adequate to moor dinghies only, some to moor a number of small to medium sized craft and others none at all. Most have mooring buoys for safe overnight mooring. Flat fees are levied for use of docks or mooring buoys. These change periodically but at present they are about $10 per mooring buoy per night, for boats under 45 feet, and the charges usually apply afer 1 pm in the San Juans and after 6 pm in Canada.

The authorities ask that parks be respected and kept clean. Garbage should not be disposed of unless there is a specific disposal station. Sewage should not be discharged in marine park anchorages and noise should be limited to daylight hours. There are marine park hosts at some Marine Parks and in BC their presence will be indicated by the flying of a BC Parks Marine Park Host burgee. The host is usually a member of a power squadron, a yacht club, a sailing association or is an individual who has volunteered to assist visitors.

In Washington State it is possible to purchase an annual moorage permit which allows use of mooring buoys and docks at the various locations throughout the year without further fee. Fees are in effect year round at some facilities while at others only between May and September. In the San Juan Islands these include Sucia Island, Stuart Island, Jones Island, James Island and Matia Island.

For more information on marine parks in US waters contact Washington State Parks Headquarters at 360-902-8844 or *www.parks.wa.gov/boating/*
In Canada, 2930 Trans Canada Hwy, Victoria BC V9B 5T9 Ph: 250-387-4363.
www.britishcolumbia.com/parks www.bcparks.com

Vancouver Island
Southern Section
Section 2

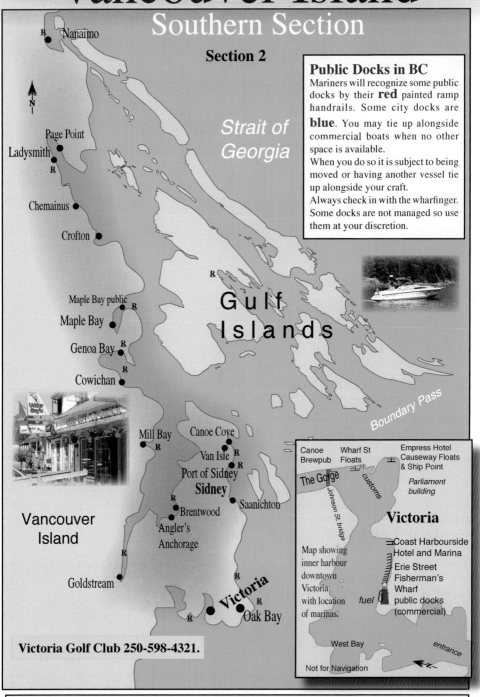

**Strait of
Georgia**

Public Docks in BC
Mariners will recognize some public docks by their **red** painted ramp handrails. Some city docks are **blue**. You may tie up alongside commercial boats when no other space is available.
When you do so it is subject to being moved or having another vessel tie up alongside your craft.
Always check in with the wharfinger. Some docks are not managed so use them at your discretion.

R Nanaimo

N

Page Point
Ladysmith
R

Chemainus

Crofton

R

**Gulf
Islands**

Maple Bay public R
Maple Bay

Genoa Bay R

Cowichan R

Boundary Pass

Mill Bay   Canoe Cove
R
            Van Isle R
        Port of Sidney
        Sidney
    R   Saanichton
    Brentwood
Angler's
Anchorage

**Vancouver
Island**

R

Goldstream

R **Victoria**
R
R Oak Bay

Victoria Golf Club 250-598-4321.

Canoe   Wharf St   Empress Hotel
Brewpub   Floats   Causeway Floats
                             & Ship Point
The Gorge   *Parliament
                             building*
Johnson St. bridge   customs

Victoria

Coast Harbourside
Hotel and Marina
Map showing
inner harbour   Erie Street
downtown   Fisherman's
Victoria   Wharf
with location   *fuel* public docks
of marinas: (commercial)

West Bay   *entrance*

Not for Navigation

● Marina locations
R Launch Ramps

Map shows marinas and public docks, this section.
Not to be used for navigation.

Victoria

Coast Marina 48° 25.420' N 123° 22.788' W

The Coast Victoria Harbourside Hotel and Marina.
VHF 66A
146 Kingston St, Victoria BC V8V 1V4
Ph: 250-360-1211 Fax: 250-360-1418
victoriamarina@coasthotels.com
www.coasthotels.com
Charts 3412, 3440, 3461, 3462, 3313
Fuel: (at adjacent fuel dock) gas, diesel.
Marina Services: Moorage. Visitors welcome. Reserve in summer. **Water** at dock. **Power:** 30, 50 amp. Pumpout. **Garbage disposal. Showers, washrooms.** Pool, spa, sauna at hotel included in moorage. Award winning restaurant in hotel. Concierge service available to marina guests. Whale watching tours and other attractions.

Complimentary shuttle from the hotel to downtown Victoria.

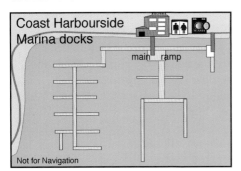

Above: Diagram of Coast Victoria marina docks. Top: Victoria's Empress (Causeway) floats in front of the Empress Hotel. Right: Docks at the Coast Victoria Harbourside Hotel and Marina.

CUSTOMS: Vessels entering Canada from foreign waters must clear Customs. The Canada Customs float in Victoria is located between the Wharf Street facility and the float plane terminals, at the foot of a 3-storey pink brick building. The Canada Customs office is located at 816 Government Street on the corner of Government Street and Wharf Street. Canada Customs can be reached by phone at 1-800-461-9999.

You must clear Customs PRIOR to arranging a berth for your vessel. A 24-hour direct phone is available on the Customs float. Once you have cleared Customs, you may hail GVHA on VHF 66A to request moorage.

Please note: The Customs dock can accommodate vessels up to 70'/21m in length. If your vessel is over 70'/21m, contact Customs to make alternate arrangements and then contact the GVHA for space availability at least 48 hours in advance.

The Causeway Floats, located in front of the Empress Hotel (bottom).

Causeway Floats
48° 25.300' N   123° 22.185' W

Vancouver Island South

Causeway Floats
107–108 Wharf St
Victoria BC V8W 3B9   VHF 66A
Ph: 250-383-8326 Fax: 250-383-8306
Toll free 1-877-783-8300
manager@victoriaharbour.org
www.victoriaharbour.org

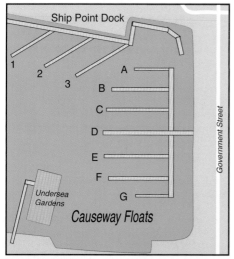

Ship Point Dock

1
2
3
A
B
C
D
E
F
G

Government Street

Undersea
Gardens

Causeway Floats

48° 25.502' N   123° 22.309' W

Charts 3313, 3440, 3412, 3461, 3462
Located in front of Fairmont Empress Hotel. Marina services: Transient moorage–3,000'. Rafting at busy times. Linear space. Reservations accepted. **Power:** 20, 30 amps. **Laundry, showers, washrooms.** Garbage disposal, recycling.
Internet access.
Customer services: Customs/phone. Nearby city downtown within walking distance.
Entertainment:
Downtown Victoria. Walking–promenade.
Adjacent or nearby services:
Ferries, seaplane services. Hospital, banks, bank machines, **Trotac Marine 800-287-6822**, car rentals, post office, swimming pool, telephone, taxi service. Museums. Summer entertainment on the promenade and in the city. This is a busy marina.
Additional moorage is available at the Wharf Street Marina.
Note: There is no moorage available at Fisherman's Wharf.
There is a Customs Dock and with a phone near Wharf Street Floats. See link on www.victoriaharbour.org
Caution: Adjacent Seaplane landing area. Check chart for caution areas. Enter and exit along yellow buoys–see diagram page 43.

Ship Point Dock

107–108 Wharf St
Victoria BC V8W 3B9
Ph: 250-383-8326   VHF 66A
Fax: 250-383-8306
Toll free 1-877-783-8300
moorage@victoriaharbour.org
www.victoriaharbour.org
Charts 3313, 3440, 3412,
3461, 3462
Located in front of Fairmont
Empress Hotel. Moorage: A
large pier for vessels up to 250'.
Power: 30 amps. Located between
Causeway Floats and Wharf
Street Floats. A float attached
to the south side of the pier is

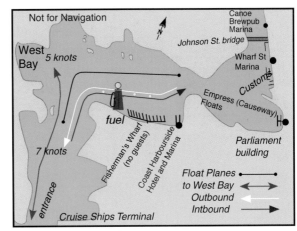

used by pleasure and commercial vessels for pick up
and drop off. Used for special events, pocket cruise
ships & large pleasure yachts. Marina services: same
as Causeway Floats.

*Caution: Seaplane landing area on approaches to Victoria Inner Harbour. Follow
the yellow markers in and out of the harbour. See the diagram above.*

Canoe Brewpub Marina

2450 Swift St
Victoria BC V8W 1S3
VHF 66A
Ph: 250-361-1940
Nearby Johnson Street Bridge
within walking distance of city
(above). Hotels nearby.

*Opposite page: The Causeway
Docks in front of Parliament and
the Empress Hotel. Alternatives are
at Wharf Street, Canoe Brewpub or
Coast Harbourside Marina,.*

*The diagram right shows Victoria
Harbour and Esquimalt Harbour.*

*Above: Ship Point is the section of docks attached to the
Causeway Floats beyond boats on the right side of photo.*

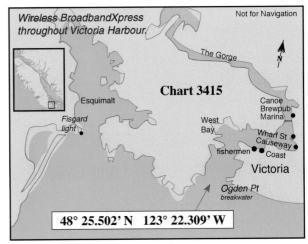

The author wishes to thank Amelia Kerr for the flight over Victoria and nearby coastal areas. Thanks also to Canadian Flight Centre, Grizzly Helicopters, West Coast Helicopters and private pilots Heinz Bold, Justin Taylor and others who have contributed to the acquisition of aerial photos for this book.

Above: In the Victoria Harbour moorage options include the Causeway Floats in front of the Empress Hotel (seen top right in the photograph). The Parliament buildings are to the right of the marina. This location gives the visiting mariner an opportunity to see the best of the city. Victoria boasts one of the top tourism billings in Canada, with its very British atmosphere highlighted by pedigree pubs, London open-top buses and High Tea at the Empress Hotel. Ship Point is the wide section of docks attached to the Causeway Floats. The Wharf Street Floats are in the centre and the Brewpub Marina is beyond the Johnson Street Bridge to the left. The Coast Hotel marina is off to the lower right. Left, top: Wharf Street Floats with a view west to the entrance of Victoria Harbour. Left, bottom: Victoria Harbour outer approaches with the fishermen's wharf in the foreground and Coast Victoria Harbourside Hotel and Marina to its right. Right: Parliament buildings from the Causeway Floats.

Above: The approaches to the Victoria waterfront with Fisherman's Wharf docks to the right. A new marina is being built on the opposite shore. Bottom: The docks at Wharf Street in downtown Victoria. Beyond the Johnson Street bridge is The Gorge. If you are in Victoria a slow cruise up there in your runabout or small boat can be a pleasant excursion.

Wharf Street Floats

107–108 Wharf St
Victoria BC V8W 3B9
VHF 66A
Ph: 250-383-8326
Fax: 250-383-8306
Toll free 1-877-783-8300
moorage@victoriaharbour.org
www.victoriaharbour.org
Charts 3313, 3412, 3440, 3461/2

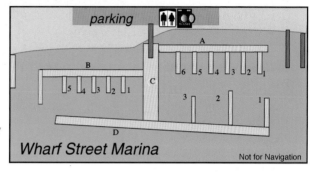

Wharf Street Marina

Not for Navigation

Marina services: Located next to the Johnson Street Bridge (blue bridge).
Moorage: Transient moorage, 2,200'. Reservations accepted for boats 65' and over. Rafting is mandatory at busy times.
Power: 20, 30, 50 amp. **Laundry, showers, washrooms.**
Garbage disposal. Recycling.
Customer services:
Customs phone on the customs dock. See *www.victoriaharbour.org* for details. Nearby city downtown within walking distance. Hotels nearby. **Munro's Books.**
Entertainment:
Downtown Victoria, Old City and China-town. Scuba diving at the Breakwater.
Adjacent or nearby services:
Ferries, seaplane services, customs. Hospital, banks, bank machines, car rentals, post office, swimming pool, public pay phone, taxi service. Museums. **Bosun's Locker 250-383-1308**.

Golf links at Oak Bay overlooking Trial Island.

Wharf Street Marina

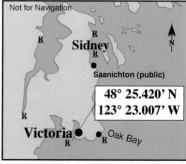

Not for Navigation

Sidney
Saanichton (public)

48° 25.420' N
123° 23.007' W

Victoria
Oak Bay

Victoria Golf Club 250-598-4321.
Uplands Golf Course 250-592-7313

Oak Bay Marina opens off Baynes Channel in the lee of Discovery Island. Watch for Lewis Reef on the northbound approaches to the entrance.

48° 25.431' N   123° 17.897' W

Oak Bay Marina

Manager Maya Gosker
1327 Beach Dr
Victoria BC V8S 2N4   VHF 66A
Ph: 250-598-3369 Fax: 250-598-1361
Toll free 1-800-663-7090
jill_smillie@obmg.com
www.obmg.com
Charts 3313, 3440, 3424, 3462
Marina services:
Fuel: Gas, diesel at marina fuel dock.
Mechanic and services available.

Moorage: Permanent moorage and some overnight slips. Reserve in summer.
Power: 15, 30 amp.
Laundry, showers, washrooms.
Customer services: Customs/phone.
Chandlery. Tackle shop. Gift shops.
Restaurant, sushi bar, coffee bar/cafe.
Nearby village–Oak Bay Avenue 6–8 blocks.
Walking on road and beach front.
Bolen Books.
Hazard: Rocky entrance. Shoals and shallows–marked with buoys. Consult charts.

Going North–from Victoria

The fabled Gulf Islands are steeped in history and folklore and there are books on many subjects dealing with these fascinating islands as well as the San Juans. As you make passage along the east shore of Vancouver Island, stopping possibly in Victoria or Sidney to clear customs, you unfold places of interest and people of charm and character that will please and intrigue you.

You may prefer to tie up at a dock and take in the local facilities. Victoria has the charm of British styled stores, pubs and restaurants. British imports are the speciality and if the atmosphere of old England does not strike you immediately go and reserve afternoon tea at the Empress Hotel. Tourists flock to Victoria each summer and the attractions include the Royal BC Museum, parliament buildings, undersea gardens, scenic London-bus tours and much more. Try also the Port of Sidney, Canoe Cove or Van Isle Marina. All three have good restaurants including places where you can sit and take in the magnificent crimson summer sunsets. Consider the fine restaurants at Tsehum Harbour, the quaint pub at Canoe Cove or any of a variety in Sidney including those at the waterfront. In Saanich Inlet stop at waterfront restaurants in Brentwood Bay or the Lodge and Spa. Take your dinghy around to Butchart Gardens for a day of strolling in one of the most magnificent masterpieces of landscaping anywhere. Anchor off Mill Bay and walk up to the local shopping centre for some tasty cappuccino or shopping at the well-stocked Thrifty Store. Continue up the coast through Genoa Bay for a safe overnight stop and fine dining, or visit Maple Bay for good moorage and a timely meal at the marina pub/restaurant.

Port Sidney

Port Sidney Marina

9835 Seaport Place
Sidney BC V8L 4X3   VHF 66A
Ph: 250-655-3711 Fax: 250-655-3771
judi@portsidney.com
www.portsidney.com
Charts 3313, 3479, 3441, 3462
Marina services:
Fuel not available. Fuel docks at Tsehum
Harbour and Canoe Cove (nearby, north)
Mechanic and services available from
local and nearby marine operators.
Marine stores in uptown Sidney.
Moorage: 300–400 slips. Permanent
moorage and plenty of overnight slips.
Reserve in summer. Excellent moorage.
Dockominium ownership resales.
Pumpout. **Power** at docks: 15, 20, 30,
50, 100 amps. **Laundry, showers, washrooms.** Activities dock–reserve for group
private functions. **Internet access.**
Nearby: Post office, general stores,
books–**Tanner's Books**, **Boater's Exchange**–250-655-3101, charts, fishing
licences, tackle, bait, fresh produce,
groceries, bakery, hardware, dry cleaning, liquor, pharmacy, clothing, gift stores,
churches all within walking distance. Numerous restaurants, coffee shops, bistros
and cafes. Walking trails or road access.
Some beachfront walks.

Inside the store/office at
Port Sidney Marina

Town streets and waterfront roads allow
views while walking.
Kayak and other small craft rentals available. Scuba diving arrangements and
charters, whale watching–ask marina for
details. Water taxi service to other marinas.
International airport nearby.
Entertainment: Nearby historic Butchart
Gardens. Sidney Museum summer hours–
7 days per week. Features whales with
murals and exhibits. Golf, tennis and other
recreation nearby.

Saanichton, Sidney
Public dock
Charts 3313, 3479, 3441, 3462
• Float length 10 m • This dock is
located south of Sidney–
Restaurants, shops, medical centre,
churches are located in Sidney. Ferries at Sidney and Swartz Bay to US
ports, Gulf Islands and BC mainland.

Not for Navigation

The Port Sidney Marina attracts many boaters from BC and Washington. It is a busy Customs port and allows access to the many shops and services in the town.

48° 39.104' N
123° 23.491' W

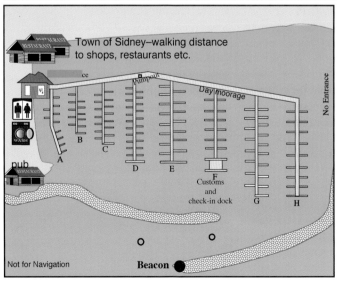

Town of Sidney–walking distance to shops, restaurants etc.

Not for Navigation

Beacon

The aerial photograph above and the diagram left show the magnitude of the marina and the layout of the docks. **DO NOT use the opening at the north side of the marina. There are rocks and reefs and only a few locals know the route and tides for that opening.** **Note: Even numbered slips on north side of docks. Odd numbered slips on south side.**

Photo courtesy of Van Isle Marina

Tsehum Harbour

48° 40.310' N
123° 24.301' W

Van Isle Marina

Dana Dickinson
2320 Harbour Rd   **VHF 66A**
Sidney BC V8L 2P6
Ph: 250-656-1138
Fax: 250-656-0182
info@vanislemarina.com
www.vanislemarina.com

Hazard–Rocks inside marked by beacons.

Enter from around the breakwater to Tsehum Harbour. Designated marina for courtesy customs clearance. Customs dock.

Large permanent marina with many overnight mooring slips. Docks can accommodate craft to 300+ feet.

Marina services:

Laundry, showers, washrooms. Visitors check in at the fuel dock. Reservations suggested. **Fuel**: Gas, diesel, stove oil. Outboard mix. Pumpout. **Power**: 15, 30, 50, 100 amp. 120, 208 volt available. Public phone–ashore and on the docks. Marine store on fuel dock 250-656-1138. Waste oil disposal, holding tanks pumpout. Ice. Charts, fishing tackle, licences, bait, life jackets etc. Yacht sales and service in marina complex.

Dining at Dockside Grill waterfront cafe. Philbrooks Shipyard adjacent: Haulouts.

Charts 3313, 3479, 3441, 3462
VHF 66A

Boatlift railway 150 tons or 120 feet. Many facilities ashore.

Nearby fine restaurants open 7 days a week. Walking trails or road access. Some beachfront walks. Views from town streets and waterfront roads.

Entertainment:

Nearby historic Butchart Gardens. Bus, taxi and rentals plus water shuttle to downtown Sidney, easy access to Victoria, airport, ferries. Golf, tennis and other recreation nearby. Walk Roberts Bay Bird Sanctuary nearby.

Nearby facilities:

Philbrooks shipyard is located adjacent to the marina complex. Also in the Sidney area: **All Bay Marine 250-656-0153**, The Boat Yard, Jensen Marine. **Tanners Books**. Various denominational churches. The Tsehum Harbour public dock is located nearby.

Above: Van Isle Marina. The fuel and Customs docks are in the left foreground. A new dock has been added alongside the breakwater.

Vancouver Island South

Right: Looking northwards over Tsehum Harbour. Westport Marina is in the upper centre of the photograph. Van Isle Marina has visitor moorage while Westport and other marinas have limited transient space.

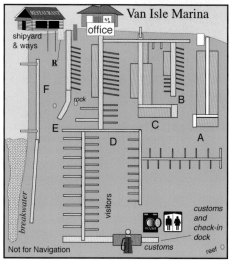

Van Isle Marina

Not for Navigation

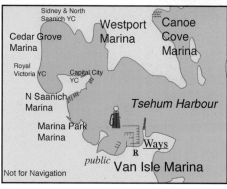

Not for Navigation

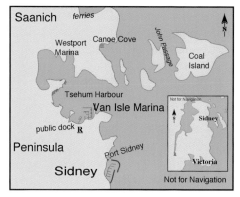

Not for Navigation

Tsehum Harbour Public dock

Sidney, Vancouver Island.
Managed • Float length: 318 m • Fully occupied with permanent tenants. No moorage available for transients. • Best use Van Isle Marina.

North Saanich Marina

1949 Marina Way, Sidney BC V8L 3S3
Ph: 250-656-5558 Fuel: Gas, diesel, private marina. Moorage by arrangement.

Marina Park Marina

2060 White Birch Rd Sidney BC V8L 2R1
Ph: 250-656-0454

Westport Marina

Division of Thunderbird Marine Corp
Manager: Ken Gowan
2075 Tryon Rd
Sidney BC V8L 3X9
Phone: 250-656-2832 Fax: 259-655-1981
westport@thunderbirdmarine.com
www.thunderbirdmarine.com
Charts 3476, 3313
Marina services: Limited guest moorage, reservations required. **Power:** 15, 30-amp, snack bar, washrooms, showers, garbage disposal, marine/fishing supplies, ice, 50-ton travel lift (max. 70'), marine repair services, marine mechanic. **Jensen's Marine.**
Nearby facilities: Restaurants, grocery store, marine chandlery, liquor store, playground, hiking trails.

fuel

Customs

Canoe Cove

Charts 3313, 3479, 3441, 3462
VHF 66A

48° 40.966' N
123° 24.025' W

Canoe Cove Marina

General manager: Don Prittie
2300 Canoe Cove Rd
Sidney BC V8L 3X9
Ph: 250-656-5566
Fax: 250-655-7197
Service department Ph: 250-656-5515
office@canoecovemarina.com
www.canoecovemarina.com

Customs services.
Designated marina for courtesy Customs clearance between docks C and D.

Moorage: Large permanent marina with limited overnight moorage slips. Reservations recommended. **Power**: 15, 30 amp.

Marina services:
Fuel: Gas. Diesel. Propane. Ice.
Marine chandlery: Charts, fishing tackle. Full service boatyard including mechanical, shipwrights, electrical, rigging, fibreglass and upholstery shops.
Haulouts. 55 ton travel lift.

Laundry, showers, washrooms.
Customer services:
Coffee shop. Artist studio.

Entertainment:
Nearby historic Butchart Gardens. Bus, taxi and rentals plus water shuttle to downtown Sidney, road access to Victoria, airport. Golf, tennis. Various denominational Churches in Sidney and nearby.

Adjacent facilities: The Stonehouse Pub open 7 days a week.

Nearby: BC Ferries Swartz Bay to Vancouver and Gulf Islands.

Hazard: Rocks in north entrance marked by poles. Narrow waterway to fuel dock. Go Slow. Use right-of-way.

Approaching Canoe Cove from Swartz Bay.

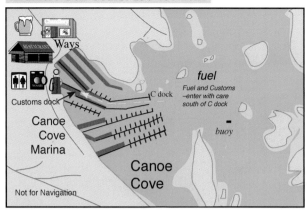

Customs and fuel dock

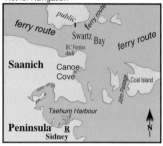

Mariners stop at Canoe Cove Marina for fuel at a dock tucked away between docks C and D. This is where you can also clear Customs. There is a homey cafe for breakfast or lunch and early light dinner in the summer. The large boat yard adjacent to the marina has haulout and dry storage space and is operated by the marina.

Piers Island, Sidney

CRD Public dock (Brief stops only)
Charts 3313, 3479, 3462, 3441
Manager • Float length 63 metres
Used primarily by local residents.
Located opposite BC Ferries Swartz Bay terminal (Sidney)–a small float near the ferries dock serves islanders.

A chandlery situated near the cafe carries a wide range of items for repairs, service and annual maintenance.

Left: Piers Island Capital Regional District float. Stops to 15 minutes–one person stay aboard.

Approaches to Swartz Bay, Piers Island and Canoe Cove from the north.

Saanich Inlet

Vancouver Island South

Brentwood Bay Lodge & Spa

Harbourmaster: Matt Smiley
849 Verdier Ave
Brentwood Bay BC V8M 1C5
Ph: 250-652-3151 Fax: 250-544-2069
Toll free 1-888-544-2079
marina@brentwoodbaylodge.com
www.brentwoodbaylodge.com
Moorage: 50 slip marina with overnight moorage to 150 feet. Reserve.
Power at docks: 15, 30, 50 amp.
Laundry, showers, washrooms.
Customer services: Wifi.
Marina services: Pumpout. Mechanic and services available from local and nearby marine operators. Ice.
Eco Adventure Centre. Wilderness Eco Cruises, kayaking, diving.
Shuttle to Butchart Gardens, wineries.
Two restaurants with outdoor patio–fine dining in Sea Grille and Sushi Bar. Casual dining in Marine Pub. Cold beer and wine

Cordova Bay Golf Course 250-658-4444

sales. Open 7 days a week. Full service spa and outdoor heated pool, hot tub. Public pay phones.
Entertainment:
Live music on select nights. Nearby historic Butchart Gardens. (Dinghy in to small dock at Butchart Gardens). Bus, taxi and rentals to downtown Sidney, Road access to Victoria, airport, ferries. Golf, tennis and other recreation nearby. Walking trails or roads. Some beachfront walks. Five wineries close by.
Adjacent and nearby facilities:
Fuel available at Goldstream Boathouse, Van Isle Marina, Canoe Cove Marina, Pier 66 Marina. Launch Ramp nearby on First Nations land.

Hazard–Reef off outer dock. Keep U22 marker to starboard. Approach dock from ferry terminal. Check your chart.

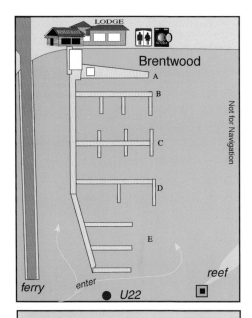

Brentwood

LODGE

A
B
C
D
E

Not for Navigation

ferry   enter   U22   reef

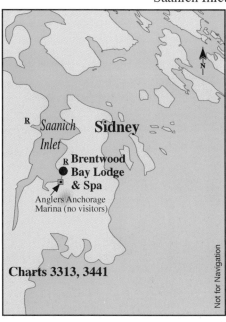

Saanich Inlet   Sidney

R Brentwood
Bay Lodge
& Spa

Anglers Anchorage
Marina (no visitors)

Charts 3313, 3441

Not for Navigation

Brentwood Bay
Public Dock
Alongside Anglers Anchorage Marina
(permanent vessels only). Nearby
Brentwood Marina and ferry to Mill
Bay on opposite side of Saanich Inlet.
Float length 22 x 60'. Part of dock re-
served for loading only. No amenities.
Day use only. Walk in adjacent park.

48° 34.617' N   123° 28.022' W
Brentwood Bay Lodge & Spa

*Opposite: Brentwood Bay Lodge and Spa
marina docks and adjacent hotel spa.
Below: The marina docks and the lodge with the
Eco Adventure Centre building at the head of
the dock. The dock next to the ferry is private.*

A Little Bit of History...Ma Miller's Pub, home of B.C.'s oldest continuous liquor licence was built on the site of the historic Goldstream Hotel which served the old wagon road to Cowichan and later the E & N Railroad since 1864. Destroyed by fire in 1873, the hotel changed hands several times before the Millers of Vancouver purchased the 33 acre property in 1910. Mrs. Mary "Ma" Miller managed the business after her husband was killed in a car accident on the Malahat in 1915. When the hotel was again destroyed by fire in 1923, the facility was rebuilt as a beer parlor. Despite opposition from, among others, the Prohibition League, "Ma" Miller opened her doors in 1931 and remained the owner-operator for another 15 years.

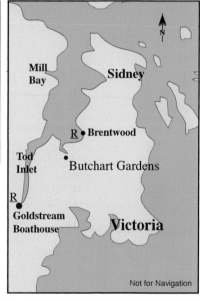

Top: Brentwood Bay lies to the left of centre in the photograph. To left of the ferry landing is a dock for a restaurant, and a private marina. To the right is Anglers Anchorage (private marina) with a public/loading dock to its left. Access to Tod Inlet is beyond the lower right of the photo. Above: Brentwood Bay from the south east side of Saanich Inlet. Below: Brentwood Bay Lodge and Spa docks.

Mill
Bay

Sidney

R • Brentwood

Tod
Inlet

Butchart Gardens

R

Goldstream
Boathouse

Victoria

Not for Navigation

Tod Inlet

Butchart Gardens

800 Benvenuto Ave
Brentwood Bay BC V8M 1J8
Toll free 1-866-652-4422
www.butchartgardens.com

Fireworks display Saturday nights in summer. Anchor in Tod Inlet and watch. Vessels anchored, or at nearby marinas or docks can use the dinghy dock and entrance to the gardens in Butchart Cove off Tod Inlet.

Goldstream Boathouse

Lida Seymonsbergen
3540 Trans Canada Hwy
Victoria BC V9B 6H6
Ph: 250-478-4407 Fax: 250-478-6882
alida@goldstramboathousemarina.com
www.goldstreamboathousemarina.com
Charts 3313, 3441, 3462   VHF 66A
Marina services:
Fuel: Diesel and gas. Oil filters. Bait, ice, tackle, snacks. Marine supplies dock.
Moorage. Transient 300' available.
Customer services: Power at docks: 20,

Above: The dock and fuel pump at Goldstream. View looks north towards entrance of Saanich Inlet.
Top: The dinghy dock (on left) at Butchart Cove.

Charts 3313, 3441, 3462

48° 29.907' N   123° 33.117' W

30 amp. **Washrooms.** Garbage disposal. 24-hour security.
Road access walking. Parkland trails at adjacent Goldstream Park. Public pay phones. (Marine repair. Haulouts to 50')
Entertainment:
Historic landmark boathouse. Ma Millers (historic hotel) pub. Crab and prawn fishing. Squid spawning, salmon run.
Adjacent facilities:
Launch ramp. Victoria General Marine Ph: 250-478-7849.

View from above the public docks.

Fisherman's Wharf
48° 44.515' N
123° 36.935' W

Cowichan Bay

Charts 3313, 3478, 3441, 3462

Cowichan Bay Fishermen's Wharf

Chuck Von-Haas
1699 Cowichan Bay Rd. PO Box 52
Cowichan Bay BC V0R 1N0
Ph: 250-746-5911 Fax: 250-701-0729
Cell 250-755-6763 VHF 66A
www.cbfwa@shaw.ca www.haabc.com
Marina services:
Moorage: Overnight available–5 docks–
being expanded. Rafting allowed. Check
in on arrival or reserve. Clubs may make
reservations. **Power** at docks 30 amp. Wifi.
Showers, laundry, washrooms. **Nearby
services:** Charters. Bed & breakfast. Ice,
fishing tackle, licences, bait. Boat lift, liquor store, post office, bank machine, pub,
hotel, restaurant, shops, swimming pool,
taxi, hardware, grocery. Mechanic and
marine service can be arranged. Garbage
disposal. **Nearby:** The Rock Cod Café fish
& chips, True Grain Mill organic bakery, Hilary's Cheese store, several coffee
houses, several restaurants, pub. Launch
ramp nearby.

Cowichan Golf and Country Club
250-746-7211 250-746-5333
Duncan Meadows 250-746-8993
Arbutus Ridge 250-743-5000
March Meadows 250-749-6241

*Top: Fishermen's Wharf in foreground. Two new fingers
were added in summer 2010. Below: The Oceanfront Grand
Resort and Marina overlooks Fishermen's Wharf and has a
dock that accommmodates hotel guest boats. The adjacent
hotel dock is reserved for the use of hotel guests only.
No entrance on the shore side of the breakwater.*

Above: New docks added at Fishermen's Wharf in 2010.
Left: Public dock and Masthead Marina to the right.
Left, below: Waterfront homes at the west end of Cowichan's marinas.

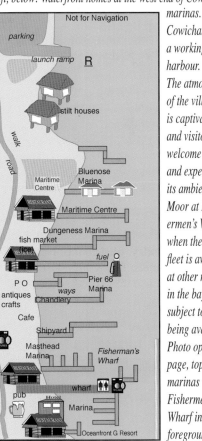

Cowichan is a working harbour. The atmosphere of the village is captivating and visitors are welcome to stop and experience its ambience. Moor at Fishermen's Wharf when the fishing fleet is away and at other marinas in the bay subject to space being available. Photo opposite page, top, shows marinas with Fishermen's Wharf in the foreground.

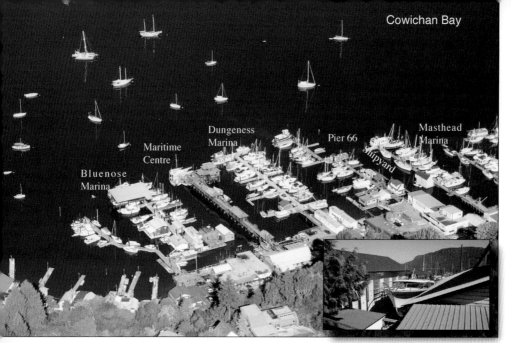

Cowichan Bay

Masthead
Marina

Dungeness
Marina

Pier 66

Shipyard

Maritime
Centre

Bluenose
Marina

Pier 66 Marina

Tom and Sharon Ingram
1745 Cowichan Bay Rd
Cowichan Bay BC V0R 1N0
Ph/Fax: 250-748-8444
sales@pier66marina.com
www.pier66marina.com
Moorage: Overnight. Check in on arrival or reserve.
Marina services:
Fuel: Gas, diesel, premix, ice, oil, bait, licences. **Garbage disposal.**
Convenience store. **Water** at dock.

Inset: On the ways at the shipyard in Cowichan.

Power: 15 amp. Multiple outlets.
Nearby and adjacent services: Showers, laundry. Take out restaurant. Fish market. groceries, liquor store, fishing tackle, bait, licenses and guides.
B&B, Oceanfront Grand Resort. Pub, restaurants. Post office. ATM. True Grains Bread organic bakery. Cowichan Bay Seafood store. Hilary's Cheese & Deli.
Showers, laundry, charters, accommodation, boat lift–mechanic and services can be arranged, post office, ATM, shops, taxi.

Pier 66

3

Easy Going

Dungeness Marina

Dungeness Marina VHF 66A

Owners: Rob & Carrie Hokanson
1759 Cowichan Bay Rd. PO Box 51
Cowichan Bay BC V0R 1N0
Ph: 250-748-6789 Fax: 250-748-9869
info@dungenessmarina.com
www.dungenessmarina.com
Marina services: Wifi **VHF 66A**
Power at docks: 30 amp. **Garbage disposal.**
Washrooms. Showers. Sewage pumpout.
Moorage: Overnight available 250' guest
dock. Check in on arrival or reserve.
Nearby: Charters. Bed & breakfast. Ice.
Marine supplies, hardware, groceries, charts,
tackle, boat rentals, fishing licences, bait.
Liquor store, post office, bank machine, pub,
restaurant, shops, taxi. Mechanic and serv-
ices can be arranged. Road access walking.
Nearby river and beach trails.

The Oceanfront Grand Resort and Marina

1681 Botwood Lane
Cowichan Bay BC V0R 1N0
Ph: 250-715-1000 Fax: 250-715-1001
Toll free 1-800-663-7898
info@thegrandresort.com
www.thegrandresort.com
Marina services: Moorage: Overnight
moorage is available only for hotel guests.
Check in on arrival or reserve. Small dock
located adjacent to the public marina–5' at
low tide. **Hotel.** Ice. Beer, wine and liquor
store. Restaurant. Pub.
Taxi service available.
Nearby services: see other listings.
Beware of the drying sandbar on the
shore side of the rock breakwater. The
opening is not an entrance to the marina.

The Oceanfront Grand Resort and Marina faces into the open basin of Fisherman's Wharf at Cowichan. NOTE: The hotel dock is reserved for the use of hotel guests only.

48° 45.468' N
123° 35.738' W

Genoa Bay

Charts 3313, 3478, 3441, 3442, 3462

Vancouver Island South

Genoa Bay Marina

Will Kiedaisch, Ben Kiedaisch
5000 Genoa Bay Rd   VHF 66A
Duncan BC V9L 5Y8
Ph: 250-746-7621 Fax: 250-746-7621
Toll free 1-800-572-6481
will@genoabaymarina.com
www.genoabaymarina.com
Marina services:
Moorage. Large marina with permanent and transient moorage. **Water** at dock (please conserve).
Power at docks: 15, 30, 50 amps.
Laundry, showers, washrooms. Ice.
Customer services:
Licensed restaurant. Breakfast, lunch, dinner. Patio service. Barbecue area. General store: groceries, fishing gear, licences. Some boat supplies, books, gifts. Fresh waffles. Ice cream. Wifi.
Video rentals. Art gallery. Gifts and fine art. Public pay phones ashore.
Courtesy van available. Float home rental–L'il Snug on the Bay.

Entertainment:
Road access cycling or walking nearby trails.
Adjacent facilities:
Anchorage. Yacht Sales. **Launch ramp**.

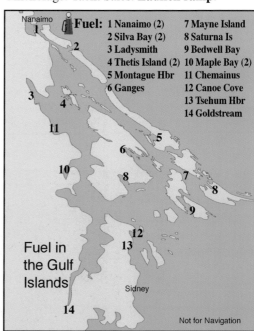

Fuel:
1 Nanaimo (2)	7 Mayne Island
2 Silva Bay (2)	8 Saturna Is
3 Ladysmith	9 Bedwell Bay
4 Thetis Island (2)	10 Maple Bay (2)
5 Montague Hbr	11 Chemainus
6 Ganges	12 Canoe Cove
	13 Tsehum Hbr
	14 Goldstream

Fuel in the Gulf Islands

Not for Navigation

Above: A busy Genoa Bay Marina, catering to yacht clubs and individual visiting boats. There is a fine restaurant on land and a well-stocked store on the docks. Bottom: An overview of the marina and the adjacent anchorage. Opposite: Aerial view of the marina in the fall of 2010.

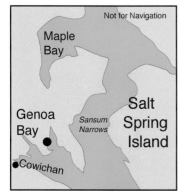

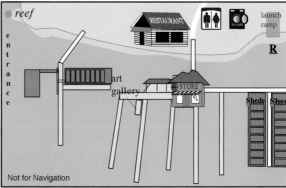

Hazard: When entering the bay keep to east of day beacon. Avoid marked shore-side reef.

48° 47.743' N
123° 36.010' W

Maple Bay

Charts 3313, 3478, 3442, 3441, 3462

Vancouver Island South

Maple Bay Marina

David and Carol Messier
6145 Genoa Bay Rd
Duncan BC V9L 5T7
Ph: 250-746-8482 Fax: 250-746-8490
Toll free 1-866-746-8482.
info@maplebaymarina.com
www.maplebaymarina.com

VHF 66A

Marina services:
Fuel: Gas, diesel, propane. Ice.
Guest moorage, about 50 slips. Reservations suggested. Yacht enclosures (houses) for a wide range of sizes.
Power: 15, 30, 50 amps. Garbage disposal. Recycling.
Laundry, showers, washrooms.
Customer services:
Internet access. The Shipyard Pub & Restaurant–licenced and open year round. Patio service. Beer/wine off-sales. ATM. Postage sold in marina office. Store. Coffee shop, light snacks. Souvenirs.
Shipwright and mechanical services.
Marine Supply chandlery 888-748-1149. 50 ton travel lift. Yacht brokerage. Float plane service. Shuttle to Duncan.

Adjacent facilities:
Golf. Rental cars. Canoe and kayak rentals and guided tours.
Entertainment:
Annual Wooden Boat Celebration every May long weekend. Groups and Rendezvous welcome–full use of Quarter Deck (covered picnic and BBQ area). Playground.
Road access walking or cycling trails. Beautiful landscaped gardens to walk through.

64

Right: The aerial view on the opposite page and this photograph show the scope of dock space at Maple Bay.

Below: The store at Maple Bay has gifts, light snacks ice cream and a lounge.

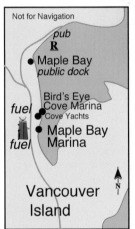

pub
R
● Maple Bay
public dock

Bird's Eye
fuel Cove Marina
Cove Yachts
● Maple Bay
fuel Marina

Vancouver
Island

Not for Navigation

Maple Bay

Municipal dock
Manager
Harmen Bootsma
Ph: 250-246-4655
Charts 3313, 3478,
3441, 3442, 3462
No Power at dock.
• Float length 46
  metres • Lights
• Launch ramp
• Water

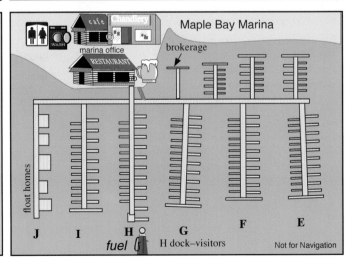

Maple Bay Marina

café Chandlery
marina office   brokerage
RESTAURANT

float homes

J   I   H   G   F   E
fuel
H dock–visitors   Not for Navigation

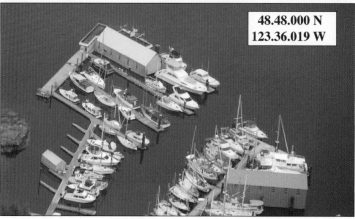

48.48.000 N
123.36.019 W

Bird's Eye Cove Marina (above and to the left) is a popular fuel stop. Service and repairs at adjacent Cove Yachts. This is a good fuel stop with a small store and available moorage. It is a short dinghy ride to the pub and public dock in Maple Bay.

Bird's Eye Cove Marina

Pat Fee & Nancy Fee   **VHF 66A**
6271 Genoa Bay Rd, Duncan BC V9L 5T8
Ph: 250-746-5686 Fax: 250-746-5685
birdseyecove@shaw.ca www.birdseyecove.ca
Marina Services: Fuel dock–diesel, gas and oils. Tackle, fishing supplies, ice, snacks.
Guest moorage–6 slips. Reservations preferred. **Power:** 15, 30 amp. **Washrooms**, garbage disposal. Boat sales. Boat rentals. The marina is open year round.
Service and repairs adjacent at Cove Yachts.
Nearby: Brigantine Pub–cold beer and wine store. Maple Bay Yacht Club. Golf. Access to town of Duncan.

Cove Yachts (1979) Ltd

6261 Genoa Bay Rd
Duncan BC V9L 5Y4
Ph: 250-748-8136 Fax: 250-748-7916
Travel lift. Ways. Commercial and pleasure craft repairs. Marine store.

Above: The Brigantine Pub dock is a short way to the north of these floats. Fuel, restaurants and facilities are available at Bird's Eye Cove Marina and Maple Bay Marina. Left: The public float at Maple Bay is in the outer bay before approaching Bird's Eye Cove.

Maple Bay to Crofton, Chemainus and Ladysmith

There is sheltered moorage at Maple Bay. Two marinas and a yacht club are the major facilities in Bird's Eye Cove. Or stop at the public dock or the Brigantine Pub for off-sales, dining or refreshment. Travelling north, an overnight stop at the sheltered harbours of Crofton and Chemainus can be a memorable experience. The public docks have room for transient boats in the summer. Off season if there is no room to tie up it is possible, preferably for not too long a stay, to come alongside a docked fishing boat. Fishermen generally do not object to having a boat moored temporarily alongside them. However you may prefer to be tied directly to the dock for easier access to and from your moored boat.

At Ladysmith, within easy walking access from the public docks, one can find many store facilities and boating requirements, supplies and services and a touch of coastal history. It is an old coal mining town named for the town in South Africa which was under siege during the Boer War and relieved by the British coincidental to the founding of Ladysmith in BC. Its naming also honoured the charitable wife of Sir Harry Smith, governor of the Cape Province of South Africa.

The Maritime Society and the public dock at the entrance to Ladysmith Harbour have visitor moorage. Farther into the harbour the docks at Ladysmith Marina or Page Point Marina are hospitable to recreational boats. During summer a steady stream of craft call at the marinas for overnight moorage. There is also good anchorage in the Dunsmuir Islands at the entrance to the harbour. From Ladysmith it is easy to access several outstanding nearby destinations. Among them are Telegraph Harbour, Wallace Island, Chemainus and Pirates Cove.

*Above: Anchoring behind the Dunsmuir Islands at the entrance to Ladysmith Harbour.
Right: Crofton has lots of room when the fishing fleet is out, but prepare to raft to other boats. The ferry terminal for Salt Spring Island is adjacent and there are stores and cafes nearby.*

Chemainus

Chemainus

Public docks Crofton to Ladysmith

Crofton Small Craft Harbour
Manager Harmen Bootsma
• Float length 1,000' • Launch ramp
• Breakwater • Garbage • Water • Lights
• **Power**: 30, 50 amps.
Note: This is a rafting dock.
BC Ferries to Vesuvius.

Vesuvius See Salt Spring Island pg 83.

Chemainus Municipal dock
Manager Harmen Bootsma
(**Fuel** adjacent) • 650' visitors float.
Ph: 250-246-4655 for reservations.
• **Power** 30, 50 amps • Water • Showers
• Washrooms • Laundry • Groceries, liquor
store, laundry, restaurant, propane, museum.
BC Ferries to Thetis Island.

Vancouver Island South

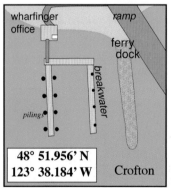

wharfinger office
ramp
ferry dock
breakwater
pilings

48° 51.956' N
123° 38.184' W
Crofton

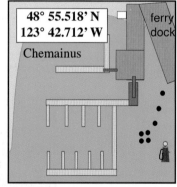

48° 55.518' N
123° 42.712' W
Chemainus
ferry dock

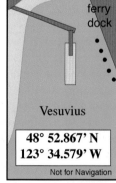

ferry dock
Vesuvius

48° 52.867' N
123° 34.579' W
Not for Navigation

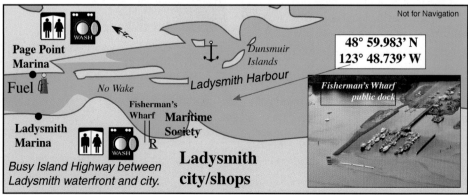

Not for Navigation

Page Point Marina
Fuel
No Wake
Ladysmith Harbour
Dunsmuir Islands

48° 59.983' N
123° 48.739' W

Fisherman's Wharf public dock

Fisherman's Wharf
Maritime Society
Ladysmith Marina
R

Busy Island Highway between
Ladysmith waterfront and city.

Ladysmith city/shops

Cottonwood Golf Club 250-245-5157

Ladysmith area

Maritime Society

launch ramp

Fisherman's

48° 59.983' N
123° 48.739' W

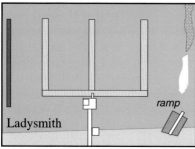

Ladysmith

ramp

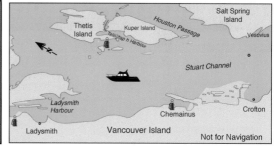

Salt Spring Island

Thetis Island

Kuper Island

Houston Passage

Telegraph Harbour

Vesuvius

Stuart Channel

Ladysmith Harbour

Chemainus

Crofton

Ladysmith

Vancouver Island

Not for Navigation

Ladysmith Fisherman's Wharf

Ladysmith, Vancouver Island
Fisherman's Wharf Association
Managers Ken Byrski, Cheryl Byrski
837 Ludlow Rd, PO Box 130
Ladysmith BC V9G 1A1
Ph: 250-245-7511 Fax: 250-245-7747
ifwa@telus.net   **Chart: 3475**
Guest Moorage: 1,200', rafting allowed
Power 15, 20 amps.
Water, washrooms, showers, laundry,
3-lane launch ramp, garbage disposal,
tidal grid, marine mechanic. Pay phone.
Nearby: Ladysmith uptown restaurants,
shops. The Maritime Society docks are
adjacent, to the south.

*Top: Ladysmith Harbour with the public dock to the
right and the Maritime Society at centre.*
*Opposite: Chemainus docks, expanded to accommodate
more pleasure boating visitors to the town.*
Below: The museum at Chemainus.

*Bottom: A mural
at Chemainus.
Bottom, left, inset:
The Ladysmith
public marina
launching ramp.*

69

Ladysmith Harbour

49° 00.615' N
123° 49.389' W

Vancouver Island South

Ladysmith Maritime Society

Wharfinger Mark Mercer
614 Oyster Bay, PO Box 1030
Ladysmith BC V9G 1A7
Ph: 250-245-1146   **Chart 3457**
wharfinger@lmmarina.ca
www.ladysmithmaritimesociety.ca
Moorage: 900' dock space. Power 15, 30 amps. Water, Ice, Garbage disposal. Large dock area for gatherings.
Maritime festival in May. Restored heritage boats and museum.
Nearby: Showers, laundry, washrooms, restaurants, groceries, post office, liquor store, propane, bank. The Ladysmith trolley stops near the marina for rapid transportation around Ladysmith.

Top: The Ladysmith Maritime Society docks are to port after entering Ladysmith Harbour.
Below: Page Point Marina offers overnight moorage, fuel and restaurant.

Trail to local swimming beach and park. The Society docks are located immediately to port after passing Sibell Bay to starboard. This bay is good for anchoring. It is also the location of the Seattle Yacht Club station in the Dunsmuir Islands. The public docks just beyond have full facilities but can be crowded when the fishing fleet is in.

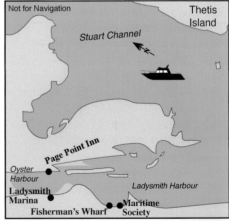

Page Point Marina

Talia Hemingway
4760 Brenton-Page Rd
Ladysmith BC V9G 1L7
Ph: 250-245-2312 Fax: 250-245-2318
Toll free 1-877-860-6866
Cell: 250-619-2312
info@pagepointmarina.com
www.pagepointmarina.com
Marina services:
Guest moorage. Reservations recommended.
Power: 30, 50 amps.
Fuel: Gas. Diesel.
Marine supplies. Ice. Mechanical service available. Garbage disposal.
Laundry, showers, washrooms.
Customer services:
Restaurant. Licenced.
Patio service. Public pay phone ashore.

Charts 3313, 3475, 3443, 3463
VHF 66A

Entertainment:
Road access walking or cycling. Golf nearby, arrangements–ask at marina for details. Car rentals. Bus or boat rides can be scheduled into nearby Ladysmith.
Adjacent facilities:
Short boat trip to Ladysmith–stores–stop at public dock opposite/south just inside entrance to Ladysmith harbour for access to the town.

Above: Page Point Marina. The property is located inside Ladysmith Harbour, at Page Point, from which it takes its name. It is not to be confused with Page's Marina in Silva Bay.

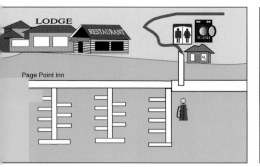

Photo courtesy Ladysmith Marina

Ladysmith Marina
49° 00.386' N
123° 49.618' W

Ladysmith Harbour

Charts 3313, 3475, 3443, 3463

Ladysmith Marina

Manager Rob Waters
12335 Rocky Creek Rd
Ladysmith BC V9G 1K4
Phone: 250-245-4521
Fax: 250-245-4538
VHF 66A
Marina Services:
Guest moorage–reservations required. **Power** at docks: 30, 50 amps. Garbage disposal. **Washrooms**.
Boat top repairs. Docking to 70 feet. New boathouses 50 to 80 feet. Host marina for Ladysmith

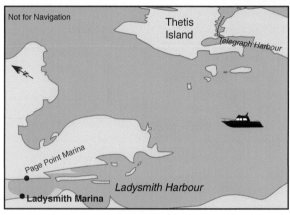

Not for Navigation

Thetis Island

Telegraph Harbour

Page Point Marina

Ladysmith Harbour

Ladysmith Marina

Yacht Club. Parking. One kilometre uptown to city of Ladysmith. Trolley transportation to town by donation.

Ladysmith Harbour

Top: Ladysmith Marina at Ladysmith Harbour.
Left: The entrance to Ladysmith Harbour with the public dock and Maritime Society to left. Ladysmith Marina lies beyond.

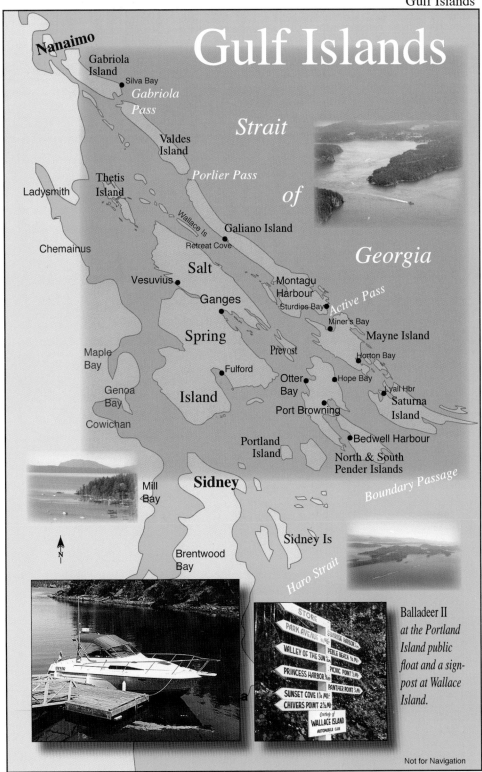

Gulf Islands

Nanaimo

Gabriola Island

Silva Bay

Gabriola Pass

Valdes Island

Ladysmith

Thetis Island

Chemainus

Vesuvius

Maple Bay

Genoa Bay

Cowichan

Strait

of

Georgia

Porlier Pass

Wallace Is

Galiano Island

Retreat Cove

Salt

Ganges

Montagu Harbour

Sturdies Bay

Spring

Prevost

Fulford

Island

Mill Bay

Sidney

Brentwood Bay

Active Pass

Miner's Bay

Mayne Island

Horton Bay

Otter Bay

Hope Bay

Lyall Hbr

Saturna Island

Port Browning

Bedwell Harbour

Portland Island

North & South Pender Islands

Boundary Passage

Sidney Is

Haro Strait

N

Balladeer II at the Portland Island public float and a sign-post at Wallace Island.

STORE
SUNRISE HARBOUR
PARK AVENUE 1/4 MI
PEBBLE BEACH 1/2 MI
VALLEY OF THE SUN 3/4 MI
PICNIC POINT 2 MI
PRINCESS HARBOR 7/8 MI
PANTHER POINT 1/4 MI
SUNSET COVE 1 1/4 MI
CHIVERS POINT 2 1/2 MI

Courtesy of
WALLACE ISLAND
AUTOMOBILE CLUB

Not for Navigation

73

Top: A popular event at Ganges is the Saturday morning farmers market in summer. Right: Special dock for the lamb roast at Saturna Island, a popular event every year.

The Gulf Islands offer many anchoring and mooring alternatives. The diagram on the previous page shows the main archipelago which makes up the group of islands that are most popular for overnight use. Note the cautions in the following text but always be mindful of weather conditions and forecasts.

Salt Spring Island is the largest of the Gulf Islands and has most facilities and amenities similar to mainland and Vancouver Island centres. Ganges holds an open air market every Saturday through the summer. The town is alive with vendors at the market and musicians in the local park.

One of the most popular events in the Gulf Islands is the annual lamb roast on Saturna Island. It is held on July 1st (Canada Day), when hundreds of boats will be found at anchor in Winter Harbour. A large dinghy dock is in place for the event.

Salt Spring Island

Fernwood

Walker Hook

Vesuvius

Salt

Trincomali Channel

Ganges

Long Harbour

Spring

Walter Bay

Burgoyne Bay

**48° 50.604' N
123° 25.034' W**

Island

Fulford

Beaver Point

Musgrave Landing

Sattelite Channel

Isabella Islets

Swanson Channel

Not for Navigation

*Top: A view over Ganges, the popular Gulf Islands destination where every Saturday morning the farmers market attracts a large crowd of visiting mariners.
Above: The farmers market and musicians at Ganges.*

● Marinas and public docks

48° 46.119' N 123° 27.161' W

Fulford Harbour

Gulf Islands

Fulford Marina

Bill and Gay Perry
5–2810 Fulford-Ganges Rd
Salt Spring Island BC V8K 1Z2
VHF 66A
Ph: 250-653-4467 Fax: 250-653-4457
fulfordmarina@saltspring.com
www.saltspring.com/fulfordmarina
NOTE: CLOSED FOR REPAIR–2010.
Please call to check if they are open again.
Marina services:
Moorage: Seasonal. Guest moorage April 1 to September 30 only. 600' plus 10 slips guest docks. Reservations suggested. Large breakwater float.
Power at docks: 20, 30 amp.
Customer services:
Showers, washrooms. Laundry at Fulford Inn, about a mile away.

Charts 3313, 3478, 3441/2, 3462/3
Entertainment:
Island tranquility. Eagles, herons, kingfishers, otters and seals. Waterfront gazebos and barbecue area. Beaches. Tennis courts.
Nearby facilities:
BC Ferries to Sidney. Government docks. Places of interest: Historic churches. Fulford settlement–gifts, art, bakery, groceries, restaurants, hotel. Walk to Drummond Park. Nearby private museum of Indian Art–Bob Akerman collection and his wife's classic doll collection. Five minutes walk to pub, beer and wine store, grocery store, coffee shop, crafts, parks, ferry. 20 minutes to lake. Salmon charters and sightseeing/eco tours.

Top: A view of the public dock and ferry landing at Fulford Harbour.

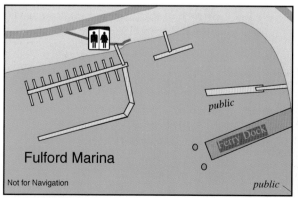

The docks at Fulford Marina have sustained damage from winter storms. In 2010 no moorage was available for transient vessels. It is hoped that the docks will be replaced in due course and that steps will be taken to build a breakwater to protect the harbour against future winter weather.

Above: The head of Fulford Harbour. The photo shows the marina, private dock to its right, the public docks in the middle of bay and the single public dock outside. The ferry landing is at the bottom left. Centre: Ferry landing and public dock. Bottom: St Paul's church is a favourite attraction at Fulford Harbour.

watercolour by the author

Public docks:

Fulford Harbour, Outside of breakwater. Harbour Authority of SSI.
• Float length 16 metres. Kayak rentals. Possible overnight moorage in calm conditions. Ferry to Sidney. Restaurants, shops. Manager Bart Terwiel Ph: 250-537-5711 Two hours free 8am to 4pm.
Charts 3313, 3478, 3441/2, 3462/3
ssha@saltspring.com

Fulford Harbour, Inner dock
Manager Ph: 250-537-5711
• Float length 36 m • Lights • Power •
Public pay phone • No guest space.

Charts 3313, 3478, 3442, 3462

Ganges

48° 51.257' N   123° 29.835' W

Ganges Marina   VHF 66A

Rick Barbieri
161 Lower Ganges Rd
Ganges BC V8K 2T2
Ph: 250-537-5242 Fax: 250-538-1719
gangesmarina@shaw.ca
www.ganges-marina.com

Marina services:
Moorage: Guest moorage about 100 slips.
Reservations taken.
Fuel: Gas, diesel, oils.
Power at docks: 15, 30, 50 amps.
Customer services:
Wifi. Public pay phone ashore. Marina
store has some supplies. Ice. Security gate.
Laundry, showers, washrooms.
Complimentary coffee, tea and muffins in
the morning–mid May to September.
Entertainment:
Ganges Saturday morning public market.
Art galleries. Walking and cycling on
island roads, Playground. Restaurants.
Nearby: Government docks. Shop-

Map labels: Salt Spring Marina; Kanaka Ganges public docks (outer harbour); Ganges Marina; breakwater dock; Mouat's; Ganges public docks (inner harbour) Commercial use; yacht club Private; R; Walter Bay; N
Caution: Aircraft activity in the harbour.
Not for Navigation

ping centre. Propane. Ganges facilities.
Fresh produce. Bakeries. **Thrifty Foods**
Phone: 250-537-1522 for groceries. **Old
Salty** 250-537-5551, **Sabine's** 250-538-
0025, **Salt Spring Books, Watermark**
and **Volume ll** book stores. Anchorages
and places of interest. Churches. Arts
and crafts. Hotels, B&Bs. Bistros. Pubs.
Nearby waterfront and beachfront access.

Top: Ganges with its marinas and anchorage.

Photograph above and below show Ganges Marina occupying a large portion of the bay. Ganges Marina is a popular venue for yacht club cruises and other boating rendezvous. No moorage is allowed on the outside of the breakwater dock.

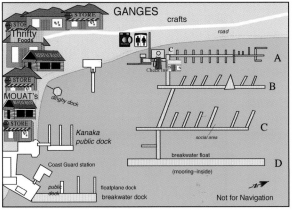

Ganges is the business centre and hub of the Gulf Islands. It is not only located on the biggest of the Gulf Islands but also it has the largest population of all communities in the archipelago. Activities on Salt Spring Island as well as art and crafts attract many visitors each summer. The morning farmers market held on the waterfront every Saturday has become a colourful attraction.

The work of local artists can be seen and bought in the several art shops and galleries in Ganges. Shopping at Mouat's historic store provides opportunity to stock up on the items you need for your boating comfort, safety and convenience.

The many other speciality, souvenir and book stores in the town will provide hours of pleasurable shopping or window shopping. The restaurants are of a variety that will enable you to select from a wide range of menus. Hastings House, rated as one of the finest restaurants in Canada, is located in Ganges.

Gulf Islands

Salt Spring Marina

Lesley Cheeseman
124 Upper Ganges Rd
Salt Spring Island BC V8K 2S2
Ph: 250-537-5810 Fax: 250-537-5809
Toll free 1-800-334-6629
Charts 3313, 3462/3, 3478 VHF 66A
Marina services:
Moorage: About 50 slips and 380' outer dock for guests and Seattle YC. **Power**: 15, 30 amp. Pumpout. Propane nearby.
Customer services:
Showers, washrooms. laundry, coffee, ice, Wifi service. Public pay phone ashore. Marine service. Chandlery, fishing licences and tackle. Haulouts, towing.
Salt Spring car rentals. Shuttle to town.
Entertainment:
Ganges Saturday public market. Art galleries. Scooter, kayak and boat rentals. Walking on island roads, some nearby waterfront and beachfront access. Whale watching.
Adjacent and nearby facilities:
Moby's Marine Pub, Rendezvous Cafe, Harbours End Marine, Gail's Hair Dressing, scuba diving store, historic Hastings House restaurant. Playgrounds. Shopping centre. Post office, banks, churches, groceries, restaurants, hotels, bed and breakfast, liquor store, auto supplies–up town.

Salt Spring Marina, right, is to left in the photo above.
Hastings House restaurant overlooks the anchorage.

Harbours End Marine & Equipment Ltd

Barry Green
email@harboursendmarine.com
www.harboursendmarine.com
122 Upper Ganges Rd
Salt Spring Island BC V8K 2S2
Ph: 250-537-4202 Fax: 250-537-4029
Honda, Mercruiser, Volvo Penta, Yanmar. Haulout to 36'. Shipwright services.

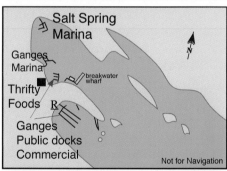

Boat services include temporary stopping if space permits, at the public dock on the south side of the town or for longer periods and overnight at any of the marinas in the harbour. The public docks, Ganges Marina and Salt Spring Marina provide overnight and extended mooring and marina services. For groceries and supplies, Mouat's and Thrifty Foods are nearby and there are restaurants and pubs in close proximity to most of the marinas.

Marylou and Courtenay at the Old Salty shop.

Above: Old Salty is one of the busy stores in downtown Ganges.
Left: The market at Ganges on Saturday mornings. Local merchants and artisans conduct business from their outdoor stalls. There is live music too. Note: Walking in and around town can be pleasant, but caution should be exercised due to seasonal heavy Saturday traffic on some of the roads and limited pedestrian sidewalks. A waterfront boardwalk has been under construction for some years but the sections have not yet been connected due to unavailability of land in one area.
Below: Many restaurants are on the Ganges Harbour waterfront.

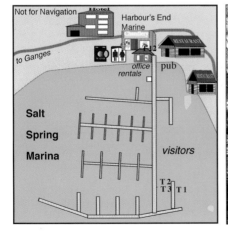

Charts 3313, 3478, 3442, 3462

Ganges Salt Spring Island Public docks
Ph: 250-537-5711   VHF 09
Harbour Authority of Salt Spring Island.

Kanaka dock
Manager–*check in at office in Inner Harbour for stays over two hours* • Two outer fingers and east side of main float for visitors • Garbage • Water • Power: 20 amps • rafting • Adjacent to restaurants and shops. School boats at inner finger.
Ph: 250-537-5711 Fax: 250-537-5353 for all public docks at Ganges.

Breakwater dock .
Breakwater: use inner fingers. • Aircraft Float • Water • Lights • Power: 20 amps • Pumpout station • rafting • **Sabine's** 250-538-0025. **Salt Spring Books** 250-537-2812. **Volume II Books** 250-537-9223. Ambulance/Coast Guard auxiliary adjacent.

Centennial Dock (Inner Harbour–commercial–below)
Ganges Boat Harbour–No guest moorage. Permanent and fishing boats harbour only. *harbour@hassi.ca*
Manager (and office for all public docks). • Float length 326 m • **Launch ramp** • Waste oil disposal • Water • Lights • Power • **Washroom** • **Showers** (serves local public docks–code available with moorage). Books–**Watermark** 250-537-9212.

The outer harbour public docks and the Ganges town waterfront. The dinghy dock is located between the public dock in the foreground and the private dock left.

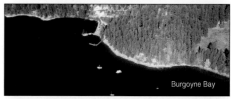

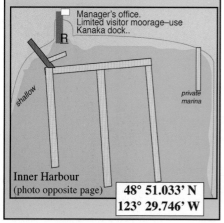

Manager's office. Limited visitor moorage–use Kanaka dock..

shallow

private marina

Inner Harbour
(photo opposite page)

48° 51.033' N
123° 29.746' W

Fernwood
Capital Regional District public dock Across the street from Raven Street Market Café. Float length 12 m • Charts 3313, 3462, 3442

Burgoyne Bay   VHF 09
Salt Spring Island public dock • Manager • Float length 10 m • Charts 3313, 3478. Ph: 250-537-5711–also:

Musgrave Landing, Salt Spring
Island public dock • Float length 12 m • dinghy dock • Charts 3313, 3441/2

48° 51.033' N
123° 29.746' W

Top: The inner harbour commer-
cial Centennial Dock lies behind
the breakwater on the southeast
side of Ganges. The small
marina alongside the breakwater
is private. Right: View of Ganges
Harbour from above the Ganges
Yacht Club at Walter Bay. The
Outer Harbour is at top left.
Ganges Marina and Salt Spring
Marina can be seen beyond Grace
Islet. Bottom: Moored alongside
the public dock at Vesuvius.

Vesuvius Bay public dock

Saltspring Island Harbour Authority
Bart Terwiel
Phone/Fax: 250-537-5711
ssha@saltspring.com
Chart: 3478
Located on the northwest side of Salt Spring Island.
VHF 09
Public dock with limited space. Exposed to westerly winds and ferry wash. When the dock is not occupied this is a good place for a short stop. Rafting at the dock can be expected.
Nearby facilities: BC Ferry to Crofton. Ferry dock is adjacent to the public dock. Small cafe a short walk along the road from the landing. Taxis are available for service into downtown Ganges and to other parts of Salt Spring Island.

Top: Looking north towards Active Pass. Port Washington opens into North Pender Island to the right. Above: Poets Cove at Bedwell Harbour. This is a popular destination with large docks, fuel and supplies as well as a resort complex with many amenities including a restaurant, pool and spa.

Left: The floats at Port Washington will accommodate several small boats but are exposed to washes from ferries and some wind conditions. The general store has served passing vessels since the early 1900s.

Bottom: View of Mount Baker from the Pender Islands.

The Pender Islands

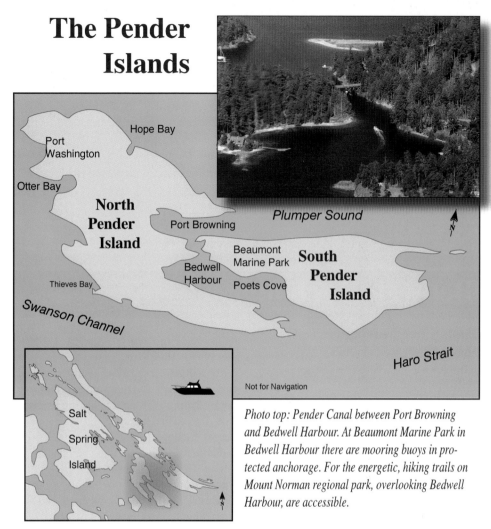

Photo top: *Pender Canal between Port Browning and Bedwell Harbour. At Beaumont Marine Park in Bedwell Harbour there are mooring buoys in protected anchorage. For the energetic, hiking trails on Mount Norman regional park, overlooking Bedwell Harbour, are accessible.*

The Pender Islands are blessed with beautiful, unspoiled and charming features and are centrally located in the Gulf Islands, providing moorage, anchorage and safe stops for all boat operators. One of the main harbours in the Penders is Bedwell Harbour with its resort, marina and adjacent anchorage.

The Pender Canal, separating South from North Pender, is a narrow passage which curves its way under a low bridge that connects the two islands. At high tide boats will clear the bridge if they are no taller than 26 feet.

Otter Bay is another of the Gulf Islands' major ports for recreational boating. It has a fully operational marina with good docks, a restaurant in summer and a store that has local crafts, fine art, clothing, books, some fresh produce, canned goods and frozen foods among other items. The marina office can provide information on local island services such as mechanical, bed and breakfast and ferries schedules. A large lawn is a playing field for children and there are several picnic tables placed along the waterfront. It has two swimming pools, one of which has hours set aside for adult usage. Watch whales swimming by or take in the magnificent sunsets from the marinas flag deck. Remember to take your gear for a game of golf at the nearby course.

Marina: 48° 44.886' N   123° 13.737' W

Bedwell Harbour

Gulf Islands

Poets Cove Marina

Marina Managers:
Jerome Rahaman, Rebecca Chivers
9801 Spalding Rd
South Pender Island BC V0N 2M3
Ph: 250-629-2111 Fax: 250-629-2110
Toll free 866-888-2683   VHF 66A
marina@poetscove.com
www.poetscove.com

Customs service. Clearance by phone for all persons May 1 through Sept 30. CANPASS only Oct. 1 through April 30.

Marina services:
Fuel: Gas and diesel. Lubricants.
Moorage. Large marina with mostly transient moorage–110 slips. **Water** at dock-limited supply. **Power** at docks: 30 amp.
Laundry, showers, washrooms. Tackle shop on dock.

Customer services:
Restaurant. Pub. Breakfast, lunch, dinner. Licensed. Also patio service. Beer and wine store. Swimming pool. ATM. Lodging. Conference center/

ballroom. Fitness centre. Spa, pool & hot tub. Playground. Wifi.
Store: ashore–fresh baked goods, gifts, deli sandwiches. Marina store: at the fuel dock– fishing gear, on line fishing licenses, bait, ice, charts, books.
Tennis racquets available. Bicycle, kayak, canoe & boat rentals. Public pay phone ashore. Garbage disposal. Pet area.

Entertainment:
Live music on weekends during the summer. Tennis courts. Seasonal barbecue.

Adjacent facilities:
Beaumont Marine Park. Camping, hiking. Road access walking or cycling. Nearby hiking trails. Nearby Mt. Norman is accessible by trail. Mooring buoys are available in the harbour.

Opposite page: Poets Cove Marina at Bedwell Harbour–also pictured right and below. Below, right: Pender Canal, the narrow passage between Bedwell Bay and Port Browning, was man made to provide an alternative route between the islands. Clearance at high tide is 26 feet. At low tide the depth of water is seven feet.

**Entrance to harbour:
48° 44.664' N
123° 13.852' W**

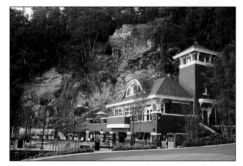

This is one of the main American entrances to Canadian waters in British Columbia. It is a popular port of entry when Customs requires vessels to stop for inspection. June through September sees large numbers of visiting vessels arriving out of the San Juan Islands and Puget Sound.

The facilities at Poets Cove are as comprehensive as you will find anywhere in British Columbian waters.

Water is available at the docks, but not for washing boats due to the relative short supply from its island source. The fuel dock serves gas and diesel and other marine products.

Showers, laundry, a small store, restaurant, snack kiosks, and a marine bar and bistro are poplar among visiting boaters. The dining room has elegant decor and fine cuisine. The elegant accommodations attract visitors by sea and by land.

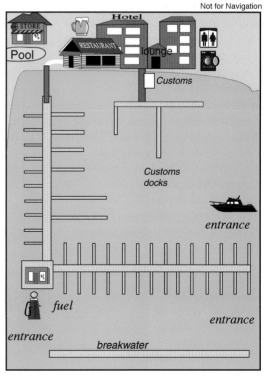

Not for Navigation

Entrance to harbour:
48° 46.191' N
123° 13.963' W

public

Port Browning

Marina:
48° 46.579' N   123° 16.249' W

Port Browning Marina

4605 Oak Rd
PO Box 126, Pender Island BC V0N 2M0
Ph: 250-629-3493 Fax: 250-629-3495
info@portbrowning.com
www.portbrowning.com

Marina services:

Moorage. Large marina with permanent and transient moorage. There is about 3,000 feet of docks space. **Power** at docks: 15, 30 amps.

Laundry, showers, washrooms.

Reservations advised in summertime. Garbage disposal.

Customer services:

Wifi. Store. Pub. Restaurant. Breakfast, lunch, dinner. Licensed. Also patio service.

Cold beer and wine off sales in the pub.

Public pay phone, water taxi, tour company. Shuttle service on summer weekends.

Entertainment:

Swimming pool (use of pool included with moorage), large lawn, camping (by reservation). Golf nearby. Saturday morning early farmers market at nearby shopping plaza and

Charts 3313, 3477, 3441/2   VHF 66A

at the island community centre. Road access walking or cycling. Take care walking the narrow island road. Good beach access.

Nearby facilities:

Shopping centre nearby at town centre–ten minutes walk. Wide range of services, liquor store, bank, post office, art, gifts, dairy products, bakery. Tru Value Foods supermarket. Delivery to marina possible. Pharmacy. Gas station. Book store. Restaurants, B&Bs, accommodations on the island. Check at shopping centre. Small craft launch ramp

Browning Harbour

North Pender Island–public dock
Claude Kennedy Ph: 250-881-2019
www.crd.bc.ca/smallcraft
Capital Regional District. Chart 3313
Float length 120'. Permanent moorage.
4 hours courtesy maximum rafting visitors dock. 15 minute walk to Driftwood Shopping Centre. Marina nearby.

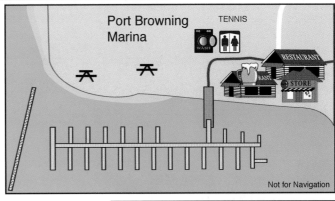

Port Browning
Marina

TENNIS

RESTAURANT

STORE

Not for Navigation

Docks and facilities at Port Browning include pub, restaurant and swimming pool. A large expanse of lawn is used frequently in summer for yacht club or group gatherings and regular weekend camping and barbecues.

located on the beach near the marina. Fishing licenses available from service station at Driftwood Mall.

Grass air strip adjacent to shopping centre. Port Browning is the nearest marina to the North Pender Island shopping centre and supermarket. Visit the well-stocked book store **Talisman Books and Gallery**–phone 250-629-6944.

Customs: Check in at Bedwell Harbour or Port Browning–designated Nexus/Canpass reporting sites.

Caution: Narrow, shallow Pender Canal divides the two Pender Islands. Check chart and tides.

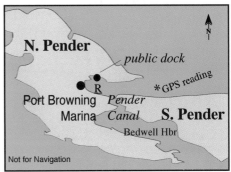

N. Pender

public dock

R

∗GPS reading

Port Browning
Marina

Pender
Canal   **S. Pender**

Bedwell Hbr

Not for Navigation

Right: Port Browning from the east. A boat is moving towards Pender Canal, opening at the left.
Below: The marina view from the restaurant.

Scooter rentals at Otter Bay

Otter Bay

Otter Bay Marina

Jess and Charlene Mansley
2311 Mackinnon Rd
North Pender Island BC V0N 2M1
Ph: 250-629-3579 Fax: 250-629-3589
info@otterbaymarina.ca
www.otterbaymarina.ca

Marina services:

Moorage. Large marina with permanent and transient moorage. Reservations advised in the summertime. **Water** at dock. Use sparingly please. **Power** at docks: 15, 30, 50 amp. **Laundry, showers, washrooms.** Public pay phone ashore. Launch ramp (small craft).

Customer services:

Garbage disposal if necessary. Store–local art and crafts. Restaurant open May long weekend to September long weekend. Coffee and deli. Dairy, fresh vegetables, fresh bread, groceries, gifts, ice, frozen foods, charts, fishing tackle, snacks. Breakfast and lunch available daily in summer. Dinner Friday and Saturday and on long weekends.

Charts 3313, 3441/2 VHF 66A

Entertainment:

Swimming pool. Children's playground and horseshoe pit. Spectacular views from flag deck on the breakwater–eagles, herons, otters and seals. Whale watching. Picnic tables. Road access walking or cycling. Take care walking the narrow island roads. Bicycle and scooter rentals. Theme events once or twice a month

Adjacent facilities:

BC Ferries dock. Picnic tables, barbecue area. Gazebo. Golf course–10 minutes walk. Shuttle service to golf course. Artists' galleries nearby. The Currents, time share homes.

Crew off anchored boats are welcomed ashore–check in with the dock manager. There is a possible fee during busy periods.

Otter Bay Marina is a very popular resort. Weekends in mid summer and on holidays are booked well in advance. For many years Otter Bay operated with minimal dock space and limited service. When Chuck Spence took over running the facility he and his late wife, Kay, set about enlarging the docks, replacing the buildings on shore and adding amenities to make a visit a more enjoyable experience. They achieved this and more with the provision of a swimming pool, coffee bar and store. There is a heated pool, with time for adult use, which is popular among those needing to relax undisturbed while they bathe.

Otter Bay was not always the laid back cruising destination it is today. At one time it flourished as a fishing centre featuring such establishments as cannery, saltery and reduction plant. In 1963 it took on a new life as a marina and by 1972 it had moved to the ownership of Bob and Karen Melville. After nearly 20 years they moved to the BC Interior when David Bromley bought the marina and the Spences took over managing it.

Today the property is managed by Jess and Charlene Mansley. The store building, including restaurant, and the marina have been rebuilt and updated.

There are world class vacation cottages at Otter Bay. The property, Currents at Otter Bay, boasts 31 architect designed fully furnished fractional ownership cottages.

Hazard: When entering keep south of green spar U57.

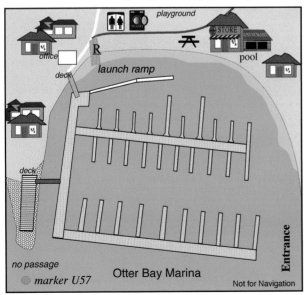

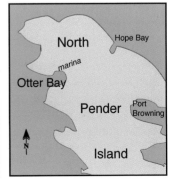

Opposite: Aerial photo of the marina, and inside the store.
Top: A view of the store and pool. Summer months at Otter Bay are busy so it is advisable to make reservations ahead of your planned arrival date.

Hope Bay, restaurant, stores and public docks in Navy Channel.

48° 48.210' N
123° 16.484' W

48° 48.756' N
123° 19.267' W

Above: Port Washington–the dock and store.
Left: Hope Bay–the dock, view from the restaurant.

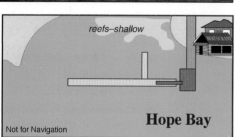

reefs–shallow

RESTAURANT

Not for Navigation

Hope Bay

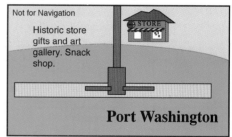

Not for Navigation

Historic store gifts and art gallery. Snack shop.

STORE

Port Washington

Hope Bay

North Pender Island
Wharfinger Peter Binner
Ph: 250-629-9990
Charts 3313, 3477, 3461, 3462, 3441/2
Public dock (CRD) • Float length–150 metres • Lights • Stores, restaurant. Two **mooring buoys** (day use) for Hope Bay customers. No garbage, water, power. Exposed to easterly and southeasterly strong winter winds.

Port Washington

North Pender Island Wharfinger: Rod MacLean Ph: 250-629-6111 (CRD-public dock) *www.crd.bc.ca/smallcraft*
Charts 3313, 3442, 3462
• Two sets of floats: 200'. Permanent moorage. Visitors may raft up. • Aircraft float • Public pay phone ashore • Nearby arts and crafts. No garbage, power or water. Galleries nearby. Taxi on island. This exposed dock is open to ferry wash.

Charts 3313, 3477, 3441, 3462

Sunset from the pub at Saturna Island. Below: The dock at Saturna Point. Bottom: The annual lamb barbecue July 1st each year attracts a lot of boats to Winter Cove on Saturna Island. The anchorage and the dinghy dock quickly fill up as boats arrive.

Saturna Point

Lyall Harbour
Government Dock

Harbour Master Gloria Manzano
102 East Point Rd,
Saturna Island BC V0N 2Y0
Ph/Fax: 250-539-2480
Marina services: Limited space–mostly drop off/pick up. **Fuel:** Gas, diesel, outboard mix, oils. (Ask at the nearby store for service.) Public pay phone. Lighthouse Pub ashore.
Adjacent: BC Ferries. Saturna Point Store–limited groceries, fishing tackle, hardware, licences, ice, bait. Boot Cove Books 250-539-5726. General Store with full groceries, post office and liquor store

one mile up the road. Use caution manoeuvering when ferry operating. Winter Cove anchorage, Boot Cove (poor anchorage).
Entertainment:
Tourism info and Saturna Lodge B&B 250-539-2254. Visit the day dock at Saturna Island Vineyards in summer for wine tasting and stay for lunch. Annual lamb barbecue July 1st at Winter Cove. Island tranquility. Eagles, herons, otters and seals.

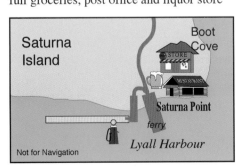

Miner's Bay

Active Pass

Gulf Islands

Galiano Oceanfront Inn and Spa

Conny Nordin
134 Madrona Drive, on Sturdies Bay
Galiano Island BC V0N 1P0
Ph. 250-539-3388 Fax. 250-539-3338
Reservations 1-877-530-3939
www.galianoinn.com   info@galianoinn.com
Moorage:180' dock space. No water, power.
Customer Services: Hotel resort: Award-winning restaurant "eat@galianoinn", licensed lounge, wine and beer store. Summer terrace has wood-fired pizza, draught beer. Spa couples massage, facials, steam rooms, hot tub. Transportation available: Smart Car rental; Resort van service to and from Montague Harbour. Local village walking distance: Galiano Books, grocery store, videos, ice cream, deli, bakery, bicycle rental, art galleries, gift shops.

Miners Bay
Mayne Island

| 48° 51.179' N |
| 123° 18.155' W |

www.crd.bc.ca./smallcraft
Public dock. Wharfinger: Larry Barker
Ph: 250-539-5808 • Two floats: 250'–
Floats are used by transport vessels, emergency vessels, loading & unloading, water taxis, float planes, all marked in yellow.
Marine Services: Active Pass Auto & Marine
Fuel: gas, diesel, propane. **250-539-5411**.
Nearby: Groceries, lodging, restaurant, pub, liquor store. Small craft moorage. No garbage disposal. No water or power on docks. Aircraft float. Taxi service. Book store, crafts stores, churches nearby. Easy walking on island roadways.
Ferry wash causes severe rolling at dock. In Sturdies Bay on the west side of Active Pass brief stops are possible at the small public dock adjacent to the ferry landing.

In Active Pass one has to be mindful of the strong current and tide rips as well as passing ferries. One should exercise caution due to the passage of ferries and slow or stationary vessels are obliged to move aside for them. Common sense calls for such action to avoid collision and to aid the ferries in their tight manoeuvering in the restrictive passage.

*Opposite page:
Galiano Inn dock and
the adjacent Sturdies
Bay ferry landing.
Inset: The fuel and
boat dock at Miner's
Bay are operated by
the community, seven
days a week. The float
is small and is not
suitable for accom-
modating overnight
visitors. The public
dock is subject to
wash from passing
vessels.*

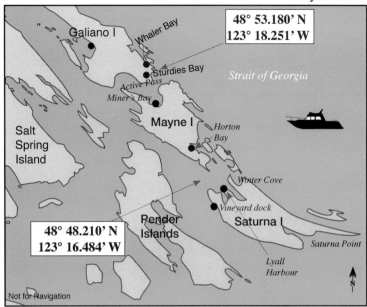

When approaching Miner's Bay for
fuel, simply steer directly towards the fuel
dock. The water shallows off towards the
shore but mooring buoys indicate adequate
water in their vicinity. Watch for the swells
created by passing ferries and other vessels
and wait for them to pass before attempting
to dock at the fuel dock or the public floats
behind the wood piling breakwater.

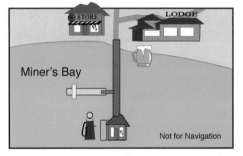

Whaler Bay
48° 53.038' N
123° 19.594' W

Public dock (Small Craft Harbours–red)
Manager Mike Westman 250-217-0910 •
Lights • Power. No facilities.
Limited dock space. Nearby convenience
store. Near ferry dock. Bakery and Deli.
Art and Soul Craft Gallery. Book store.

*Left, top: The ferry terminal and the docks
at Sturdies Bay (a float has been added since
the aerial photo–above, left).*
*Above, right: Whaler Bay with Sturdies Bay
just showing at the top of the picture.*

Montague Harbour

Montague Harbour Marina

Marilyn Breeze
3451 Montague Rd
RR 1 S-17, C-57, Galiano Island BC V0N 1P0
Ph: 250-539-5733 Fax: 250-539-3593
info@montagueharbour.com
www.montagueharbour.com
VHF 66A
Marina services:
Fuel: Gas, diesel, oils. Marine supplies. Open
May through September–guest moorage.
Limited water. Power: 15, 30 amp.
Customer services:
Grocery store, books, charts, clothing and
gifts, fishing supplies. Harbour Grill restau-
rant–licensed family sundeck serving hot
meals all day. No off-sales. Public pay phone.
Seasonal garbage disposal boat.
Adjacent facilities and entertainment:
Marine park at Montague Harbour. Mooring
buoys and dock. Extensive walks and camp
ground, beaches and picnic facilities.
Kayak rentals and tours. Scuba diving good
in Active Pass and nearby reefs. Use charter
services. Golf. Floating bakery in summer.

Public docks on Galiano:

North Galiano

Summer only. Public dock. Small Craft Harbours (red) Ph: 250-539-5420. Joy Wilson.
Charts 3313, 3443, 3463
Float length–12 metres. Public pay phone
ashore. Adjacent the old Spanish Hills Store.

Retreat Cove (photo opposite page)

Galiano Island. Public dock (CRD).
Wharfinger Kiyo Okuda 250-539-5557
www.crd.bc.ca/smallcraft. Charts 3313,
3442, 3463. Moorage 80' rafting dock.
No garbage, power or water.

Montague Harbour

Galiano Island Public dock (CRD)
Wesley Gross Ph: 250-222-0124
www.crd.bc.ca/smallcraft Float length 50
metres. Reserved space for emergency
vessels and float planes. Moorage: Summer
resident boats. Rafting allowed for visitors.

Sturdies Bay

Galiano Island. Public. (CRD) Near shops.
Jean Jones *www.crd.bc.ca/smallcraft*
Ph: 250-539-5053. Moorage 30' Reserved
space for emergency vessels and float planes.

48° 53.465' N
123° 23.545' W

Opposite: Montague Harbour on a quiet day in late summer. Trincomali Channel with Wallace Island lie beyond the harbour. Top and above: Montague Harbour Marina. To the left is the small public dock. The fuel dock is easy to access.

Centre, right: Store and espresso bar overlooking the docks. Patio service at the restaurant. The marina has a well stocked store and a kayak rental office.

Right: Retreat Cove public dock and anchorage on the west side of Galiano Island.

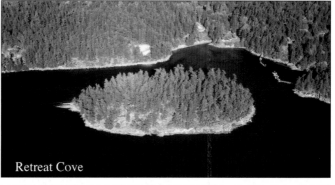

Retreat Cove

Nanaimo

Sidney

Victoria

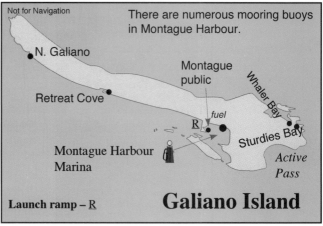

Not for Navigation

There are numerous mooring buoys in Montague Harbour.

N. Galiano

Retreat Cove

Montague public

Whaler Bay

fuel

R

Sturdies Bay

Active Pass

Montague Harbour Marina

Launch ramp – R

Galiano Island

Above: En route up the coast towards Thetis Island and its popular marinas many stop at Princess Bay on Wallace Island. Nearby is Conover Cove where you can stop at the dock and go ashore to hike the easy trails that run the length of the island. Opposite: Telegraph Harbour looking north. It occupies a central location in the Gulf Islands. Preedy Harbour on the west side of Thetis Island offers conditional anchorage.

Gulf Islands

Left: The Cut at low tide. It divides Thetis Island and Kuper Island. It is passable in small to medium size boats at high tide, but care must be taken to follow the narrow channel. It is wise to explore it first in a dinghy.

Bottom: At the dock in Horton Bay, Mayne Island.

Horton Bay

Mayne Island
Small Craft Harbours (red)
Charts 3313, 3477, 3442, 3462
Wharfinger Larry Barker Phone
250-539-5808 • Float length 60
metres • Lights • No garbage, no
power or water.
Moorage: mostly summer permanent boats. Visitors may raft. Be
mindful of the currents and reef at
the entrance to Horton Bay from
the direction of Lyall Harbour.

Thetis Island

There's a waterway in the Gulf Islands that draws boats to the challenge of its shallows. One which lures sailors like the legendary sirens to an ignominious fate of running aground if not onto the rocks, to reach the prize beyond of sheltered anchorage and a fair haven from unexpected squalls and wind. The shallow, narrow passage that separates Thetis Island from Kuper is the eastern entrance to one of the most centrally located and popular anchorages in the Gulf Islands. The canal (known as 'The Cut') lets shallow draft boats through at medium to high tides and denies passage to all but the tiniest of craft at medium tides. It dries at a one foot tide. But despite the quirks and whims of the famous passage, it is the waterway that experienced cruising yachtsmen associate with Telegraph Harbour. Explore the area. Take a dinghy ride through "The Cut" and see the shallows for yourself before taking your boat through. The alternative route into Telegraph is around the south end of Kuper or the north of Thetis. If you are coming from a Vancouver Island base and returning to Vancouver Island after a stay at Telegraph Harbour, the passage is not an issue. But if you are crossing the Strait of Georgia and entering the Gulf Islands through Porlier Pass then the canal is the short way in. Choose a high tide to approach the canal or plan a longer, but pleasant detour around Thetis or Kuper.

Make reservations before arriving at a marina if you are seeking moorage. When you arrive in Telegraph Harbour look for moorage at Thetis Island Marina or at Telegraph Harbour Marina. At the former you may look for the pub, at the latter you will want to moor quickly and head up the dock for one of

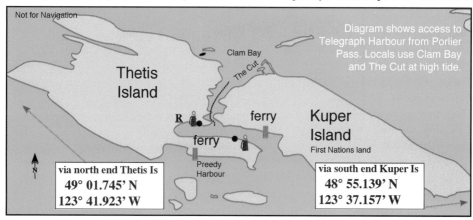

Not for Navigation

Diagram shows access to Telegraph Harbour from Porlier Pass. Locals use Clam Bay and The Cut at high tide.

Clam Bay

The Cut

Thetis Island

R

ferry

ferry

Kuper Island

First Nations land

Preedy Harbour

N

via north end Thetis Is
49° 01.745' N
123° 41.923' W

via south end Kuper Is
48° 55.139' N
123° 37.157' W

Owners of the marina: Tara Kaulback and Ron Faoro

Telegraph Harbour

Telegraph Harbour Marina
Tara Kaulback, Ron Faoro
PO Box 7-10 Thetis Island
BC V0R 2Y0
VHF 66A
Ph: 250-246-9511 Fax: 250-246-2668
Toll free: 1-800-246-6011
sunny@telegraphharbour.com
www.telegraphharbour.com

Marina services:

Moorage. About 2,500' visitor dock space. Guest moorage open Easter to Thanksgiving. Reservations suggested.

Fuel: Gas. Diesel. Oils.

Water. Limited supply–use sparingly.

Power at docks: 15, 30 amp.

Customer services:

Laundry, showers, washrooms for overnight moored guests.

Store with groceries, ice. Dinner specials. Bistro and '50s style soda fountain serves pizza, salads, sandwiches, espresso–Thetis Island Pot of Gold coffee, milkshakes,

48° 58.890' N
123° 40.225' W

Charts 3477, 3313, 3442, 3463

sundaes, ice cream cones, produce, gifts, art and crafts, books, snacks. Catering services available.

Boating groups book events/rendezvous. Playground. Picnic/barbecue facilities ashore. Book ahead in summer.

Nearby:

Road access walking or cycling.

Some nearby parkland and beach trails.

Public pay phones ashore.

Daily float plane service to Thetis Island with float at Thetis Marina.

Fresh roasted coffee available on island.

Entertainment:

Volleyball, shuffleboard, horseshoes.

Short ferry trip to Chemainus shops, restaurants and the town's famous murals.

Adjacent facilities:

Bed & breakfast accommodations nearby.

the delicious old fashioned milkshakes for which the marina store has become famous. Owners at Telegraph Harbour Marina are Ron Faoro and Tara Kaulback, who promise a warm welcome to all mariners.

Across the harbour, Paul Deacon and his staff at Thetis Island Marina, go to great lengths to welcome you and make you feel at home. In fact, so relaxing is the atmosphere at the two marinas at Thetis Island that we have found ourselves cancelling our continuation plans in favour of just staying around longer than planned. And extending a visit is a logical choice considering the advantages of being there. The harbour is very protected from winds and weather and moorage is sometimes available without reservations even in the busy summer period.

Opposite: The Cut and Telegraph Harbour Marina. Above and below: A friendly gathering place.

When rounding Thetis Island the western entrance to Telegraph Harbour is via Preedy Harbour where seals can be seen sometimes sunning themselves on the rocks just off Foster Point. Thetis Island Marina juts out into the main passage and posted signs effectively call on boats entering Telegraph Harbour to slow down. Thetis Island Marina has a pub and serves meals from a more varied menu than that at Telegraph Harbour Marina. The regular clientele at the two marinas can be quite different, naturally, the pub being typically a congregating place for those who enjoy the pub atmosphere. Telegraph Harbour

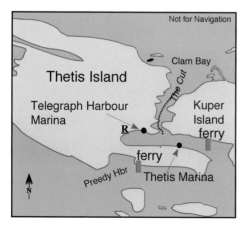

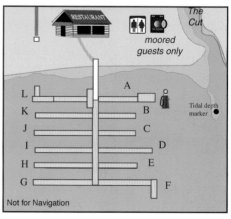

48° 58.661' N
123° 40.135' W

Thetis Island

Charts 3477, 3313, 3442, 3463

Thetis Island Marina and Pub

VHF 66A

Paul Deacon
General Delivery
Thetis Island BC V0R 2Y0
Ph: 250-246-3464 Fax: 250-246-1433
marina@thetisisland.com
Web: www.thetisisland.com

Marina services:

Fuel: Gas, diesel, propane. Some marine supplies, tide tables, ice. Liquor store.

Transient moorage. About 3,000'. Reservations suggested.

Power at docks: 15, 30 amp–multiple outlets.

Water. Limited supply–use sparingly.

Outlet for 18 litre Columbia Ice water jugs.

Laundry, showers, washrooms.

Customer services:

Rental suites. Post Office. ATM. Store–groceries, deli items, clothing, dairy treats, ice cream, bakery products. Frozen foods, gifts, books, snacks, toiletries. Restaurant/pub–meals available inside or on large sunny patio. Boating groups book weekend events/rendezvous. Playground. Swings, two horseshoe pits. Picnic/barbecue facilities ashore. Arrange/book ahead in summer.

Public pay phones ashore and at fuel dock. Daily float plane service. Fresh roasted coffee available on the island.

Entertainment:

Short ferry trip to Chemainus shops and famous murals. Live entertainment in the pub on long weekends through summer months. Major sporting events available on satellite TV.

Adjacent facilities:

A variety of comfortable bed & breakfast accommodations are located nearby. Good scuba diving nearby. Nearby church.

Road access walking or cycling.

Nearby: Island art and crafts, knitted goods.

Right: At Thetis Island Marina. The pub and restaurant are busy year round, with a sundeck that is particularly popular in summer.

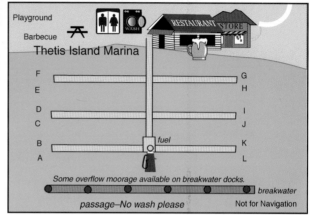

Thetis Island Marina

Playground

Barbecue

RESTAURANT STORE

F   G
E   H
D   I
C   J
B fuel K
A   L

Some overflow moorage available on breakwater docks.

breakwater

passage–No wash please   Not for Navigation

Opposite: Aerial view, fuel dock and patio at Thetis Island Marina. Many clubs hold their annual rendezvous at the marinas in Telegraph Harbour. Above: Comfy accommodations are available at the marina.

is more suitable for families and family activities. Like most of the Gulf Islands water is in short supply on Thetis and boat owners are asked to use only what they need for their fresh water tanks. Garbage is a problem for marinas but they do allow disposal of garbage by moorage customers. The Thetis Island post office and a propane filling station is located at Thetis Island Marina. The convenience stores at both marinas carry some souvenirs, charts and books as well as a selection of items for replenishment of boating supplies. Other than these stores at the two marinas there are no shops or shopping centres on the island. However, Chemainus on Vancouver Island, which is a short ferry ride away, has a selection of stores and restaurants to please everyone. It is worth the ferry ride to stroll around this artistic Vancouver Island centre. The passenger ferry leaves Thetis Island for the run across Stuart Channel eight times a day.

Not far from Telegraph Harbour Marina is a well-known supplier of fresh roasted coffee. *Pot of Gold* is open at most times to sell their rich aromatic beans or freshly ground coffee to islanders and visitors alike. Just stroll up to the entrance of their property and make your purchases at the gate stall and self-service bakery.

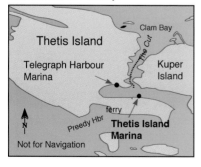

Thetis Island

Clam Bay

The Cut

Telegraph Harbour Marina

Kuper Island

ferry

Preedy Hbr   Thetis Island Marina

N

Not for Navigation

Thetis Island is known for its art and crafts. Crafts on sale on the island represent the works of various islanders and prices are generally more favourable than those for similar items in the cities. Look for their wares and details at the two marinas.

If you enjoy strolling, a walk along any of the Thetis Island roads is relaxing and easy without any significant hills and traffic. Or at low tide you can don your boating boots and go beachcombing along the dry but marshy flats of the canal between the two islands and watch your fellow boat owners trying their luck through The Cut.

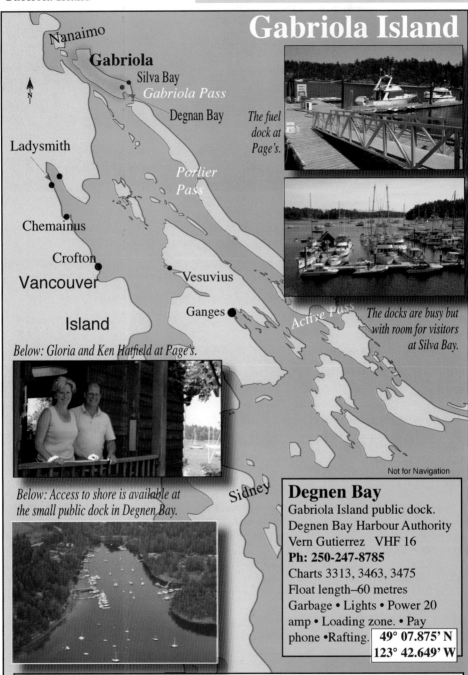

Gabriola Island

Nanaimo

Gabriola

Silva Bay

Gabriola Pass

Degnan Bay

The fuel dock at Page's.

Ladysmith

Porlier Pass

Chemainus

Crofton

Vancouver

Vesuvius

Ganges

Island

Active Pass

The docks are busy but with room for visitors at Silva Bay.

Below: Gloria and Ken Hatfield at Page's.

Sidney

Not for Navigation

Below: Access to shore is available at the small public dock in Degnen Bay.

Degnen Bay

Gabriola Island public dock.
Degnen Bay Harbour Authority
Vern Gutierrez   VHF 16
Ph: 250-247-8785
Charts 3313, 3463, 3475
Float length–60 metres
Garbage • Lights • Power 20
amp • Loading zone. • Pay
phone •Rafting. **49° 07.875' N
123° 42.649' W**

Anchoring in Silva Bay is popular but beware of strong northerlies or north-westerlies that tend to blow into the bay at times causing the need for a watch during the night, when anchors may tend to drag. Page's Marina, which has been around a long time, is known as a fuel stop and offers transient overnight moorage. It has expanded docks and some interesting art and books available at the office.

Gulf Islands

*Commodore Pass
49° 09.080' N
123° 40.962' W

Silva Bay

Page's Marina

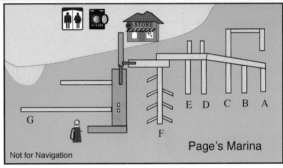

Not for Navigation

Page's Marina

Page's Resort & Marina

Gloria and Ken Hatfield

3350 Coast Rd   **VHF 66A**
Gabriola Island BC   V0R 1X7
Ph: 250-247-8931 Fax: 250-247-8997
Charts 3475, 3310

mail@pagesresort.com
www.pagesresort.com

Marina services:
Fuel: Gas. Diesel. Outboard oil.
Moorage: 300' added for boats to over 65 feet. Reservations suggested. **Water** at dock.
Power: 15 amps. **Showers, laundry, washrooms.** Public pay phone. Garbage disposal. Rental cottages. Campground. Picnic area. Office/store has CHS charts, books (local authors featured), ice etc.

Cottages for rent–one and two bedroom.
Entertainment:
Fishing and dive charters. Kayak, canoe rentals to explore the Flat Top Islands and bicycle rentals for touring Gabriola. Beautiful hikes including Drumbeg Provincial park nearby.
Adjacent facilities: Restaurant. Grocery, liquor and art stores. Sunday Market. Shipyard and mobile boat repair. Taxi service to golf course, shopping and more restaurants.

Top: Page's Marina fuel dock is easy for docking. It is located at the end of the passage south of Sear Island. Watch depths at low tide and use your chart.

*Commodore Pass is one of the entrance passages to Silva Bay. **Pass clear of Ship Rock at entrance.**

The Silva Bay Inn, foreground.
The Resort and Marina (centre)
with the Royal Vancouver YC
station on the opposite side of
the bay. Page's at far right.

Silva Bay

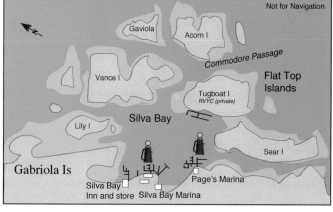

Not for Navigation

Gaviola

Acorn I

Commodore Passage

Vance I

Flat Top
Islands

Tugboat I
RVYC (private)

Lily I

Silva Bay

Sear I

Gabriola Is

Silva Bay
Inn and store

Page's Marina

Silva Bay Marina

Silva Bay Resort and Marina

Jenny Ireland

3383 South Rd   **VHF 66A**
Gabriola BC V0R 1X7
Ph: 250-247-8662 Fax: 250-247-8663
Charts 3475, 3313, 3463, 3443
info@silvabay.com www.silvabay.com
Marina services: Fuel: Gas. Diesel.
Outboard mix. **Power:** 30, amp. **Moorage**.
37 slips–reservations suggested. **Water** at
fuel dock only. Garbage disposal for a fee.
Washrooms, laundry, showers,
Silva Bay Bar and Grill. Liquor store.
Customer services: Tennis courts, Float

plane service. Fishing charters. Sight see-
ing charters. Water taxi. Kayak rentals.
Sunday market.
Adjacent: Silva Bay Shipyard. Ph: 250-
247-9800. 12 ton travel lift, 100 ton ways.
Nearby: Golf, grocery store, inn.

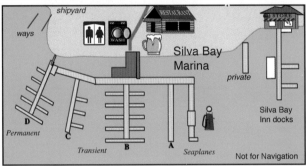

Top: The docks and restaurant at Silva Bay Marina are busy in summer. The fuel dock is to the right.
Opposite, bottom: Silva Bay Inn. It is served by the small dock north of Silva Bay Marina, above right.

Silva Bay Inn
3415 South Rd, Silva Bay
Gabriola BC V0R 1X7
Ph: 250-247-9351 Fax: 250-247-9390
info@silvabayinn.ca www.silvabayinn.ca
Inn has 7 self-contained kitchenette suites.
Marina services:
Dinghy dock at foot of ramp on "A" dock serves customers to **Silva Bay Grocery Store, Silva Bay Inn** and art store.
Moorage: Reservations recommended.

Charts 3475, 3313, 3443, 3463
Primarily used by hotel guests.
Customer services:
Grocery store–meat, cheeses, organic fruits & veggies, ice.
Entertainment:
Fishing charters, sailing charters, kayak rentals can be arranged.
Adjacent facilities:
Nearby restaurant, liquor store, marine mechanic, fuel.

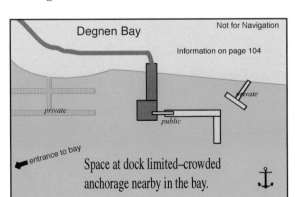

Nanaimo Boat Basin

Nanaimo

Charts 3447, 3458, 3313, 3443, 3463

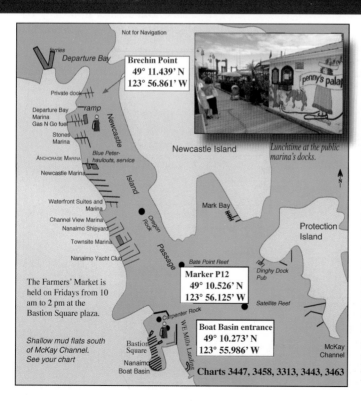

Not for Navigation

ferries
Departure Bay

Brechin Point
49° 11.439' N
123° 56.861' W

Private dock

Departure Bay
Marina
Gas N Go fuel

ramp

Stones
Marina

Blue Peter-
ANCHORAGE MARINA haulouts, service

Newcastle Marina

Newcastle Island

Newcastle

Island

Passage

*Lunchtime at the public
marina's docks.*

Waterfront Suites and
Marina

Channel View Marina
Nanaimo Shipyard

Townsite Marina

Nanaimo Yacht Club

Oregon
Rock

Mark Bay

Protection
Island

N

The Farmers' Market is
held on Fridays from 10
am to 2 pm at the
Bastion Square plaza.

Bate Point Reef

Marker P12
49° 10.526' N
123° 56.125' W

Dinghy Dock
Pub

Satellite Reef

Shallow mud flats south
of McKay Channel.
See your chart

Carpenter Rock

Bastion
Square

Nanaimo
Boat Basin

W.E. Mills Landing

Boat Basin entrance
49° 10.273' N
123° 55.986' W

McKay
Channel

Charts 3447, 3458, 3313, 3443, 3463

Nanaimo
and vicinity

Growth of the city of
Nanaimo continues at
a fast rate. Marinas and
docks are plentiful with
several having been
upgraded substantially
but with little, if any, permanent moorage avail-
able. The waterfront has
undergone a massive
face lift and new restau-
rants and public areas
have evolved. There is
a regular ferry service
between Newcastle Is-
land Marine Park and
Nanaimo and a foot ferry
that serves the famous
Dinghy Dock Pub on
Protection Island.

Nanaimo Boat Basin

Port of Nanaimo Boat Basin

David Mailloux **VHF 67**

10 Wharf St, Nanaimo BC V9R 2X3
Ph: 250-754-5053 Fax: 250-754-4186
W.E. Mills Landing & Marina, formerly Cameron Island Marina **250-755-1216.**
marina@npa.ca   www.npa.ca

Marina services: Fuel, Petro Canada: Gas, diesel, mixed gas, ice. Wi-fi Internet access.

Moorage: Large civic marina with pleasure boat moorage in summer. In winter docks are heavily used by fishermen.

Reservations taken for 600 foot floating breakwater pier for large vessels and adjacent **W.E. Mills Landing Marina Ph: 250-755-1216** seasonal May to Sept. **Power**: 15, 20, 30, 50 and 100 amp. **Laundry, showers, washrooms.** Ice machine. Sani-station pumpout. Hydraulic crane to 1000 lb.

Customer services: Customs/phone 24 hour service. Maps, brochures, dining guide. Road access walking or cycling or vehicle rentals. Downtown Nanaimo at doorstep of marina.

Grocery stores, shops. Regular scheduled float plane service to Vancouver.

Entertainment:

Restaurants, pubs and theatres, arts and crafts exhibits, stores and galleries. Bathtub race every July. Many festive activities.

Adjacent and nearby facilities:

Marine service available. Walkway, plaza and shops. Farmers' Market Fridays 10am to 2pm. Fish and chips and Penny's Palapa Mexican Restaurant on dock. Casino nearby. DVD rentals. For books and charts visit **The Chart Shop** on Church Street Phone: 250-754-2513, **Harbour Chandlery** on Esplanade Street Ph: 250-753-2425 and **Nanaimo Marine Centre** Ph: 250-753-1244. Shipyards, ways, all marine services. Bistro/Pub. Newcastle Island Marine Park–docks, walking trails, camping, picnics, BC Ferries to mainland nearby. Walk on ferries to Newcastle or Protection Islands.

Protection Island: Dinghy Dock Pub–anchor off and go by dinghy to the dock.

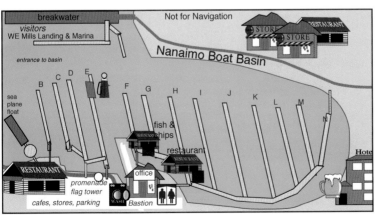

No wake speeds are enforced in the Harbour. Mind the reef and shallows in mid Newcastle Island Passage marked by a piling with a sign indicating correct passage. Avoid the mud flats to the south.

Above: Nanaimo Harbour with the entrance to the visitor docks to the left past the outer breakwater. Below: The Bastion looms over the marina during the annual Nanaimo Boat Show. Bottom: Nanaimo Boat Basin.

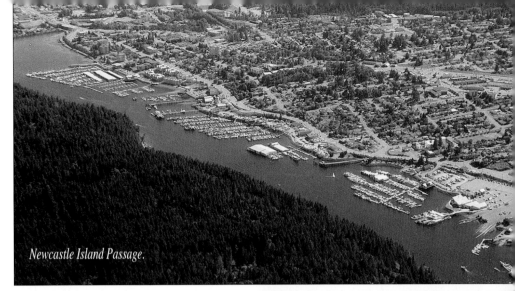

Newcastle Island Passage.

Nanaimo Shipyard Group
1040 Stewart Ave, Nanaimo BC V9S 4C9
Ph: 250-753-1151 Fax: 250-753-2235
rvw@nanaimoshipyard.com
www.nanaimoshipyard.com
Marina services:
Haulouts. Repairs. Vessels to 200 feet. Nanaimo Marine Chandlery Ph: 250-753-1244.

Waterfront Suites & Marina
1000 Stewart Ave
Nanaimo BC V9S 4C9
Ph: 250-753-7111 Fax: 250-753-4333
Toll Free: 1-800-663-2116
mobydicklodge@shaw.ca
www.mobydicklodge.com
Formerly called Moby Dick Oceanfront Lodge and Marina.

Above: The market at Nanaimo on Fridays.

WE Mills Landing and entrance to Boat Basin in downtown Nanaimo.

Petro Canada
Ph: 250-754-7828 Gas, diesel, oil, bait, filters, candy, fishing licences.
Charts at The Chart Shop, nearby up town.

Blue Peter Marine Services
1520 A Stewart Avenue
Nanaimo BC V9S 4E1
Ph: 250-754-7887 Fax: 250-754-7885
Shipyards, haulouts. all marine repairs, refits and service. Near Nanaimo Marine Centre. Near launch ramp and ferries.

Hazard: Enter Nanaimo via south of Protection Island. From the north/Departure Bay watch correct channel when proceeding past Oregon Rock. Use passage on Newcastle Island side, indicated by the sign on the mid-channel marker at Oregon Rock.

Dinghy Dock
Marine Pub & Bistro

8 Pirate's Lane, Protection Island BC
Nanaimo BC V9R 6R1
Ph: 250-753-2373
Charts 3447, 3458, 3313, 3443, 3463
www.dingydockpub.com

Marina Services

Tie up space for family restaurant/pub.
Open year round. No overnight moorage.
Pub restaurant dining, washrooms.
Walking on Protection Island.
There is moorage and anchoring at the

Below: The Dinghy Dock Marine Pub.

Newcastle Island Marine Park nearby.
The ferry between the Nanaimo Boat Basin and Protection Island leaves the docks hourly, from 9:00 am to 11:00 pm.
Ferry information Ph: 250-753-2373

Newcastle Island
Marine Provincial Park

The park dock is a short distance away from the Dinghy Dock Pub or a 10 minute ferry ride from Nanaimo Boat Basin. There are several slips for medium to larger sized boats as well as numerous slips for smaller boats and dinghies. Going ashore at Newcastle Island is a treat, providing lots of treed pathways for hiking, walking or cycling.

An interpretive centre functions in summer for students, groups and others interested in the use of the facilities. There are overnight facilities, including washrooms and a concession and camp store. See *www.env.gov. bc.ca/bcparks/explore/parkpgs/newcastle/* also *www.newcastleisland.ca*

Newcastle Marina
1300 Stewart Ave
Nanaimo BC V9S 4E1
Ph: 250-753-1431 Fax: 250-753-2974
Toll free 1-866-883-2628
newcastle@shaw.ca
Marina services:
Haulouts. Repairs. Welding. Yard. Storage.
Mostly permanent moorage.

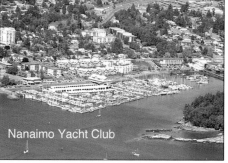

Nanaimo Yacht Club

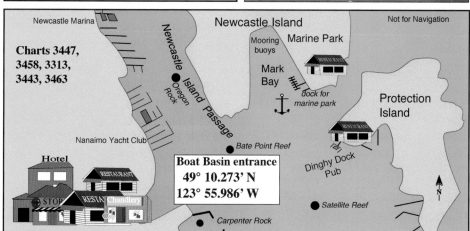

Top: Newcastle Island docks, Mark Bay and Nanaimo beyond. Above, right: Nanaimo Yacht Club and adjacent marinas. Above diagram: Newcastle Island Marine Park and docks, Mark Bay anchorage and marinas that line Newcastle Island Passage. Opposite page: Aerial view of Dinghy Dock pub location on Protection Island.

Nanaimo Golf Club 250-758-6332

Stones Marina

Departure Bay Marina

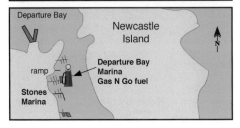

Not for Navigation — Stones Marina

Departure Bay

Newcastle Island

N

ramp

Departure Bay Marina
Gas N Go fuel

Stones Marina

Stones Marina & Boatyard

Carol Stone
1690 Stewart Ave
Nanaimo BC V9S 4E1
Ph: 250-753-4232 Fax 250-753-4204
email@stonesmarina.com
www.stonesmarina.com
Charts 3447, 3458, 3443, 3463
Launch ramp adjacent.
Marina services: Moorage:
Limited guest moorage, by reservation.
Power: 15, 30 amp.

Customer services: Ice. Laundry, showers, washrooms. Public pay phone. Garbage disposal. 83 ton travel lift. Large fenced boatyard. Marine sales.
Entertainment:
Walking: Road access walking or cycling. Road or water access to ferries to Galiano Island, Newcastle and Protection Islands.
Adjacent facilities:
Muddy Waters Pub & Restaurant, Beefeater Restaurant, Miller's Landing Pub.
ATM. Liquor store. Yacht sales. Sailing school. RV park.
Boat repairs: 83 ton travel lift.
Nearby: BC Ferries. Seair float plane service. Skipper's Marine Centre, Nanaimo Shipyard & Chandlery. Screaming Reel.

Departure Bay Marina

Owner Mike Seargant
1840 Stewart Ave, Nanaimo BC V9S 4E6
Ph: 250-741-4444
mike@ msel.ca
Fuel: Departure Bay Gas N Go: gas, diesel, snacks (250-591-0810) on the south side of the launch ramp.
Marina services: Limited guest moorage.
Power: 30, 50 amps. Sani-dump. **Water.**
Ice. **Laundry, showers, washrooms.**
Nearby: Ferry terminal, launch ramp, pubs, restaurant, marine stores, repairs.

Vancouver Area

Section 3

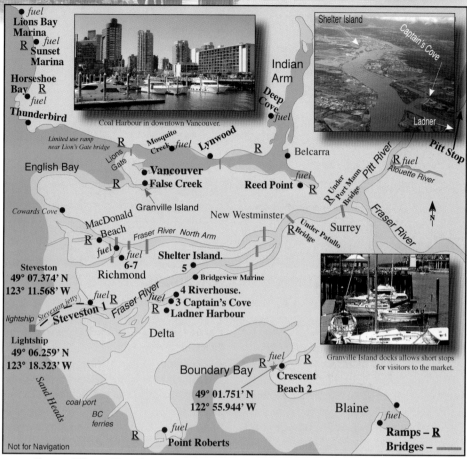

Coal Harbour in downtown Vancouver.

Lions Bay Marina • fuel
R • fuel Sunset Marina
Horseshoe Bay R
• fuel
Thunderbird

Shelter Island
Captain's Cove
Ladner
Pitt Stop

Indian Arm
Deep Cove • fuel

Limited use ramp near Lion's Gate bridge R
Mosquito Creek • fuel Lynwood R
Lions Gate
Belcarra
R fuel Alouette River

English Bay
R • Vancouver
• False Creek
Reed Point • R
fuel
Under Port Mann Bridge
Pitt River

Cowards Cove •
Granville Island
New Westminster
R Under Patullo Bridge
Surrey
Fraser River

MacDonald Beach R
fuel
Fraser River North Arm
• fuel
Steveston
49° 07.374' N
123° 11.568' W
Richmond
• fuel
6-7
Shelter Island.
5 •
• Bridgeview Marine

lightship Steveston jetty
R
Fraser River • fuel
R
Steveston 1
4 Riverhouse.
• 3 Captain's Cove
Ladner Harbour
Delta

Lightship
49° 06.259' N
123° 18.323' W

Boundary Bay
R • fuel R
Crescent Beach 2
49° 01.751' N
122° 55.944' W

Sand Heads
coal port
BC ferries
R • fuel
Point Roberts

Blaine
• fuel

Granville Island docks allows short stops for visitors to the market.

Ramps – R
Bridges –

Not for Navigation

Fraser River: Use charts 3490, 3463 (South Arm) and 3491 (North Arm)

1. Steveston Harbour

Near the mouth of the south arm of the Fraser River. Steveston Harbour Authority **Ph: 604-272-5539 Fax: 604-271-6142** *info@stevestonharbour.com* *www.stevestonharbour.com* Charts 3490, 3463 Float length–200' transient. • Water • Parking • Lights • Waste oil disposal • Garbage • Power: 20, 30 amp • Public pay phone • Washrooms • Public fish sales float • Showers • Adjacent city restaurants, shops, marine stores, chandleries, repair facilities. Auxiliary Coast

Guard. **Chevron Fuel.** Additional public docks (Paramount) for fishing and commercial vessels. 50 ton Travelift. Call for visitor dock space. **Launch ramp.**

Steveston waterfront.

Nico-wynd Golf Course 604-535-9511

Crescent Beach Marina is tucked in behind the railway line, in the curve of Boundary Bay.

2. Crescent Beach Marina

Carol Charles
12555 Crescent Rd
Surrey BC V4A 2V4

49° 03.367' N
123° 53.475' W

Ph: 604-538-9666 Fax: 604-538-7724
info@crescentbeachmarina.com
www.crescentbeachmarina.com
Fuel: Gas, diesel. Chandlery, bait, fishing supplies. 30-ton trailer. Haulout to 50'.
Launch ramp. Washrooms, laundry and showers. Ice.
Guest moorage (phone for reservations).
Power: 15, 30 amp. public pay phones.
Entrance: Follow red right returning markers in channel through Boundary Bay.
Nearby: Restaurants, shops, bakery, golf.

3. Captain's Cove Marina

Manager Grace Bukowsky
6100 Ferry Rd, Ladner BC V4K 3M9
Ph: 604-946-1244 Fax: 604-946-1246
info@captainscovemarina.ca
www.captainscovemarina.ca
Fresh water moorage. Visitors dock. **Water.**
Power: 30 amps. **Fuel:** Gas, diesel, engine and outboard oils.
Showers, laundry, washrooms. Public pay phone. Rusty Anchor Pub. Travelift 60 tons, repairs, service, storage and workyard, power wash, painting. **Launch ramp** adjacent.

Cove Links Golf Course 604-946-1839

Captain's Cove Marina.

Top: Crescent Beach Marina shows the launch ramp to the right between two fingers. The fuel dock is centre foreground. Inset: Crescent Beach Marina is on the Nikomekl River.
Left: View of the docks at Captain's Cove Marina in Ladner on the Fraser River.

Chart 3490

Captain's Cove and River House
entrance off Fraser River.

Captains Cove
49° 06.921' N
123° 04.933' W

4. River House Marina (South Arm)

5825 60th Ave, Ladner BC V4K 3E2
Ph: 604-940-4496 Fax: 604-940-7502
marina@riverhousegroup.com
www.riverhousegroup.com
Manager Walter Greene. Some guest moorage. **Water. Power**: 15, 30 amps. Garbage disposal. River House Restaurant & Marine Pub. Low bridge beyond Captain's Cove Marina. 9'9"– 21'9" tidal clearance.

Docks and restaurant at River House.

Bridgeview Marine (South Arm)
604-946-8566 *www.bridgeviewmarine.com*
Boat storage, haulouts, service and repairs.
Brand name outboards, marine supplies.

Top: Captain's Cove Marina lies at centre top with access off the Fraser River or Ladner Slough. The main arm of the river is at upper left. Above: River House Marina.

Most marinas in the Greater Vancouver area offering moorage for overnight customers are dedicated to providing permanent moorage. Some have many slips during summer when customers' boats are away. Many boat operators in transit from southern ports to places such as the Sunshine Coast and Desolation Sound miss the river in favour of Vancouver's downtown area or False Creek where there are many attractions. In the Fraser River, one can cruise all the way up to Mission or turn off on the Pitt River and enjoy a splendid run into Pitt Lake.

Entering the Fraser River is safe provided you do so when winds are relatively calm and the tide is right. At about maximum low tide with a northwesterly wind you are well advised to wait. Beware of the shallows off the mouth of the river, especially if you do find yourself running into some wind and waves. It is well marked but the shallows actually extend somewhat beyond the markers, especially around the beacon to the south of the lightship.

Stopping at Steveston is a treat if you can find moorage. Call the number posted on the main dock as you arrive. The variety of shops, cafes and restaurants will keep you busy for hours.

Farther up the south arm is Captain's Cove Marina for haulouts, repairs and service as well as some overnight moorage, fuel, ice and a pub, The Rusty Anchor, which serves good meals seven days a week. Beyond Captain's Cove past the low bridge of Highway 99 is the River House Marina with adjacent restaurant and pub.

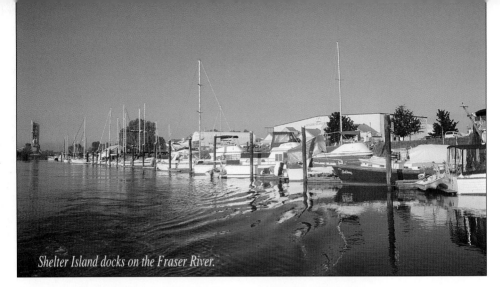
Shelter Island docks on the Fraser River.

5. Shelter Island Marina & Boatyard
120–6911 Graybar Rd (South Arm)
Richmond BC V6W 1H3
Ph: 604-270-6272
Fax: 604-273-6282
Toll Free: 1-877-270-6272
infodesk@shelterislandmarina.com
www.shelterislandmarina.com

Moorage: Fresh water permanent and transient. **Power** 30, 50 amps. **Showers, laundry, washrooms.** Marine hardware and supplies, repairs, service. Two travel lifts to 150 tons–vessels to over 130', 30' beam. Workyard for up to 500 boats. Tugboat Annies Restaurant and pub on the waterfront. Beer and wine store.

6. Delta Marina   Chart 3491
Manager Rick Cockburn
3500 Cessna Dr (Fraser Middle Arm)
Richmond BC V7B 1C7
Ph: 604-273-4211
Fax: 604-273-7531
deltacharters@telus.net
www.deltacharters.com

Fresh water permanent and limited transient moorage–reservations required.
Customs clearance.
Power: 20, 30 amps. Full service shop, 50 ton lift. Free shuttle to Vancouver International Airport. Hotel facilities and services.
Near Richmond city facilities, restaurants and shopping centres.

The village of Ladner is tucked away down Ladner Reach which opens off the south arm of the Fraser River at the entrance to Captain's Cove (where fuel and transient moorage are available). A large public dock at Ladner accommodates visiting mariners when the fishing fleet is away. Phone 604-946-8430 for information. Another good facility with marine pub and restaurant is at Shelter Island a little farther up river. If you need a haulout or a workyard in which to block it up Captain's Cove or Shelter Island Marina can provide the necessary facilities. Marine service is available also at Bridgeview Marine near Shelter Island.

You could cruise to New Westminster and return to the Strait of Georgia by going down the north arm of the Fraser. Part way down you will come to Richmond's marinas just after passing under Knight Street bridge and Oak Street bridge. Fuel is available at Vancouver Marina just beyond the swivel bridge on the Middle Arm or just under the Arthur Laing bridge. Haulouts and repairs are available at Shannon Buoys Ph: 604-231-0599.

Visit the facilities in False Creek or stop right downtown in Vancouver. There is a Customs dock in the harbour on approaches to Coal Harbour Marina.

New Westminster

Above: The waterfront at New Westminster. While there are no facilities for mooring at this Fraser River waterfront city, it affords a spectacular view as you cruise by, perhaps en route to the Pitt River or Mission.
Right: Delta Marina docks opposite Vancouver Marina in the Middle Arm.
Right: Vancouver Marina includes the gas dock, prominently located at the west end of the docks and boathouses.
Opposite: Shelter Island Marina in Richmond.

Delta Marina

Vancouver Marina

Marine Drive Golf Course 604 261-3212
Mayfair Lakes Golf Course 604-276-0505
Green Acres Golf Course 604-273-1121

7. Vancouver Marina (Middle Arm)

Michael Short
200-8211 River Road
Richmond BC V6X 1X8
Chart 3491 VHF 66A
Ph: 604-278-3300 Fax: 604-278-7444
mooring@vancouvermarina.com
www.vancouvermarina.com

Some transient moorage–up to 85' open, to 80' covered. Call to reserve. Check in at fuel dock. Water, power: 15, 20, 30, 50 amps. **Fuel:** gas, diesel, oil, repairs, service, books, snacks. Walking distance to Richmond city facilities, shops and restaurants. Close to airport. **Galleon Marine** boat sales at top of dock. **Adjacent bridge maximum clearance 10 m (33').**

Vancouver waterfront

1. Harbour Cruises Marina

Fred Hercules   **Charts 3311, 3493**
1 North Foot Denman St
Vancouver BC V6G 2W9
Ph: 604-605-6019 Fax: 604-605-6006
fred@harbourcruises.com
www.boatcruises.com
Moorage. **Power:** 15, 20, 30 amp. **Fuel**
(nearby): Gas, diesel, stove oil, engine and
outboard oils. Public pay phone. Chandlery, repairs, service, nearby. Located next
to Stanley Park and charter vessel basin.

2. Bayshore West Marina

Managed by Thunderbird Marina
450 Denman, Vancouver BC V6G 3J1
Ph: 604-689-5331 Fax: 604-689-5332
bayshorewest@thunderbirdmarine.com
www.thunderbirdma-rine.com
Marina Services:
Limited transient
moorage, security.
Power: 30, 50,100
amp. Pumpout. **Fuel**
nearby at fuel barge.
Washroom. Garbage
disposal. Ice. Broad-
band Wifi. Yacht
sales. Next to Westin
Bayshore Resort. Near
Stanley Park. Nearby
laundry, restaurants,
coffee shops and
shopping.

In Coal Harbour the marinas are easy to locate after rounding Brockton Point and passing the fuel barges. Visit downtown Vancouver within easy walking distance of the marinas.

North Vancouver

49° 18.941' N
123° 08.422' W

4

N

Lions
Gate
Bridge

Stanley Park

Brockton Pt.

Fuel

RVYC

Barge

Coal Harbour

Convention Centre

1
2
3

Burrard
Yacht Club

5

Burrard
Inlet

Continue east on
Burrard Inlet to
Indian Arm or
Port Moody–dia-
gram page 125.

*Watch for seaplane
operations in this area
of Coal Harbour*

Vancouver

Not for Navigation

Opposite and right: Views of Coal Harbour. Below: Coal Harbour Marina is to the left and Harbour Cruises and Bayshore West marinas are in the lower right.

Photo: Justin Taylor.

3. Coal Harbour Marina

VHF 66A

Marina administrator Danielle Brown

1525 Coal Harbour Quay
Vancouver BC V6G 3E7
Ph: 604-681-2628 Fax: 604-681-4666
info@coalharbourmarina.com
www.coalharbourmarina.com

Marina Services:

Moorage. Some transient space–reservations recommended. Cable vision.
Washrooms. Power: 30, 50, 100 3 phase

Use charts 3311, 3493, 3494, 3495

amps. **Showers** nearby. Ice, garbage disposal. **Fuel** (nearby): Gas, diesel, stove oil, engine and outboard oils. Pumpout system. Courtesy telephone and internet. Broadband Xpress Wireless Internet available. Coffee shop, convenience store.
Nearby: Stanley Park, **Wright Mariner Supplies** (chandlery), city centre with all amenities, hospital, restaurants, shops. Promenade. Easy walking to downtown Vancouver. Nearby medical services.

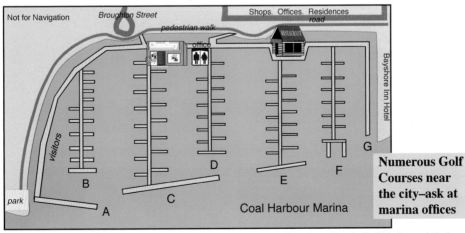

Numerous Golf Courses near the city–ask at marina offices

Diagram above: The basin at Coal Harbour Marina. To its right (not shown) are Thunderbird Marina and Harbour Cruises Marina. The Royal Vancouver Yacht Club is across the waterway.

Coal Harbour.

Stanley Park Pitch & Putt 604-681-8847

4. Thunderbird Marina

Manager Fred McDonald
5776 Marine Dr. West Vancouver BC V7W 2S2
Ph: 604-921-7434 Fax: 604-921-7486
Limited moorage. **Power** 15, 30 amp.
Marine store, tackle, bait, fishing licences.
Repairs, service. 25 ton travel lift to 50
feet. Workyard, storage.
Fuel at Sewells Marina, Horseshoe Bay
Ph: 604-921-3474. Gas, diesel, engine and
outboard oils.

5. Mosquito Creek Marina

Donny Mekilok
415 W Esplanade Ave
North Vancouver BC V7M 1A6
Ph: 604-987-4113 Fax: 604-987-6852
info@mosquitocreekmarina.com
www.mosquitocreekmarina.com
Limited moorage. **Power**: 15 amp.
Fuel: Gas, diesel, oils. **Washrooms, showers, laundry.** Marine supplies, repairs,
service. Crane. 55 ton travel lift. Cafe.
Near North Vancouver restaurants, shops.

6. Lynnwood Marina

1681 Columbia St
North Vancouver BC V7J 1A5
Ph: 604-985-1533 Fax: 604-985-8892
Visitor dock for restaurant only. Perma-
nent moorage marina. Work yard with 60
ton travel lift to boats 75'. Repairs. Mast
rigging. Wood and f/g repairs. Painting.
Open six days a week. Marisol Marine
chandlery. Covered storage. **Washrooms**.
Chandlery, repairs, painting. Covered stor-
age, work yard: service–six days a week.
Hazard: strong currents at times.

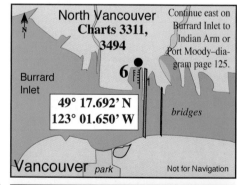

North Vancouver
**Charts 3311,
3494**

N

Burrard
Inlet

6

Continue east on
Burrard Inlet to
Indian Arm or
Port Moody–dia-
gram page 125.

**49° 17.692' N
123° 01.650' W**

bridges

Vancouver *park*

Not for Navigation

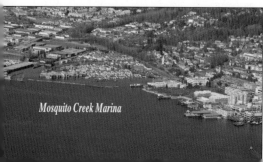

Mosquito Creek Marina

Lynnwood Marina

Granville Island

entrance to False Creek

Maritime Museum

False Creek

welcome@fcyc.com
blueways@Vancouver.ca

Call the Welcome Centre for Transient Moorage on VHF 66A, or phone 604- 648-2628. Also permits to anchor–for up to 14 days in summer, 21 days in winter.

1. Cooper Boating

Ph: 604-690-2628 Fax: 604-687-3267
marla@cooperboating.com
www.cooperboating.com
Limited moorage–reservations required. **Power, showers.** Located near the Granville Island Market and restaurants.

2. Blue Pacific Yacht Charters

1519 Foreshore Walk, Granville Is
Vancouver BC V6H 3X3 Ph: 604-682-2161
www.bluepacificcharters.ca
Limited moorage. Reservations required.

3. Fishermen's Wharf   VHF 66A

False Creek Harbour Authority
False Creek, 1505 W 1st Ave
Vancouver BC V6J 1E8. Ph: 604-733-3625
fchaf@telus.net   www.falsecreek.com
Moorage–reservations recommended, Power: 20, 30 amp. Showers, laundry. Ice, garbage disposal. Cafe–fish and chips.

4. False Creek Yacht Club

1661 Granville St, Vancouver BC V6Z 1N3
Ph: 604-682-3292 Fax: 604-682-3614
fcyc@fcyc.com   www.fcyc.com
Water, power, showers. Pumpout.

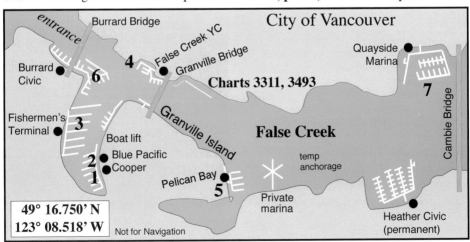

City of Vancouver

entrance

Burrard Bridge

False Creek YC

Granville Bridge

Quayside Marina

Burrard Civic

Charts 3311, 3493

Cambie Bridge

Fishermen's Terminal

Boat lift

Granville Island

False Creek

Blue Pacific

Cooper

Pelican Bay

temp anchorage

Private marina

Heather Civic (permanent)

49° 16.750' N
123° 08.518' W

Not for Navigation

From east of Cambie Bridge looking Southwest.

Quayside

5. Pelican Bay Marina

1708 W 6th Ave, Vancouver BC V6J 5E8
Ph: 604-729-1442 Fax: 604-683-3444
Pelican.bay.marina.van@gmail.com
www.globalairphotos.com/pelican_bay_marina
Visitor Moorage. Power: 30, 50 amps.
Washrooms. Water.
Wifi. Phone, cable hookups. Ice.
Located at Granville Island Hotel, near
Granville Island Market, theatres, restaurants
and shopping.

6. Burrard Bridge Civic Marina

1655 Whyte Ave, Vancouver BC V6J 1A9
Ph: 604-733-5833 Fax: 604-733-9413
burrard.marina@vancouver.ca
www.vancouverparks.ca
Limited moorage, phone for reservations.
Pumpout, power: 15 amp. Washrooms, laundry,
garbage. Located near Granville Island.

7. Quayside Marina (pronounce 'Keyside')

Dockmaster Dave Bird
1088 Marinaside Cres Vancouver BC V6Z 3C4
Phone: 604-681-9115 Fax: 604-681-1932
qsmarina@ranchogroup.com www.quaysidemarina.CA
Guest moorage–reservations recommended.
Power: 30, 50, 100 2 phase amps. Space for
large yachts. Located on False Creek north side.

Indian Arm

Deep Cove North Shore Marina & Rentals Ltd

2890 Panorama Dr
North Vancouver BC V7G 1V6
www.deepcovemarina.com
Ph: 604-929-1251 Fax: 604-929-7862
Moorage: call ahead, **water, power**: 15, 20,
30 amp. **Fuel**: Gas, diesel. **Washrooms.**
Pumpout. Chandlery, mobile repairs, service. Ice, snacks, bait, fishing supplies. Boat
rentals, certified marine technician on site
and mobile. Walking distance to Deep Cove
village, restaurants, stores.

Indian Arm

Deep Cove

Belcarra Park

Cates Park

Belcarra Park

Phone: 604-520-6442 Parks Board park
and public dock. Seasonal concession
stand. Washrooms. Water. Picnic shelter.
Launch ramp at Cates Park.

Vancouver Area

Charts 3495, 3311
Deep Cove Marina

49° 19.701' N
122° 56.128' W

Above: The Deep Cove North Shore Marina is located at the north side of Deep Cove. It has a fuel dock and snacks. Nearby, in the cove, is the Deep Cove public dock (photo right) which allows convenient metered stops and excursions into the nearby village.

Deep Cove
public dock

Deep Cove Public dock

Diane and Roy Alton-Kaighin
Ph: 604-990-3800 Dock for day use only.
Float length 44 m. Boats to 36'–pay at meter. Village–Restaurants, groceries, stores.
Adjacent: Deep Cove Yacht Club.

Deep Cove public dock and Yacht Club   Not for Navigation   **R = ramp**

Charts 3311, 3495

N

Deep Cove
Marina
fuel

Twin Islets
park and dinghy dock

Deep
Cove

Bedwell Bay

North Vancouver
Mosquito Creek
R
fuel
Lynnwood

Cates
Park

Indian Arm

Stanley
Park
fuel

Burrard Inlet

R

Belcarra

R
fuel
Vancouver city

Reed Point
fuel
R

R
fuel
False Creek
Granville
Island
Pelican Bay
Heather Civic

Port Moody

Boat lift on Granville Island

125

49° 17.562' N
122° 53.307' W

Charts 3311, 3494/5

Reed Point

Reed Point Marina

Dave Harris
850 Barnet Hwy
Port Moody BC V3H 1V6
Ph: 604-937-1600   Fax: 604-937-1607
office@reedpoint.com
www.reedpoint.com
Marina services:
Fuel barge: Gas, diesel. Ph 604-937-1606.
Moorage: Short and long term for boats of all sizes. **Washrooms. Power:** 20, 30 amps.
38 ton travelift, dry storage and major workyard. Full mechanical, fibreglass, woodwork and canvas work. Restaurant. Ample parking, full time security. Public pay phone. New and used boat sales. Chandlery, marine supplies, service, repairs.

Views of Reed Point Marina (top) and the fuel dock just inside the centrally located entrance (bottom). This is a major repair and service centre. Vessels launching at Rocky Point in Port Moody (above) can fuel up at nearby Reed Point Marina.

For close up diagram of Burrard Inlet, Indian Arm and Reed Point Marina please refer to the previous page.

Reed Point Marina

Howe Sound

Sewell's Marina

Horseshoe Bay

Horseshoe Bay	49° 22.635' N 123° 16.364' W

West Vancouver
Public dock adjacent to Sewell's Ocean Adventure Centre. • Manager • Lights • Float length 64 m, south of pier, day use 2-3 hours. Adjacent restaurants, shops, ferries to Vancouver Island and the Sunshine Coast via Langdale/Gibsons.

Sewell's Ocean Adventure Centre

6409 Bay St
West Vancouver BC V7W 3H5
Ph: 604-921-3474 Fax: 604-921-7027
info@sewellsmarina.com
www.sewellsmarina.com

Marina Services
Moorage–limited space. Reserve.
Fuel: Gas, diesel, stove oil, engine and outboard oils.
Power: 15, 30 amp.
Washrooms. Public phones, launch ramp. Fishing charters, licences, bait, tackle, rentals. Restaurants, Horseshoe Bay village, **The Boat Centre** marine store adjacent–propane, boat sales, marine repairs, service. Adjacent to the ferry terminal.

Howe Sound is one of the most active playgrounds for summer boating. It is the nearest relatively sheltered cruising area to Vancouver and a popular stop for vessels en route south/north. Several large marinas offer sheltered guest moorage and some smaller docks can accommodate boats for short durations while visiting local places of interest.

Charts 3534, 3311, 3526, 3512

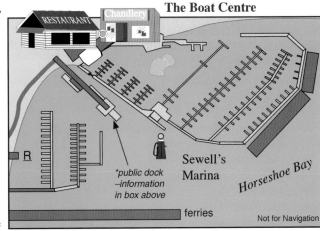

The Boat Centre
RESTAURANT
Chandlery
R
*public dock –information in box above
Sewell's Marina
Horseshoe Bay
ferries
Not for Navigation

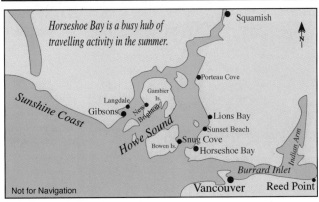

Horseshoe Bay is a busy hub of travelling activity in the summer.

Squamish
Porteau Cove
Sunshine Coast
Langdale
Gibsons
New Brighton
Gambier Is.
Lions Bay
Sunset Beach
Snug Cove
Howe Sound
Bowen Is.
Horseshoe Bay
Indian Arm
Burrard Inlet
Vancouver
Reed Point
Not for Navigation

Howe Sound

Snug Cove

Not for Navigation

Howe Sound

Gambier I

Bowen I

Union Steamship Co. Marina

VHF 66A

Rondy and Dorothy Dike

PO Box 250 431 Trunk Rd
Bowen Island BC V0N 1G0
Ph: 604-947-0707 Fax: 604-947-0708
Charts 3534, 3311, 3526, 3512
ussc@shaw.ca
www.steamship-marina.bc.ca
Hazard: Shallows near beach beyond marina docks. Watch for ferry operations.
Marina services:
Moorage: Many slips. Maximum to 200 feet. Reservations suggested. **Power** at docks: 30, 50 amp. **Laundry.**
Showers, washrooms.

49° 22.834' N
123° 19.501' W

Customer services:
Chandlery–boating supplies, gifts, novelties, charts, snacks. Free wifi and TV. Boaters' lounge. Garbage disposal. Nearby fresh produce, frozen foods, pharmacy, liquor, tackle, bait, hardware, ice and most supplies–at marina or in village. Also restaurants, pubs, art shops, bistro, bakery, health food, gift and specialty stores. ATM, Post office, medical services nearby.
Entertainment.
Annual summer events include live entertainment, (pub Saturday nights), Bowen Island parade and festival (Saturday prior to Labour Day). Dog Days of Summer (Second Sunday in August). Walking roads and trails on island. Crippen Regional Park has many trails and walks. including 600 acres surrounding Snug Cove and marina. Golf. Farmers market.
Adjacent facilities:
BC Ferries to Horseshoe Bay. Crippen Regional Park. Picnic ashore. Walking trails. Killarney Lake in Crippen Park area. Anchorage in Mannion Bay (temporary).

Opposite: Snug Cove's Union Steamship Marina. The public dock acts as a breakwater with the ferry landing and a small private marina in front. Mannion Bay is to the north of Snug Cove. Opposite bottom: Inside the store at the marina.

Right: The Union Steamship Marina at Snug Cove is a busy place. Every summer, boats converge on this popular destination from all parts of the coast. The restaurants, bakery, farmers market, gift shops and specialty stores give this quaint village its particular charm.

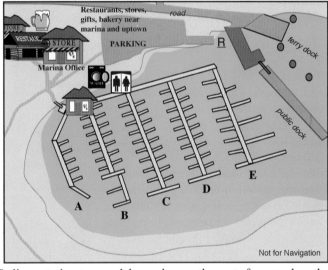

The village

One of the busiest boating centres on the coast, Snug Cove is a high profile marina and boating haven. It is a multi-slip dock facility with over 170 slips catering to boats up to 200 feet in length. The public dock that serves as a breakwater will dock about ten more boats depending on size. The ferry from Horseshoe Bay lands right alongside the public dock. Its wake and turmoil from the substantial propellers causes a stream that washes against boats moored to the dock, so caution should be exercised when coming or going. When tying up, be sure to secure your boat adequately before leaving it for a walk up to the stores or the regional park and lake nearby.

The walk through the park is an easy one with well worn pathways, as is the stroll up to Killarney Lake. Hiking around the lake is also not too taxing, unless you choose to do so in the middle of summer. Lots of shade helps reduce the discomfort in summertime and the cooler weather out of season does the same. Follow the trail up through the park, along the paved road a short distance to the right and then pick it up again for the stroll to the lake.

The village at the ferry landing is simply known as Snug Cove. There are several gift, handicraft and souvenir stores as well as cafes and refreshment establishments for dining or light meals and coffee shops for beverages, cappuccino and latte.

A bakery nearby serves coffee to go along with any of the freshly baked bread and pastries available. There is a restaurant at the top of the main road, serving a variety of meals.

Other restaurants near the main Union Steamship landing boardwalk offer a wide selection of fine dining and pub fare.

Union Steamship Marina

Bowen Island Marina docks

Snug Cove public dock

ferry

Bowen Island Marina

Mannion Bay

Left: Union Steamship Marina occupies most of Snug Cove. Bowen Island Marina, left of centre, has restricted overnight moorage and facilities but the shore attractions include crafts and gift shop, bicycle rentals and a kayak shop–accessible from the roadway.

Charts 3534, 3311.

Howe Sound

49° 27.257' N   123° 14.476' W

Lions Bay Marina

Ken Wolder

60 Lions Bay Ave, Lions Bay
West Vancouver BC V0N 2E0
lionsbaymarina@telus.net
www.lionsbaymarina.com
Ph: 604-921-7510 Fax: 604-921-0782
Charts 3311, 3526, 3512
Guest moorage, water, power: 20 amps.
Fuel: gas, diesel, engine and outboard oils.
Washrooms. Garbage disposal. Public phone.
Launch ramp, store–marine supplies. Haul out. Ice, snacks, bait. Recycling.

Sunset Marina

49° 24.312' N
123° 14.821' W

Sue Rauter
34 Sunset Beach
West Vancouver BC V7W 2T7
Ph: 604-921-7476 Fax: 604-921-7477
sunset marina@shawlink.ca
Charts 3311, 3526, 3512
Visitors–call ahead. Open Feb 15 to Nov 15.
Wet and dry moorage, power at gas dock.
Launch ramp, marine store. Fuel: Gas, engine and outboard oils. Tackle, fishing licences. Washrooms. Repairs, service, power wash. Bait, ice. Snack bar. Parking.

Caulfeild Cove

West Vancouver Public dock
Charts   3311, 3526, 3463
Float length 12 m • Lights •
see number 10 on map

Bowen Island Marina

Norma and Dennis Dallas
Bowen Island BC V0N 1G0
Ph/Fax: 604-947-9710 Cell: 604-880-2282
norma@bowen-island.com
www.bowen-island.com
Marina located to starboard approaching Snug Cove ferry landing, public dock and Union Steamship Marina. Limited moorage–reservations required. Tackle and bait shop. Ice cream, tacos. Gift shop, kayak, bicycle rentals. Nearby hiking trails, shops, liquor outlet, grocery store, B&Bs, beach. Musicians. *Hazard: Ferry dock alongside.*

Snug Cove publilc dock

Above: The public dock at Snug Cove forms a breakwater to Union Steamship Marina. Tie up on a first come basis. Rafting allowed.

Not for Navigation

Howe Sound

Squamish

Porteau Cove

Gambier Island

New Brighton

Helkett Bay

Sunset Marina

Lions

R

R

Plumper Cove

R

Snug Cove

Lions Bay Marina

Gibsons

Bowen Island

Horseshoe Bay

Caulfeild Cove

130

For more information on marine parks see **Anchorages and Marine Parks.**

Top: Looking north up Queen Charlotte Channel. Horseshoe Bay is in the foreground and Squamish is up the channel to the right, beyond Lions Bay.
Right: A warm summer day at the marine park docks in Plumper Cove on Keats Island. Above: The Plumper Cove docks and anchorage.

Plumper Cove marine park

rock

Parks in Howe Sound

Halkett Bay
Fair weather anchorage (some wind conditions).
Dinghy dock.
Camping sites, toilets, hiking.

Porteau Cove
Temporary moorage.
Buoys mark location of artificial reefs.
camping/picnic sites, water, toilets, beach, scuba diving (wrecks as artificial reefs).

Plumper Cove anchorage provides shelter from most conditions but occasional westerly winds blow in, causing some discomfort when anchored in the cove or tied to mooring buoys. Best use docks if space available.

Plumper Cove
This is a popular all weather anchorage (some unsettling wind conditions do occur).
Mooring buoys. **Boat docks,**
camping/picnic sites, water, toilets, beach.
Hiking. Fishing nearby at The Cut.

131

Howe Sound Public Docks

1. Squamish public dock
Ph: 604-815-8035
Charts 3311, 3534, 3526, 3512
Manager • Float length 118 m • Garbage • Water • Lights • Power 20 amp • Public phone ashore • Near city restaurants, shops, churches, service and facilities. Adjacent yacht club offers some transient moorage. Launch ramp. Pumpout.

2. Hopkins Landing public dock
Charts 3311, 3526, 3512
Manager • Float length 17 metres • Lights on the dock.

Above: Gibsons Landing to the left. The marine park at Plumper Cove includes the docks in the nook on Keats Island opposite Gibsons Landing.

3. Keats Island public dock
Charts 3311, 3526, 3512 Manager • Float length 15 m Water • Lights •

4. New Brighton Thornborough Bay Gambier Island public dock
Charts 3311, 3526, 3512
Float length 120 m • Lights • Public pay phone • Walking–island roads.
Nearby store. Ferry service to Langdale/ Gibsons Landing.

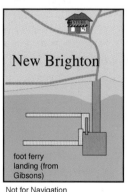

New Brighton

foot ferry landing (from Gibsons)

Not for Navigation

Gambier Harbour

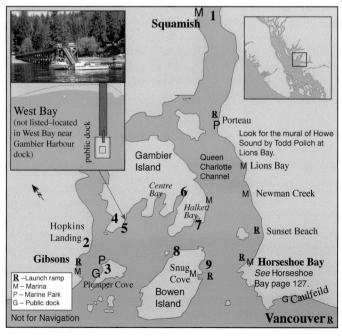

M 1 Squamish

West Bay (not listed–located in West Bay near Gambier Harbour dock)

public dock

Gambier Island

Queen Charlotte Channel

R Porteau
P

Look for the mural of Howe Sound by Todd Polich at Lions Bay.

M Lions Bay

Centre Bay 6
Halkett Bay 7
M

M Newman Creek

Hopkins Landing 2
4
5

R Sunset Beach

Gibsons R
M
P
G 3
Plumper Cove

8
Snug Cove M
R

Bowen Island

9 R

R M Horseshoe Bay
See Horseshoe Bay page 127.
G Caulfeild

R –Launch ramp
M – Marina
P – Marine Park
G – Public dock

Not for Navigation

Vancouver R

Sunshine Coast Golf and Country Club 604-885-9212

Above: The dock at New Brighton in Thornborough Bay. on the west side of Gambier Island.

5. Gambier Harbour

Gambier Island
public dock
Charts 3311, 3526, 3512
Float length 30 m
Lights • Showers.

6. Port Graves

Gambier Island
public dock
Charts 3310, 3512, 3526
Manager • Float length 10 m

7. Halkett Bay

Gambier Island
public dock
Charts 3311, 3526, 3512
Float length 17 m
Adjacent marine park.

8. Mount Gardner Park

Bowen Island
public dock
Charts 3311, 3526,
3512. Float length 17 m

9. Snug Cove

Bowen Island
public dock
Charts 3534, 3311,
3481, 3512, 3526
Manager •
Float length 105 m
Garbage • Lights • Power • Public pay phone ashore •
Washrooms ashore • Adjacent Union Steamship Marina.
Near village arts and gifts, bakeries, restaurants, shops.
All services. Ferry to Horseshoe Bay.

Above: Waterfront pub at Gibsons. Bottom: There are busy permanent and transient facilities behind the breakwater at Gibsons.

Gibsons Landing Harbour Authority

PO Box 527, Gibsons BC   V0N 1V0
Ph: 604-886-8017 Fax: 604-886-1347
glha@telus.net   Bill Oakford   **VHF 66A**
Fee for brief stops at marina. Overnight as space
permits. Pumpout. Washrooms, showers, laundry.
Rafting allowed • Garbage drop. Power: 15, 30 amps
• Nearby restaurants, shops. *Launch ramp and good
overnight moorage at Gibsons Marina, next page.*

49° 23.963' N
123° 30.213' W

Gibsons Marina at left. Public docks to the right.

Gibsons Landing

Howe Sound

Gibsons Marina   VHF 66A

Art McGinnis
675 Prowse Road, PO Box 1520
Gibsons BC V0N 1V0
Ph/Fax: 604-886-8686
Charts 3534, 3311, 3526, 3512
Marina services:
400 permanent and transient berths.
Reservations suggested for visiting boats.
Dock A – main visitor dock.
Portable pumpout. Garbage disposal.
Power at docks: 15 amp at all slips.
Launch ramp.
Customer services:
Laundry, showers, washrooms.
Marine supplies at chandlery/marina office.
Fishing gear, licences, charts, bait,
ice, accessories, books, binoculars.
Nearby churches multi-denominational.
Post Office. Walk to stores in village, also
pharmacy and other necessities.
Scuba diving at Sechelt up the Sunshine
Coast. Ask for information.

Not for Navigation

N

Howe

Gibsons

Gambier
Island

Sound

Bowen
Island

Horseshoe Bay

Vancouver

Walking: Road access walking or cycling.
Waterfront walk, partial around bay. Walk,
cab or bus up to main shopping centre.
*Bus service between Langdale ferry, Gibsons
and Sechelt.*
Entertainment.
Fishing at The Cut a short run from the
marina. Museum, local stores. Art galleries.
Book store (**Coast Books**).
Adjacent facilities:
Fuel: Gas, diesel, oils. Service. **Hyak Ma-**
rine fuel dock Ph: 604-886-9011. Marine
repairs available–mechanic on call. Banks,
ATM, gifts, arts and crafts, snacks. Vehicle
rentals.

Top and inset: The public docks at Gibsons Landing. Above: The store at Gibsons Marina and a view from the gazebo on the outer breakwater. Opposite: Gibsons Marina behind the long breakwater.

Gibsons to Squamish

The town of Gibsons is a busy community of residents, transient ferry travellers, business people and boat operators docking their craft at Gibsons Marina. This large facility is one of the biggest of its kind in local coastal waters. At the marina and nearby can be found most services required by mariners, from the chandlery at the head of the dock to nearby stores and restaurants. In the waterfront village of Gibsons Landing there are stores, restaurants, a pub, post office, museum and convenience stores. Craft and art stores have become a major attraction.

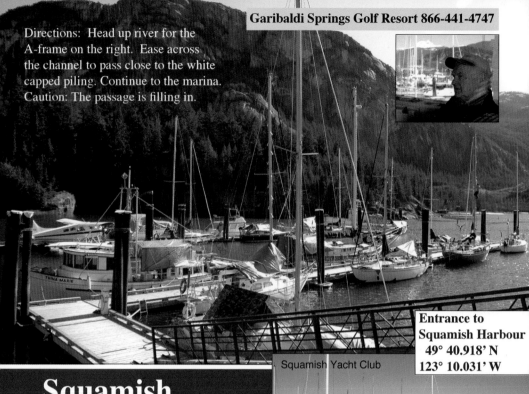

Directions: Head up river for the A-frame on the right. Ease across the channel to pass close to the white capped piling. Continue to the marina. Caution: The passage is filling in.

Entrance to
Squamish Harbour
49° 40.918' N
123° 10.031' W

Squamish Yacht Club

Squamish

Howe Sound

Squamish Harbour Authority
Bill McEnery – See also page 132
PO Box 97, Squamish BC V8B 0A1
Ph: 604-815-8035
Use the float at the foot of the red ramp. Check also for moorage at the yacht club.

Squamish Yacht Club
Les Smith
37116 Loggers Lane, PO Box 1681, Squamish BC V0N 3G0
Phone 604-892-3942   604-898-4101.
commodore@squamishyachtclub.com
Mostly reciprocal moorage, but some available when members are out. Up to 50'.
Moorage. Power 15 amps. **Water. Washrooms. Showers**. Launch ramp. Club house. Visitors are welcome to join in club events.
Nearby: Howe Sound Brewing Company. Short walk to uptown Squamish–shops.

Top and right: From the wharf at Squamish. The public dock and the Yacht Club, to the north of it. Inset, top: Wharfinger Bill McEnery has a good view from his office.

From Gibsons to Squamish takes you either up the eastern shore of Howe Sound, where you can see numerous waterfront homes and small settlements, or up the western side with its islands and passages. One of the major landmarks on the steep-sloped eastern shore is Britannia Beach with its hillside mining museum. The dock there, unfortunately, is inadequate for access ashore other than by dinghy.

The passage up the western shore passes from Gibsons via New Brighton on Gambier, privately owned club facilities of Thunderbird Yacht Club and Burrard Yacht Club at Ekins Point, and McNab Creek on the opposite shore.

Sunshine Coast
Howe Sound to Desolation Sound

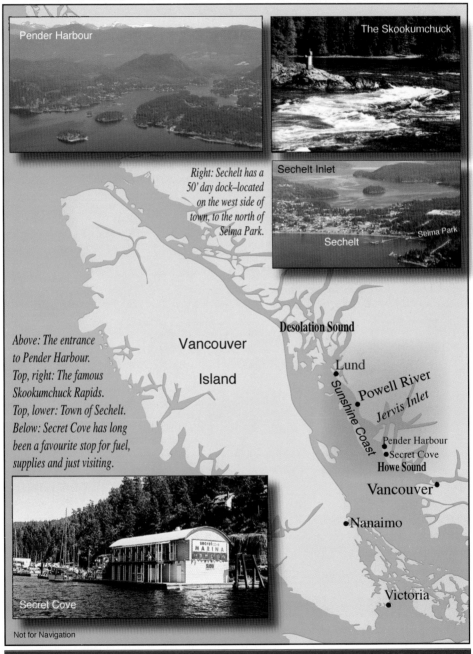

Pender Harbour

The Skookumchuck

Right: Sechelt has a 50' day dock–located on the west side of town, to the north of Selma Park.

Sechelt Inlet

Sechelt

Selma Park

Desolation Sound

Above: The entrance to Pender Harbour.
Top, right: The famous Skookumchuck Rapids.
Top, lower: Town of Sechelt.
Below: Secret Cove has long been a favourite stop for fuel, supplies and just visiting.

Vancouver

Island

Lund

Powell River

Jervis Inlet

Sunshine Coast

Pender Harbour

Secret Cove

Howe Sound

Vancouver

Nanaimo

Victoria

Secret Cove

Not for Navigation

The official VHF channel for BC marinas is 66A (US mode)

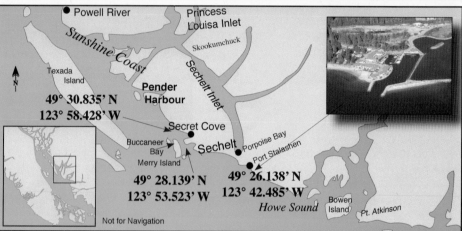

Powell River · Princess Louisa Inlet · Skookumchuck · Sunshine Coast · Texada Island · Sechelt Inlet · Pender Harbour · 49° 30.835' N 123° 58.428' W · Secret Cove · Buccaneer Bay · Sechelt · Porpoise Bay · Port Stalashen · Merry Island · 49° 28.139' N 123° 53.523' W · 49° 26.138' N 123° 42.485' W · Howe Sound · Bowen Island · Pt. Atkinson · Not for Navigation

Top: Secret Cove Marina. Opposite page: The fuel dock at Secret Cove and boats alongside at the marina store. Inset, above: Below: The small public dock at Vaucroft in Buccaneer Bay provides access to the beach. The adjacent anchorage is popular in season. Port Stalashen (small inset photo above right) is located off Sechelt. It is fully occupied with permanently moored boats and no berths are readily available for visitors. But it could serve as a refuge in an emergency. Use chart 3311.

Vaucroft public dock
Sunshine Coast Regional District
Buccaneer Bay Provincial Park (Seen below). Ph: 604-885-6800

Secret Cove

49° 31.620' N
123° 58.102' W

Charts 3535, 3311, 3512

Secret Cove Marina

Scott Rowland & Nicole Hagedorn
5411 Secret Cove Rd, PO Box 1118
Sechelt BC V0N 3A0   VHF 66A
Ph: 604-885-3533 Fax: 604-885-6037
Toll free 1-866-885-3533
info@secretcovemarina.com
www.secretcovemarina.com
Marina services: (Seasonal)
Fuel: Gas, diesel, oil. 30 transient slips
& permanent 150 berths. Seasonal Easter
to Thanksgiving. Website on line reserva-
tions. **Power** at docks: 15, 30, 50 amps.
Customer services:
Showers. Washrooms. Fish cleaning
tables, picnic tables, garbage disposal for
moorage customers only.
Full grocery store, marine supplies.
Fishing gear, licences, charts, bait, ice,
electronics, repairs, accessories, books,
gifts, wireless internet access. Fax service.
Restaurant upstairs with patio, building
located on dock.
Liquor agency. Water Taxi available.
Walking: Road access walking or cycling.
Cab or bus to main shopping centres.
Nearby:
Good fishing a short distance from the
marina. Hotels, restaurants and facilities
located in and around the harbour.
Golf. Swimming at Thormanby Island's
white sandy beach.

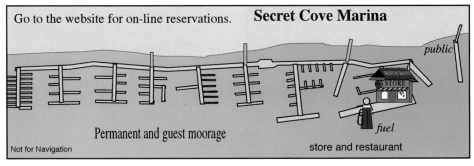

Go to the website for on-line reservations.   **Secret Cove Marina**

public

Permanent and guest moorage   *fuel*

Not for Navigation   store and restaurant

Sunshine Coast

Buccaneer Marina
Bob, John, Jerry Mercer
5535 San Souci Rd
Halfmoon Bay BC V0N 1Y2
Ph: 604-885-7888 Fax: 604-885-7824
Toll free: 1-877-885-7888
buccaneermarina@telus.net
www.buccaneermarina.com
Charts 3311, 3512, 3535   VHF 66A
Marina services: Fuel: Gas, diesel, oil,
propane. Guest moorage as available. Marine centre and store. Sales & service. Parts
and repairs. Repair dock.
Mercury Marine service. Boat rentals.
Fishing gear, licences, charts, live and
frozen bait, ice, groceries, snacks. Marine

*Above: Buccaneer Marina and its fuel dock are located
at the head of the east arm of Secret Cove.*
*Below: Hotels, their docks and the busy, narrow water-
way to Buccaneer Marina.*

ways 40'. Hull repairs, pressure washing,
bottom painting. Water taxi to Thormanby
Island. Road access walking.
Nearby: Buccaneer Bay Provincial Park
and Cove Provincial Park.

Secret Cove
Public dock (Managed by the Harbour
Authority Pender Harbour)
Manager Ian McNee Ph: 604-883-2234
Charts 3311, 3535, 3512 • Float length
44 m • Lights • Power 20, 30 amp •
Adjacent to or near marinas, provisions,
fuel, service and repairs.

Halfmoon Bay
Sunshine Coast Regional District
Public dock
Manager
Ph: 604-885-6800
Charts 3311, 3512
Float length 26 metres • Lights.

Pender Harbour from the southeast. Painted Boat and Coho marinas in the foreground, Hospital Bay beyond.

**Entrance to Pender Harbour
49° 37.808' N 124° 03.986' W**

Pender Harbour

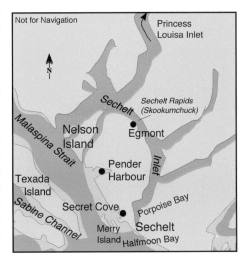

The dock at Princess Louisa. Pender Harbour is an ideal stop en route to Princess Louisa Inlet.

The location of Pender Harbour is central to many coastal areas, a favourite of which is nearby Princess Louisa Inlet (right). As a base to launch from or cruise from, Pender Harbour's 32 miles of shoreline has anchorages and facilities to meet most needs of cruising mariners.

Entering Pender Harbour use your charts and pass between Martin Island to port and Charles and William Islands to starboard.

Yachts tying up at marinas in Hospital Bay, Madeira Park or Garden Bay will not be far from most facilities. Visit Fisherman's Resort & Marina, The Pilothouse Marina or try for space at the Madeira Park public docks.

The former hospital at Hospital Bay has functioned in more recent years as a lodge and restaurant. A short trip away is the famous Skookumchuck where the Sechelt Rapids tumble wildly over themselves during tidal changes. Pender Harbour or Egmont are staging areas for viewing the magnificent natural sight. There is good fishing nearby.

141

Garden Bay

Hospital Bay

Fisherman's Resort

Pender Harbour

Entrance to Pender Harbour
49° 37.808' N 124° 03.986' W

Sunshine Coast

Fisherman's Resort & Marina

David Pritchard, Jennifer Love
4890 Pool Lane PO Box 68   VHF 66A
Garden Bay BC V0N 1S0
Ph/Fax: 604-883-2336
fishermans@dccnet.com
www.fishermansresortmarina.com

Marina services:
Moorage. 2,200 feet. Reservations suggested. **Power** at docks: 20, 30 amp. Water.

Customer services:
Seasonal: April - October. Laundry, showers, washrooms, ice, marine charts, books, clothing. Waterfront cottages and RV sites. Secure parking. Launch ramp. Float plane service. Free wi-fi internet access.

Entertainment:
Music & other festivals from June to October. Charters available for fishing & scuba diving. Road access walking or cycling. Four lakes nearby, swimming, golfing, mountain biking, animal and marine life.

Charts 3535, 3311, 3512   VHF 66A

Adjacent and nearby facilities:
Groceries, liquor and **fuel at John Henry's** general store. **Ph: 604-883-2253.** Post office, pub and restaurants nearby. Public marina. Anchorage in Garden Bay.

Below: Hospital Bay and Fisherman's docks.

Above: Boats moored safely at Fisherman's Resort and Marina. Opposite page, top to bottom: Overview of Pender Harbour, the dock at Fisherman's Resort, approaches to Hospital Bay. Right: An aerial view of Fisherman's Resort. Beyond can be seen John Henry's, the public dock and Garden Bay on the far side of the isthmus with its marinas and anchorage. Opposite RVYC are Garden Bay Hotel and the Pilothouse marinas.

Garden Bay

Pilothouse Marina

RVYC

Garden Bay Hotel & Marina

John Henry's fuel and store.

public dock

Hospital Bay

Fisherman's Resort

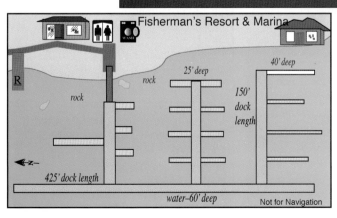

Fisherman's Resort & Marina

WASH

R

rock

rock

25' deep

40' deep

150' dock length

425' dock length

water–60' deep

Not for Navigation

Above: Fisherman's Resort owner David Pritchard takes time out from a busy marina to chat to Carla.

Above: Hospital Bay and the fuel dock at John Henry's store and marina. Opposite: Garden Bay Hotel and Marina docks. The marina is adjacent to the Royal Vancouver Yacht Club outstation at Pender Harbour.

John Henry's Marina

Lucy & Wayne Archbold
4907 Pool Lane, PO Box 4907
Garden Bay BC V0N 1S0
Phone: 604-883-2253 Fax: 604-883-2147
Marina services: No moorage. **Fuel:** gas, diesel, 50:1 mix, oil; propane; ice; full grocery supply store/liquor/marine/fishing, small café, bank machine. Internet access.
Nearby facilities: Restaurants; playground; hiking trails; post office. Gift shop and art gallery. **Nearby:** LaVerne's Grill. Launch ramp (at Fisherman's Resort).

Above: The store at John Henry's Marina.

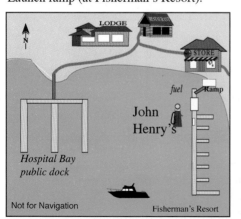

Hospital Bay
public dock

John Henry's

fuel

Ramp

LODGE

STORE

Not for Navigation

Fisherman's Resort

Hospital Bay

Public dock
Pender Harbour Authority
Manager Ian McNee   VHF 66A
Ph: 604-883-2234
Charts 3535, 3311, 3512
Dock length 200 metres.• Garbage •
Water • Lights • 20, 30 amp power •
Close to restaurants, groceries, liquor, boating needs. Anchorage.
Fuel at John Henry's.

Pender Harbour Golf Club 604-883-9541

Garden Bay Hotel and Marina has a popular pub and restaurant. This marina is directly adjacent to the Royal Vancouver Yacht Club outstation at Pender Harbour. Madeira Park can be seen below.

Garden Bay Hotel & Marina

Owner: Ron Johnston

4985 Lyons Rd, PO Box 90   VHF 66A
Garden Bay BC V0N 1S0
Ph/Fax: 604-883-2674

gbhm@dccnet.com
www.gardenbaypub.com

Marina services:

Guest moorage: 1,200', reservations suggested, seasonal March-Oct. Water at dock. **Power**: 15, 30 amp. **Washrooms, showers.**

Customer services:

Fine dining at pub and waterfront restaurant. Kayak and canoe rentals, on dock.

Entertainment. Live entertainment in pub. Jazz Festival in September. Good fishing and scuba a short run from the harbour, hiking, easy walking or cycling.

Nearby facilities: Fuel: At **John Henry's Marina** in Hospital Bay. Gas, diesel, outboard fuel, propane, tackle.

Garden Bay

Madeira Park

Post office, liquor agency, restaurants. LaVerne's Grill (seasonal).

Nearby: Fishing charters. Air charters. Churches. Golf course. Public pay phone. Anchorage in the bay. Marina located adjacent Royal Vancouver Yacht Club out station.

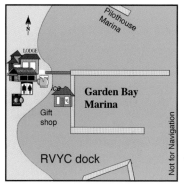

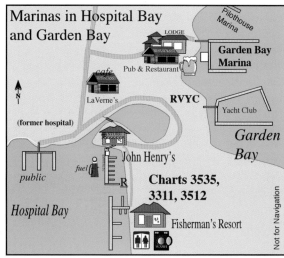

Charts 3311, 3535, 3512

Above: Aerial photo shows The Painted Boat marina, left, and Coho Marina to the right.

The Pilothouse Marina
VHF 66A
Owner Ronan Oger
13172 Sexw Amin, PO Box 6
Garden Bay BC V0N 1S0
Ph: 604-883-2479 Fax: 604-608-2968
Toll free 1-877-856-2479
ronan.roger@roitsystems.com
www.thepilothousemarina.com
Moorage: Dock 1,400 feet. Maximum
boat length 125'. Multihulls welcome.
Fourth night is free. **Power**:15, 30 50 amp.
Water, garbage. **Washrooms,**
Showers, laundry.
Wifi. Rental cabin. Fishing
charters, boat rentals.
Nearby: John Henry's store
with fuel, liquor agency, post
office, ATM. LaVern's Grill.
Garden Bay Marine Provincial
Park. Garden Bay Pub and
restaurant.

Right: The Pilothouse Marina

The Painted Boat
Resort Spa and Marina
Manager Marlene Cymbalist
12849 Lagoon Rd., PO Box 153
Madeira Park BC V0N 2H0
Ph: 604-883-2456 Fax: 604-883-2122
Toll free 1-888-527-7776
admin@paintedboat.com
www.paintedboat.com
Moorage: Reservations recommended.
Maximum 6' draft. **Water. Power** 15, 30,
50 amps. Accommodation. **Nearby:** IGA,
Oak Tree Market, liquor store, pharmacy,
art gallery, book store. health clinic,
RONA, coffee shops.

49° 37.39' N 124° 01.5' W

Pender Harbour Resort at Duncan Cove

Pender Harbour Resort

Walter Endert & Tammy Endert
4686 Sinclair Bay Rd., Garden Bay
BC V0N 1S1 Toll free 1-877-883-2424
Ph: 604-883-2424 Fax: 604-883-2414
info@phrm.ca
www.phrm.ca
Charts 3512, 3535, 3311
Marina services: Showers, laundry, washrooms. Ice. **Water. Power:** 15, 30 amps. Groceries, licences, garbage disposal, rental boats, kayaks and canoes. Access to heated pool. Cabins, yurts and motel rooms. Fire pit. Walking. Launch ramp.

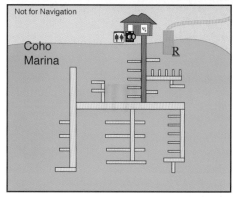

Coho Marina Resort

Dwayne and Brenda Balon
12907 Shark Lane, PO Box 160
Madeira Park BC V0N 2H0
Ph: 604-883-2248 Fax: 604-883-2237
cohomarina@dccnet.com
Hazard: Rocks in bay–marked by beacons. Consult charts.
Marina services: Limited visitor moorage. Launch ramp. **Showers. Washrooms. Power** 15 amps.

Coho Marina

Pender Harbour Hotel & Marina

Manager: Bik Brar
12671 Sunshine Coast Hwy
Pender Harbour BC V0N 2H0
Phone: 604-883-9013
bikrambrar@hotmail.com
www.penderharbourhotel.com
Marina services: Guest moorage. **Power:** 15, 30, 50 amps, Grasshopper Pub & Restaurant. Hotel. Liquor store. **Chart 3535.**

Pender Harbour Hotel & Marina

Inset courtesy Sunshine Coast Resort & Marina

Sunshine Coast Resort

Sunshine Coast Resort, above and below, is located opposite Garden Bay, to the east of Madeira Park.

Photo courtesy Sunshine Coast Resort & Marina

Sunshine Coast Resort & Marina

Ralph Linnmann **VHF 66A**
PO Box 213 12695 Sunshine Coast Hwy
Madeira Park BC V0N 2H0
Ph: 604-883-9177 Fax: 604-883-9171
Toll free 1-888-883-9177
vacation@sunshinecoast-resort.com
www.sunshinecoastresort.com
Marina services: Guest moorage. Water. Power: 15, 30 amp. **Laundry, washrooms, showers.** Garbage disposal. Boat rentals, accommodations. Sundeck and hot tub. Playground. Free Wifi. Free transportation to and from golf course for marina guests.
Nearby: Shopping centre, restaurant, **launch ramp** at Madeira Park.
Marina locations shown on previous page.

Irvines Landing (private)

This was the original Union Steamship stop at Pender Harbour. It is located at the entrance to Pender Harbour and was a favourite stop for sports fishermen with its close proximity to the entrance of the harbour. Its marina, fuel and pub are gone.

Madeira Marina

Karen and Rick King
12930 Madeira Park Rd Madeira Park
Ph: 604-883-2266 Fax: 604-883-9250
Location: next to Madeira Park public docks and ramp. No transient moorage.
Marina services: Haulout to 35'. Marine repairs. Marine store. charts.

Sunshine Coast

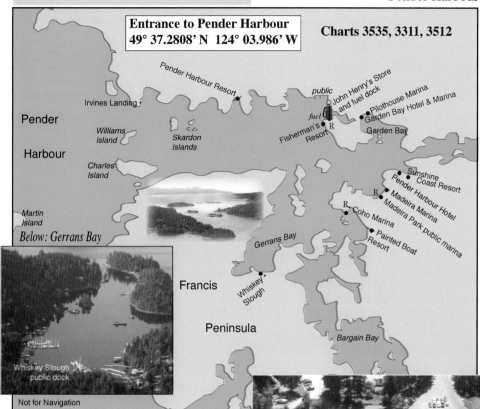

| Entrance to Pender Harbour |
| 49° 37.2808' N 124° 03.986' W |

Charts 3535, 3311, 3512

Pender Harbour Resort

Pender

Irvines Landing

Williams
Island

Skardon
Islands

Harbour

Charles
Island

Martin
Island

Below: Gerrans Bay

Francis

Whiskey
Slough

Peninsula

public

John Henry's Store
and fuel dock

fuel

Fisherman's
Resort

Pilothouse Marina

Garden Bay Hotel & Marina

Garden Bay

Sunshine
Coast Resort

Pender Harbour Hotel

Madeira Marina

Coho Marina

Madeira Park public marina

Painted Boat
Resort

Gerrans Bay

Bargain Bay

Whiskey Slough
public dock

Not for Navigation

Whiskey Slough public dock
Harbour Authority of Pender Harbour
Ian McNee
Ph: 604-883-2234   VHF 66A
Charts 3535, 3311, 3512
Moorage, 20, 30 amp power, water.
Two fingers–300' plus in summer.
*See location of Whiskey Slough in Gerrans
Bay in photo and on diagram above.*

Madeira Marina (to left) and Madeira Park docks.

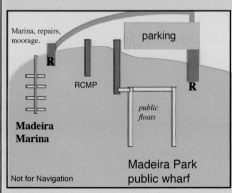

Marina, repairs,
moorage.

parking

R

RCMP

R

public
floats

**Madeira
Marina**

Madeira Park
public wharf

Not for Navigation

Madeira Park public dock
PO Box 118, Madeira Park V0N 2H0
Harbour Authority of Pender Harbour.
Manager Ian McNee
Phone: 604-883-2234 VHF 66A.
• Float length 500' • Launch ramp • Air-
craft float • seasonal snack bar • Garbage
• Washrooms • showers • Water • Lights
• Power: 15, 30, 50 amps • Pumpout •
Nearby restaurants, supermarket, liquor
store, pharmacy. Marine mechanic.

entrance to
Bathgate Marina
docks and fuel

49° 44.989' N
123° 55.689' W

Not for Navigation
Charts 3512, 3535, 3514

Bathgate Marina

Public
Dock

It is very important to consult your charts and tide tables when navigating in this area. "Red Right Returning."

Sechelt Inlet

Sunshine Coast

Bathgate General Store Resort & Marina

Doug and Vicki Martin
6781 Bathgate Rd, Egmont BC V0N 1N0
Ph: 604-883-2222 Fax: 604-883-2750
bathgate@lincsat.com
www.bathgate.com

Marina services:
Fuel: Gas, diesel, propane, oils.
Moorage. Visitor moorage–reserve. Marine ways to 40 tons. **Power** at docks: 15, 20, 30 amp. **Water** at dock. Ice. Washrooms for Bathgate Marina customers, **showers, laundry.** Wireless internet access. Liquor agency. Grocery store–fresh meat and vegetables. Fishing tackle, licences. ATM.

Customer services:
Deluxe waterfront motel–wheelchair accessible. RV tent sites. Boat, cabin, video rentals. Automobile fuel ashore.

Entertainment: Water taxis to Princess Louisa Inlet. Kayaking. Scuba diving and fishing in the immediate vicinity. Trail to the Sechelt Rapids viewpoint in Skookumchuck Rapids Provincial Park. The trail head is located opposite Egmont Heritage Centre. Ferry to Princess Louisa Inlet and Malibu Club, Young Life *www.mailbuyachts.com*.

Adjacent facilities:
Public dock. Egmont–nearest base before trip to Princess Louisa Inlet.

Hazard: Drying reef in middle of bay on approaches to fuel dock and another off the government dock. Check your chart.

Store at Bathgate Marina.

Left: Two views of Backeddy Resort and Marina. Inset: Nearby Skookumchuck. Below: Suzanne Laurie and Carla. Opposite Top: Bathgate Marina and the public docks. Opposite, bottom: The store at Bathgate Marina.

Backeddy Resort and Pub

Peter and Suzanne Laurie
16660 Backeddy Rd
Egmont BC V0N 1N0   VHF 66A
Ph: 604-883-2298   Fax: 604-883-2239
Toll free: 1-800-626-0599
Charts 3312, 3512, 3514
info@backeddy.ca   www.backeddy.ca
Marina services:
Fuel: Gas diesel, oils, two stroke oil. Garbage disposal. Guest moorage available 500'.
Laundry, showers, washrooms. Power: 15, 30 amp. Potable water, ice, book exchange. ATM. On call marine mechanic. Gravel Launch ramp.
Entertainment: Back Eddy Pub–limited winter hours. Summer long-weekend live entertainment. Pool table. Nearby restaurant, trails to Skookumchuck rapids. Tours to Princess Louisa Inlet. Boat US participating marina. Approach the docks, stay west of the beacon. West Coast Wilderness Lodge–dining etc–next door to Backeddy Resort.

Egmont public dock

Egmont Harbour Authority.
Wharfinger Betty Silvey
Ph: 604-883-9652. Float length 500' •
Lights. Power: 20, 30 50 amps.
Free 4-wheel drive launch ramp
West Coast Wilderness Lodge nearby has fine dining and occasional dock space.

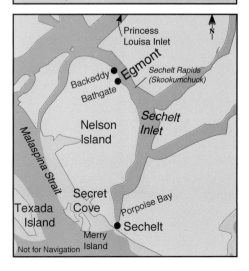

Saltery Bay

Sunshine Coast public dock
Chart 3514
• Float length 133 metres • Garbage •
Lights • Adjacent ferry dock to Egmont.

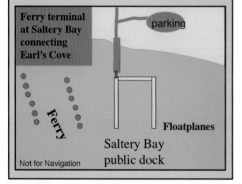

Ferry terminal at Saltery Bay connecting Earl's Cove

parking

Ferry

Floatplanes

Saltery Bay public dock

Not for Navigation

Photo Justin Taylor

Above: The dock at Saltery Bay.

Top: Saltery Bay, showing the public dock as well as the ferry landing. Avoid the commercial area shown to the right (east) of the public dock.
Bottom: Porpoise Bay at the head of Sechelt Inlet and the town of Sechelt.

Porpoise Bay

Choquer

Lighthouse Marina

Public dock

Porpoise Bay, Sechelt

Public dock. Charts 3311, 3512
Manager Bruce Haynes
District of Sechelt
Ph: 604-885-1986
• Float length 132 metres •
Launch ramp • Tidal grid •
Garbage • Water • Lights •
Power 20, 30, 50 amps • Pay
phone ashore • Adjacent pub •
Washrooms, showers and laun-
dry available at adjacent pub.
Hotels. Nearby shops, scuba
diving charters, kayak rentals.

Charts 3312, 3512

Porpoise Bay
49° 29.045' N
123° 45.525' W

Lighthouse Marina

Pub and Beer and Wine store
Manager: Dale Schweighardt
5764 Wharf Rd PO Box 137
Sechelt BC V0N 3A0
Ph: 604-885-9494 Fax: 604-885-3382
info@lighthousepub.ca www.lighthousepub.ca
Marina services: Fuel: gas, diesel.
Guest moorage 4-5 slips. Ice, l**aundry,**
showers, washrooms, pumpout, garbage
disposal, Wifi, ATM, rental cottages, pub.
Large **launch ramp**.
Nearby: Floatplane service, golf, hospital.

Choquer & Sons Marina

5977 Sechelt Inlet Rd
Sechelt, BC.
Ph: 604-885-9244 Fax 604-885-2576
choquerandsons@telus.net
300' dock. Boats to 75'. Haulouts to 40'
launch ramp. 15, 30 amp power.

*Above: The public docks at Porpoise Bay in Sechelt
Inlet are adjacent to the launch ramp and Lighthouse
Marina. Below: Lighthouse Marina docks at Porpoise
Bay in Sechelt Inlet. Time your passage through the
Skookumchuck Rapids with care.*

Lighthouse Pub has rental cabins available for the
day or week. Check www.bednboatcottages.com

Lighthouse Marina

49° 47.974' N
124° 31.308' W

Powell River

Beach Gardens Resort and Marina

Joan Barszczewski
7074 Westminster Street
Powell River BC V8A 1C5
Ph: 604-485-6267 Fax: 604-485-2343
Toll free 1-800-663-7070
beachgardens@shaw.ca
www.beachgardens.com
Charts 3563, 3311, 3513 VHF 66A
Marina entrance is at the breakwater just south of Grief Point.

Marina services:
Fuel: Gas, diesel, oil. ice (in season). Mechanic and services available from local and nearby marine operators.
Moorage: Large permanent marina with overnight moorage slips. Reserve.
Power at docks: 15, 30 amp.
Laundry, showers, washrooms.
Customer services:
Hotel with deluxe oceanfront accommodations. Indoor pool & fitness centre.
On site Seaside Restaurant and the Savoury Bight pub. Liquor store.

Alpha Dive & kayak. Public pay phones.
Entertainment: Fishing charters. Cooper Yacht Charters–sail boats. Sightseeing charters. Sea kayaking. Wilderness canoe routes. Fishing charters. Getaway packages for golf, scuba diving, kayaking and biking.
Adjacent and nearby facilities:
Grocery store, post office, city bus, bus service to Vancouver. Free shuttle to the Town Centre Mall in July and August. Shopping, golf and hiking in the area. Medical services in town.

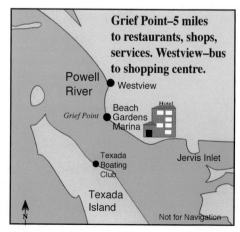

Grief Point–5 miles to restaurants, shops, services. Westview–bus to shopping centre.

Beach Gardens Resort

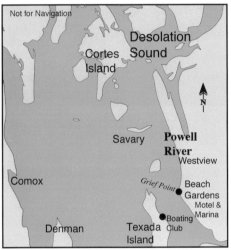

Not for Navigation

Desolation
Cortes Sound
Island

N

Savary **Powell River**
Westview

Comox   Grief Point   Beach Gardens
                                  Motel & Marina
                            Boating Club
Denman   Texada
              Island

Motel
RESTAURANT
WASH

winter
summer

A B C D E F G H

Not for Navigation

Texada Boating Club
Wharfinger
PO Box 196
Van Anda BC V0N 3K0
Phone: 604-486-6774
Chart: 3513
Located on northeast side of Texada Island.
Marina Services: Guest moorage, power: 15-amp, garbage disposal, launch ramp.

Nearby facilities: Hotel nearby offers showers, restaurant, ATM, ice, grocery store with liquor agency, laundry at the garage, hiking club on Saturdays, old mine on opposite beach. New RV park with showers and laundry nearby
The bay is rough in strong SE winds. Moorage for boats to 80' when wind conditions prevent safe anchorage in the bay.

The Boating Club at Sturt Bay on Texada Island. Visitors are welcome to the guest dock at the far end of the marina. Boat size restricted by the type of anchored dock moorings. Good anchorage opposite in favourable winds.

Fuel dock inside south breakwater

49° 50.055' N
124° 31.766' W

North harbour

South harbour

fuel

Westview South Harbour

Manager Jim Parsons.

6910 Duncan St, Powell River V8A 1V4
Ph: 604-485-5244 Fax: 604-485-5286
jparsons@cdpr.bc.ca www.powellriver.ca

• Float length 625 m • Garbage • Waste oil disposal • Water • Lights • Power: 15, 30 amp. Rafting required. Near ferry landing, city restaurants, shops.

Moorage: No reservations. **Washrooms, laundry, showers**. Enter south marina past the fuel dock located inside breakwater, on the south side of the ferry dock. Fuel–see Westview Fuel Dock below. Free shopping shuttle bus to mall in July and August Small boat rentals. Internet access.

Nearby: Marine Traders chandlery–fishing tackle, marine supplies. Les Koleszar's

Koleszar Marine and Power Equipment
Powell River, BC V8A 2M6
Ph: 604-485-5616 at Westview
Adjacent to marina and marine store.

marine services. Near city restaurants, shops, hotels. Golf course. Seafair in July, Blackberry Festival in August, Int'l Choral Kathaumixw held bi-annually. Community events–Visitors Bureau **Ph: 604-485-4701.** Ferries to Texada Island and to Comox on Vancouver Island. **Powell River–Vancouver flights daily on Pacific Coastal Airlines Phone: 1-800-663-2872.**

Westview North Harbour

Ph: 604-485-5244 No transient moorage.
Launch ramp located at north end.

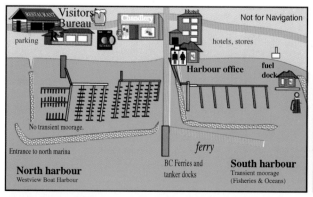

Not for Navigation

Visitors Bureau

Chandlery

parking

hotels, stores

Harbour office

fuel dock

No transient moorage.

Entrance to north marina

ferry

North harbour
Westview Boat Harbour

BC Ferries and tanker docks

South harbour
Transient moorage (Fisheries & Oceans)

Charts 3311, 3563, 3513
VHF 66A

Westview Fuel dock
(located in South Harbour)
Ph: 604-485-2867
Fax: 604-485-7238
Fuel: Gas, diesel, outboard mix, naptha, water, ice.

The dock at False Bay has very limited space.
It is used primarily for the local water taxi.

Food services: Burgers / Pizza / Appys + daily specials–at the old hotel. Phone 250-333-8506.

Texada and Lasqueti Islands

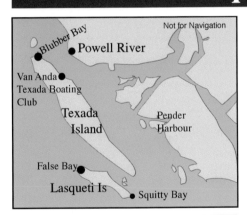

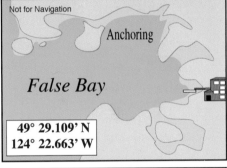

Blubber Bay
49° 47.924' N
124° 37.134' W
Texada Island dock
BC Ferries. Chart 3311. Ph: 250-978-1307
Limited facilities and moorage at 13 m float.
Shore access by dinghy. Try the Boat Club
docks at Van Anda to the south.

Squitty Bay
49° 27.110' N
124° 09.762' W
Lasqueti Island
Public dock. Chart 3512 Float length
47 meters • Aircraft float. Scheduled
passenger ferry service. No facilities.
Walking island roads and trails.

False Bay public dock
Lasqueti Island (adjacent old hotel)
Charts 3536, 3512, 3513. Float length
36 m • Aircraft Float • Food at old hotel.
No facilities at dock. Transport Canada.
Food service–Phone: 250-333-8506.

Hotel dock

Fuel dock

north entrance

south entrance

Note: The north float at the busy public dock is reserved for pleasure craft. The southern one serves commercial vessels. Expect racfting. Tie-up on the inside of the breakwater is allowed–no link to shore.

49° 58.891' N
124° 45.827' W

Lund   Charts 3311, 3538, 3513

Sunshine Coast

Lund Small Craft Harbour

Manager Fran Lacey

Ph: 604-483-4711   VHF 73

Marina services:

Moorage: Over 500 feet for transient use.
Water. Power: 20, 30 amp. Public pay phone.
Washrooms. Showers. Launch ramp.
Rafting permitted at public docks.

Adjacent and nearby facilities: Board-walk. Fishing charters. Water taxi service. Kayak rentals. Scenic cruises. Lund Hotel, shops. ATM. Laundry. Stores, coffee house, souvenirs and gifts. Restaurants. Ice cream. Pizza. Clothing store. Walking trails and road access. 30-ton travel lift at service dock. New breakwater being installed fall of 2010.

Above: Stores, bakery and tea room at Lund.
Below: The south entrance to the harbour.

The Historic Lund Hotel, Lund Fuel dock

Ph: 604-414-0474 Fax: 604-414-0476

Fuel: Gas, diesel. Some moorage after 9 pm in summer. Paid garbage drop. Hotel accommodation, pub restaurant–open 7 days a week May–Sept. Day dock with 2-hour limit.
Showers, laundry. Ice. Art store at hotel. General store: groceries, tackle, marine sup-plies. Some hardware. Liquor agency. Deli, bakery, fresh produce, butcher. Post office.

Okeover Inlet

Okeover dock
49° 59.511' N
124° 42.643' W

Public dock
Charts 3512, 3514, 3312, 3559
Manager • Two decked breakwater docks providing 240' of guest
moorage. • Lights • Power 15
amps • Public pay phone ashore
• Outhouse ashore.• This public
dock provides access to the Laughing Oyster restaurant a short way
from it. Okeover Provincial Park.

Savary Island

Public dock
Charts 3311, 3538, 3513
Float length 85 feet. Regular
water taxi service from Lund.
No moorage–for loading only.
Riggers Restaurant and General Store,
located up the hill from the public dock.

Photograph above shows a view of the Lund Hotel. It overlooks the wharf and fuel dock. The fuel dock can be seen in the foreground. The one to the left is the hotel dock. Bottom: The wharf at Savary Island.

Public docks

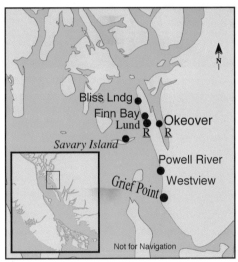

Not for Navigation

Lund is an interesting place, existing as the northernmost town on the Sunshine Coast road. It has an historic hotel, restaurants and numerous facilities including a well-stocked grocery store selling a fair selection of marine hardware, fishing gear, clothing, books and charts. There is a waterfront marine service centre, catering year-round to the local community. Lund is a busy fuel stop before entering Desolation Sound. It is also a major boat launching place and water access point with water taxi service to Savary Island.

49° 56.940' N
124° 46.433' W

Above: The Copeland Islands provide a protected waterway from Lund to the entrance of Desolation Sound.

Finn Bay at Lund is an interesting spot, but there is no shore access and seldom space for tie-up at the public dock.

Bliss Landing   Chart 3311

Managers Marl and Mac Eyre
Ph/Fax: 604-414-9417   **VHF 16**
Cell phone: 604-483-8098
bliss@twincomm.ca
Located at the north end of Thulin Passage.
Marina services: Limited guest moorage. Power 30, 50 amp. Limited water. Washrooms, showers, laundry. Garbage disposal.
Nearby: Water taxi. Air service at Lund.

Top: Bliss Landing, north of Lund, marks the entrance to Desolation Sound. Visitor docks at right. Overnight moorage is available as space allows.

After Lund, pay a visit to Okeover (right,) where the cuisine at the Laughing Oyster–Ph: 604-483-9775 (right, top) is exceptional. Many mariners anchor in Grace Harbour and dinghy down to Okeover for dinner at the restaurant. The public docks accommodate dinghies or a few small boats.

Vancouver Island

Central East Coast

Section 4

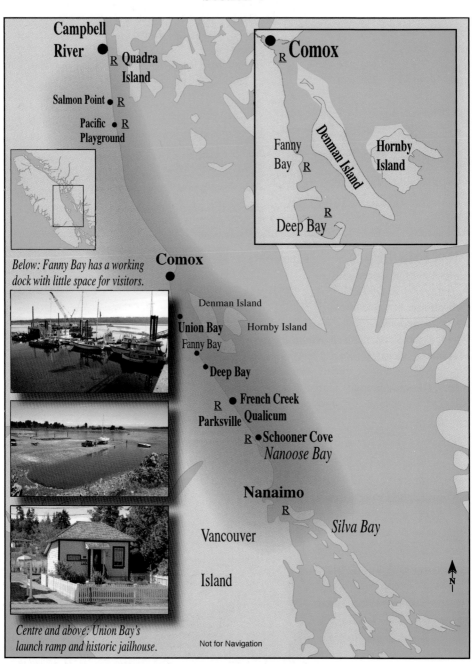

Campbell River ● R Quadra Island

Salmon Point ● R

Pacific ● R Playground

R Comox

Fanny Bay R

Denman Island

Hornby Island

Deep Bay R

Below: Fanny Bay has a working dock with little space for visitors.

Comox ●

Denman Island

Union Bay
Fanny Bay

Hornby Island

● Deep Bay

R ● French Creek
Parksville Qualicum

R ● Schooner Cove
Nanoose Bay

Nanaimo
R

Silva Bay

Vancouver

Island

N

Centre and above: Union Bay's launch ramp and historic jailhouse.

Not for Navigation

49° 17.238' N
124°08.003' W   Schooner Cove Marina

Fairwinds Golf & Country Club 250-468-7666

Schooner Cove   Charts 3512, 3459   VHF 66A

Fairwinds Schooner Cove Marina

Manager Greg Dunn
3521 Dolphin Dr   VHF 66A
Nanoose Bay BC V9P 9J7
Marina Ph: 250-468-5364
Toll free 1-800-663-7060
gdunn@fairwinds.ca   tcdavies@fairwinds.ca
www.fairwinds.ca
Marina services:
Fuel: Gas, diesel, oils, 30 plus visitor slips. **Water** at all docks. **Power**: 15, 30, 50 amp. Some 125, 240 amp. Pumpout station–at end of G dock.
Customer services:
Access to internet in café.

Public pay phone. **Laundry, shower, washrooms.** Dockside Café and Pub. Fishing licences, **ice.** Cold beer, wine and spirits store.
Entertainment:
Tennis court, fitness centre. Walking trails. Courtesy shuttle to golf course.
Hazard: Drying rock in entrance to marina. Keep red marker to starboard and keep close to floats inside the basin.

Top: Schooner Cove. It has a nearby golf course and a well located launch ramp (right).

From Nanaimo to Campbell River take time to stop at Schooner Cove. This is a large permanent moorage marina with guest moorage, and adjacent to a fine golf course.

Farther north up Vancouver Island's east coast is Deep Bay, a pleasant place to visit and sheltered from windy conditions. If it is too long a stretch from Schooner Cove to Deep Bay drop in at French Creek, not the easiest entrance in adverse conditions, but shelter from rough seas and a place to break a long stretch along the coast.

After Deep Bay, passing along Baynes Channel comes **Fanny Bay** and **Union Bay** then Comox with its vast set of docks, private and public. Fanny Bay has a working dock with little suitable overnight moorage. It has an historic inn and pub nearby. Union Bay has a launch ramp for small boats. Comox Marina or those adjacent have lots of transient moorage. There are restaurants ashore and a park and stores nearby. Other facilities along with events such as Nautical Days each August will keep you entertained and enthused about the stop-over.

Fairwinds Golf & Country Club
Phone: 250-468-7666 Toll free 1-888-781-2777

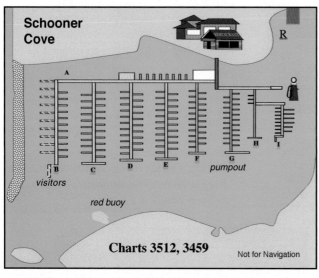

Charts 3512, 3459

Not for Navigation

Beachcomber Marina

In the lee of Cottam Point, north of Schooner Cove, there is a permanent moorage marina with a small store and a launch ramp. There is conditional anchorage in the bay, opposite.
Refer to charts for reefs. Enter between the red and green buoys.

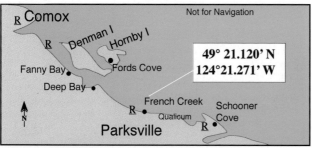

49° 21.120' N
124°21.271' W

Top: The entrance to French Creek. This is a well-situated harbour along an exposed stretch of coast. Enter with caution when sea conditions are deteriorating. Opposite: Deep Bay. Use caution in adjacent shallow waters.

French Creek harbour

French Creek to Comox

French Creek

Managed by Harbour Authority
of French Creek
1055 Lee Rd, Parksville BC V9P 2E1
Ph: 250-248-5051 Fax: 250-248-5123
hafc@frenchcreekharbour.com
Charts 3512, 3513
Breakwater. Garbage. Waste oil disposal.
Water. Lights. **Moorage**. Rafting harbour.
No reservations. **Fuel:** Gas, diesel. **Laundry. Showers.** Washrooms, water, garbage,
lights, launch ramp. Breakwater. Security
gate. Waste oil disposal. Seafood sales,
mechanic, Coast Guard station.
Power: 20, 30 amp. Adjacent: Convenience store: ice, fishing gear and licenses.
Restaurants, pub, off sales. Foot ferry to
Lasqueti Island. **Launch ramp.**

Deep Bay   Chart 3527

Deep Bay Harbour Authority
Bill Falkiewicz
Ph: 250-757-9331 Fax 250-757-9319
deepbay-mgr@shawcable.com
www.dfo-mpo.gc.ca
Protected marina near Hornby and Denman Islands. Guest moorage–about 20
slips available. **Launch ramp.** Tidal grid.
Trailerable boats. Store and restaurant.
Water. Power: 20, 30 amp. Pumpout,
washrooms, showers, water, lighting, tidal
grid, 3 ton emergency crane.
Adjacent: Ship and Shore Campground:
Launch ramp, **fuel**–mobile gas pump, coffee shop, marine & general supplies, RV
park. There is a private marina on the other
side of the public marina.

49° 27.806' N
124°44.047' W

Deep Bay

Hornby Island

49° 29.811' N 124°40.704' W

Ford Cove Hornby Island

Harbourmaster Una Keziere
PO Box 2-6, Ford Cove BC V0R 1Z0
Ph: 250-335-2141 Fax: 250-335-2121
www.hornbyisland.com

Charts 3527, 3513

Float length 1,200 linear feet, rafting allowed • Breakwater • Tidal grid • Garbage • Lights • **Power:** 15, 20, 30 amps • Toilets • Also available: Grocery store, ice, fishing supplies. Art gallery • Boat rentals •. Diving charters.

It is safe to anchor to the north of the docks in most conditions except in a northwesterly wind. This anchorage is generally used in preference to the harbour which is usually occupied by commercial vessels.

The village and community centre on the island is near Tribune Bay where anchoring is popular in summer. It is a short walk from the beach and offers restaurants, art and craft stores and a grocery store. A large number of talented artists reside on Hornby Island and their work can be seen at the village centre and elsewhere on Hornby.

Top: Ford Cove docks. Left: There is a wide range of crafts available include items such as those shown at this boutique in the shopping centre.

Ford Cove

Store
Smaller boats
Pleasure boats
Commercial
Charter

Dock layout is shown in above diagram.

Ford Cove on Hornby Island. Anchorage can be taken to the north of the docks and shallows.

The Thatch Pub dock on Hornby Island

The Thatch

Not for Navigation

Strait of Georgia

Comox
Denman I
Hornby I
Ford Cove
Fanny Bay R R
Deep Bay
R
French Creek
Parksville
R Schooner Cove
Nanoose Bay
Vancouver Island
Nanaimo

Fanny Bay
Fishing Harbour
Ph: 250-887-5049
Charts 3513, 3527
Manager–Maureen Nordstrom •
Float length 42 m • Breakwater •
Power 20 amps • Yacht sales.
Historic Inn across the road.
Plans for 2011 included expanding
the docks and adding a drive-on
ramp for loading and unloading.

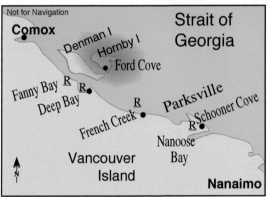

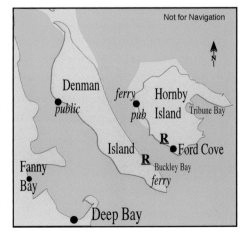

Not for Navigation

Denman
public
ferry
Hornby Island
Tribune Bay
pub
Island
R
R Ford Cove
Buckley Bay
Fanny Bay
ferry
Deep Bay

Top: Ford Cove views showing also The Thatch pub dock at Hornby Island ferry landing. Diagrams show the sequence of harbours between Nanaimo and Comox. Above: A wide selection of local art is available at the gallery at Ford Cove.

The outer dock has space available for visitors. Comox Municipal Marina lies in the centre of the complex, with Comox Bay Marina and Gas N Go docks to its left. Bottom: A view from shore of the public outer visitors' dock (far right this photo).

Entrance to harbour 49° 39.155' N 121° 54.973' W

Comox–Courtenay

Central East Vanc I

Comox

Comox Harbour is home to over 500 pleasure boats and a well organized charter boat fleet. It offers plenty of moorage for boaters visiting the Comox Valley. The marinas are protected by a rock breakwater which in turn is protected by Goose Spit making it one of the safest harbours on Vancouver Island.

For fishing enthusiasts there is a large launch ramp adjacent to Marina Park with lots of parking, washrooms and a play area for children. At the harbour, well-maintained

Visitor docks at east side of the harbour.

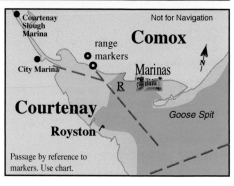

Courtenay Slough Marina
range markers
Comox
City Marina
Marinas
R
Courtenay
Goose Spit
Royston
Not for Navigation
N
Passage by reference to markers. Use chart.

guest floats are accessed around the east end of the breakwater on D and H floats.

The harbour managers and staff are usually on hand to meet arriving vessels, but mariners can also check in at the office on the wharfhead. No reservations are required but a phone call ahead to 250-339-6041 will determine availability of space.

The Comox harbour puts on a warm welcome to visitors. There are nearby restaurants, shops and a golf course.

It is worthwhile arriving for the annual Nautical Days Filberg Festival, held in July-August and the Shellfish Festival in June.

Not for navigation

Gas N Go Marina   VHF 66A

Manager Christine Marshall
132 Port Augusta St, PO Box 1296
Comox BC V9M 7Z8
Phone: 250-339-4664 Fax: 250-339-4662
info@gasngo.com www.gasngo.com
Two or three slips available at times for visitors. **Fuel Dock:** Gas, diesel, ice. Marine and convenience store. Webcam security, Wifi.
Nearby facilities: Launch ramp, The Pier Pub & Bistro, Black Fin Pub, Comox with all amenities.

Comox Bay Marina   VHF 66A

Manager Brad Jenkins
1805 Beaufort Ave, Comox BC V9M 1R9
Ph/fax: 250-339-2930 cell: 250-218-2827
manager@comoxbaymarina.com
www.comoxbaymarina.com
Moorage: Reservations suggested for overnight. **Water. Power** 15, 30, 50 amps.
Showers, laundry, washrooms. Garbage disposal. Float plane service to Vancouver.
Entertainment:
Nautical Days celebrated every August.

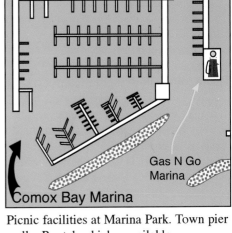

Picnic facilities at Marina Park. Town pier walk. Rental vehicles available.
Adjacent facilities:
Pub restaurant, yacht club. Comox town with all amenities. Liquor store.

Comox Bay Marina

VHF 66A

Fisherman's Wharf
Comox Valley Harbour Authority
121 Port Augusta St, Comox BC V9N 7Z8
Ph: 250-339-6041 Fax: 250-339-6057
info@comoxfishermanswharf.com
www.comoxfishermanswharf.com
Charts 3527, 3513
Guest moorage, rafting allowed.
Power: 20, 30, 50, 100 amps.
Washrooms, showers, free internet access, laundry, pumpout, garbage disposal, ice, hydraulic winches, dogs welcome.
Nearby facilities: Comox: golf course, restaurants, grocery store, marine chandlery, marine mechanic, liquor store; pubs, playground, hiking trails, medical services, post office, banks, airport, float plane service, golf, adventure charters.
Canadian Armed Forces base.
HMCS Quadra camp at Goose Point.
Ferry to Powell River departs Comox.

Above: Fisherman's Wharf east side visitors docks.
Enter the marina to the east of the breakwater.
Inset: The launch ramp at Comox Bay Marina.

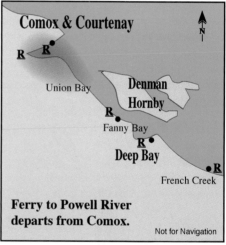

Caution: There are drying flats in the lee of Goose Spit, to the east of the harbour.

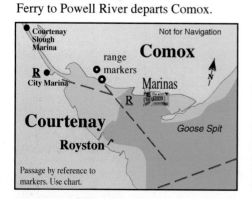

Comox Municipal Marina
Ph: 250-339-3141 Fax: 250-339-7110
Charts 3527, 3513

No transient docks. Pier and promenade. Launch ramp. This is the large dock behind the breakwater, with fingers extending from the causeway inside the main basin at Comox. Two boat grids for vessels to 40'.

170

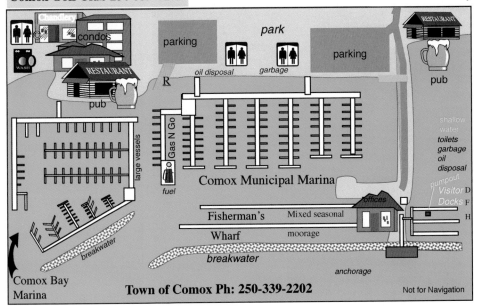

Comox Golf Club 250-339-7272

Chandlery
condos
parking
park
parking
RESTAURANT
WASH
RESTAURANT
pub
oil disposal
garbage
pub
R
shallow water
toilets
garbage
oil disposal
Gas N Go
large vessels
fuel
Comox Municipal Marina
pumpout
Visitor D
Docks F
H
offices
Fisherman's
Wharf
Mixed seasonal
moorage
breakwater
breakwater
anchorage
Comox Bay Marina
Town of Comox Ph: 250-339-2202
Not for Navigation

Courtenay Slough Marina

Comox Valley Harbour Authority.
Ph: 250-339-6041

Limited moorage for small boats. Walking distance to Courtenay. Lift bridge–phone 250-339-6041. This marina is accessible only for small boats with shallow draft. The river delta dries at places at low tide. Range markers indicate the channel. Check with harbour authority before attempting to navigate the river. Note: Magnetic dis-turbance affects compass readings by two degrees in excess of normal in the vicinity of Comox. Another facility, City Marina (map page 170), is part way up the river. It has a launch ramp and an adjacent airfield. *Hazard: Shallow river. Depths allow boats with shallow draft only– about 4 feet.*

Below: Courtenay River drops to about four feet. There are range markers. Small craft only. City Marina (inset) has a launch ramp.

Use chart 3527. See diagram opposite.
Use chart, tide tables and caution.

There is a launch ramp at City Marina.

49° 51.897' N
125°06.505' W

Pacific Playgrounds

*Pacific Playgrounds.
Hazard–Channel may be
entered at 4 foot (plus)
tides. Follow pilings.*

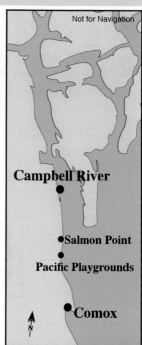

Not for Navigation

Campbell River

●**Salmon Point**

Pacific Playgrounds

●**Comox**

N

Comox to Campbell River
Charts 3527, 3513

Central East Vanc I

Pacific Playgrounds
Resort & Marina
9082 Clarkson Dr
Black Creek BC V9J 1B3
Ph: 250-337-5600 Fax: 250-337-5979
info@pacificplaygrounds.com
www.pacificplaygrounds.com
(Alongside Oyster River Mouth.)
Call marina for guidance.

Marina: Moorage. Reservations recommended. Sheltered basin. Slips to 40 feet.
Power: 15 amp.
Showers, laundry, washrooms.
Marine store: Tackle, charts, groceries,
public pay phone.
Garbage disposal.
Entertainment and nearby facilities:
Golf, mini-golf, trails. Take-out pizza, pub,
medical centre. Grocery, liquor and video
stores.Scenery, sunsets and eagles. Nearby
beach walks, bird watching. Fishing guides
available.

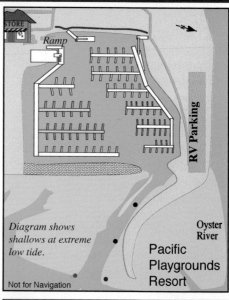

STORE

Ramp

RV Parking

*Diagram shows
shallows at extreme
low tide.*

Oyster
River

Pacific
Playgrounds
Resort

Not for Navigation

49° 53.428' N
125°07.489' W

Salmon Point Resort & Marina

Monica Best
2176 Salmon Point Rd
Campbell River BC V9H 1E5
Ph: 250-923-6605 Fax: 250-923-7572
Toll free 1-866-246-6605
sales@salmonpoint.ca
www.salmonpoint.ca

Marina: Sheltered boat moorage for power vessels up to 32'. No stayaboards.
Fuel: Gas. Propane.
Water, power: 30, 50 amp. **Laundry.**
Services: Accommodation and tenting available. Restaurant, marine pub. Store: tackle, bait, ice, fishing licenses, public pay phones, wireless internet. Garbage disposal. Resort facilities include swimming pool, hot tub, recreational halls. Launch ramp.
Entertainment and nearby:
Golf, mini-golf, nature trails. Stores. Scenery,

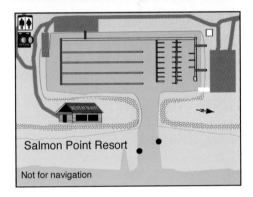

Salmon Point Resort

Not for navigation

sunsets and eagles. Nearby beach walks, bird watching. Fishing.

Hazard: Narrow, shallow channel into Salmon Point Marina. Boats need a minimum of a 5' tide. Proceed between floats off breakwater. Call marina for guidance.
Phone: Toll free 1-866-246-6605

Pacific Playgrounds entrance

Top: Salmon Point Marina (with diagram below it).
Opposite, top: Pacific Playgrounds with its open water entrance. Its approaches are shallow but clearly marked. NOTE: It dries at zero tide. Line up with the channel about 100 yards out. Check with marina.
Left: Pacific Playgrounds marina's entrance at high tide. Its launch ramp–opposite page, bottom.

50° 01.917' N
125° 13.273' W

Campbell River

April Point Resort & Spa

50° 03.927' N
125° 14.149' W

900 April Point Rd
Quadra Island BC V0P 1N0
Ph: 250-285-2222 Fax: 250-285-2411
aprilpointmarina@obmg.com
www.aprilpoint.com
Charts 3312, 3540, 3539   VHF 66A

Moorage. Large permanent marina with 4,000' year-round overnight or permanent moorage. Reservation requests by email or phone. Cable TV. Laundry, showers, washrooms. Ice. Garbage drop. Launch ramp.
Power at docks: 15, 30, 50 amp.

Customer services:
Wifi. Lodge with full numerous amenities. Fishing guides and charters. Restaurant. Breakfast, lunch, dinner. Open 7 days a week. Lounge, sushi bar. Coffee shop. Gift shop. Spa. Conference rooms. Walking trails or road access. Some beachfront walks. Scuba diving arrangements and charters–ask at the lodge for details.

Many visiting boats in Campbell River head for the April Point Marina tucked into Quadra Island on the east side of Discovery Passage. The guest marina is located beyond April Point. Inset: The resort and spa are located right at the point. When travelling from the lodge to the marina keep well off shore and pass the red buoy to your starboard to avoid shallows in the passage. No moorage at the Resort docks on the point.

Scooter rentals. Kayak rentals, eco-tours. Accommodations at lodge and bungalows. Transport to golf courses. Airport limo. Shuttle to and from Painters Lodge in Campbell River and access to their facilities including dining room, Sushi bar, gift shop, pub, swimming pool, exercise room.

Adjacent facilities:
Kenmore Air regular flights.
Liquor, grocery, arts and crafts and other stores including post office nearby.

Keep red channel marker close to starboard when approaching marina, red right return.

Above: Campbell River Fisherman's Wharf.

Fishermans Wharf   VHF 66A

Ph: 250-287-7931

Fax: 250-287-8495

fishermans@telus.net

| 50° 01.516' N |
| 125° 14.274' W |

Open all year • Commercial and pleasure boats welcome–reservations suggested • Three tidal grids • Hydraulic winches • Garbage disposal • Pumpout • Power 20, 30, 50, 100 amps • Washrooms • Showers • Ice, bait, tackle, seafood sales, charts. Wireless internet access. Marine service, mechanic, repairs, stores nearby. Near ferry to Quadra Island. Visit the Campbell River Maritime Museum, uptown.

Below: April Point visitor docks.

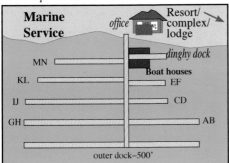

Above: The April Point Resort gift shop.

Cape Mudge

(Yaculta) Boatworks access.

Ph: 250-285-3622 Charts 3540, 3539

The float is north of the tip of Cape Mudge, on First Nations land. Kwakiutl Museum on the headland above–best visit by road.

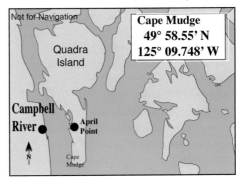

Above: Diagram shows location of Cape Mudge.
The small community dock in Discovery Passage is exposed to wind and tidal currents.

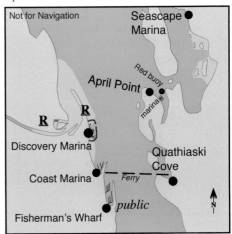

Seascape Marina

Mark & Jennifer Wanstall
774 Cliff Rd   PO Box 250
Quadra Island BC V0P 1N0
Ph: 250-285-3450 Fax: 250-285-2101
Toll Free 1-888-893-1626
info@seascapewaterfrontresort.com
www.seascapewaterfrontresort.com
Charts 3312, 3540, 3539   VHF 66A (10)
Marina services: Guest moorage, 1,000'
dock, reservations preferred. **Power:** 15,
30-amp. **Washrooms, showers,** laundry,
ice, wireless internet, kayaking, power boat
rentals, sauna, DVD rentals. Paviliion.
Nearby facilities: Vineyard, restaurants,
grocery store, post office, bank, adventure
tours, liquor store, float plane service.

Freshwater Marina

2705 N. Island Hwy
Campbell River BC V9W 2H4
Ph: 250-286-0701 Fax: 250-286-1343

Above: Freshwater Marina on the Campbell River.

*Above: Seascape Resort Marina dock. Seascape is located
in Gowlland Harbour as seen in the diagram and the
photograph below. Shallows at north end.*

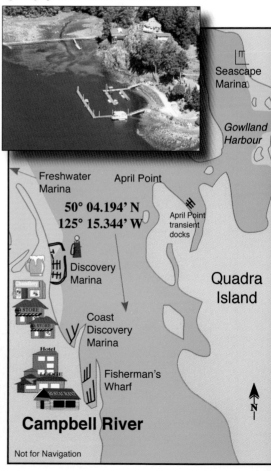

50° 01.743' N   125° 14.380' W

Coast Discovery Inn & Marina
975 Shoppers Row
Campbell River BC V9W 2C4
Ph: 250-287-7455 Fax: 250-287-2213
www.coasthotels.com
Charts 3540, 3539, 3312   VHF 66A
Marina Services:
Moorage. 1,900 feet docks. Boats to 150'. **Power:** 30, 50, 100 amps.
Customer services:
Showers, ice. Cold beer, wine and spirits store. **Washrooms**, restaurant, pub, fitness centre, hot tub. At marina: Floating restaurant, fishing charter boats, boat rentals, tours, scuba diving charter boats, water taxi, garbage disposal. At hotel: **Showers,** ice, cold beer, wine and spirits store, restaurant, pub, fitness centre, hot tub.
Adjacent facilities:
Opposite the marina is the Coast Discovery Inn and adjacent downtown shopping centre. Adjacent to the marina is the ferry landing for Quathiaski Cove on Quadra Island. Medical services nearby. **Laundry**. Charts, books, fishing gear, licences and boat supplies are available at **Ocean Pacific Marine Supply** in Discovery Harbour Centre, a large, modern shopping centre adjacent to Discovery Marina. There are more shops and reataurants in the city centre.

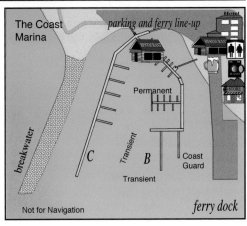

Entertainment:
Foreshore Park with walkway to scenic downtown Campbell River. Fishing is excellent in the general area.

Below: Coast Marina docks are near the ferry terminal.

Charts 3540, 3539, 3312

50° 02.5162' N
125° 14.571' W

Discovery Harbour Marina

Discovery Harbour Marina

Manager Tara Henderson

392-1434 Island Hwy   **VHF 66A**
Campbell River BC V9W 5T7
Ph: 250-287-2614 Fax: 250-287-8939
Charts 3540, 3539, 3312
tara@discoveryharbourmarina.com
www.discoveryharbourmarina.com

Marina services:

Moorage: 150 berths, 1,600 feet side tie for guests. Boats to 160 feet. **Water** at dock. **Power:** 20, 30, 50, 100 amps. Single phase and three phase. Water, laundry,showers, ice, bail, garbage disposal.

Customer services: Dockside marine service. **Laundry, showers,** ice, bait. Garbage disposal. Vehicle rentals in town. All amenities. Travelift and shipyard adjacent. The launch ramp is nearby, north of the marina. **Entertainment:** Wireless Internet. Road access walking or cycling. Sport fishing and scuba diving are excellent in the area. There are strong tidal currents and it is suggested that divers use local dive operators as guides. House of Treasure native art gallery next door. **Ocean Pacific Marine Supply** is convenmiently located at the marina.

Discovery Harbour Fuels: Gas, diesel, oils. Fuel is also available at Brown's Bay, Heriot Bay and at Blind Channel.

Riptide Marine Pub

Manager Dick Walton

1340 Island Hwy
Campbell River BC V9W 8C9
Ph: 250-830-0044 Fax: 250-830-0055
riptide@connected.bc.ca
www.riptide.homestead.com

Marina services: Limited moorage–use K dock slips 1 and 3 and the long finger against the shore, which is marked to identify the Riptide Marine Pub. **Power** 30, 50 amp. **Water. Washrooms, showers, laundry.** Pub and restaurant. Liquor store. Located at the Discovery Harbour Shopping Centre.

Fuel: Adjacent–Gas, diesel, oils.

Quathiaski Cove

Quadra Island Harbour Authority
Public dock (DFO)
Dawn Ross manager
Ph: 250-285-3622
qiha@island.net

• Float length 195 metres • Launch ramp • Garbage drop for a fee • Lights • **Power**: 20, 30 amps • Public pay phone. Showers, washrooms, wifi, rafting dock, commercial & pleasure boats Shops nearby. Adjacent BC Ferries to Campbell River.

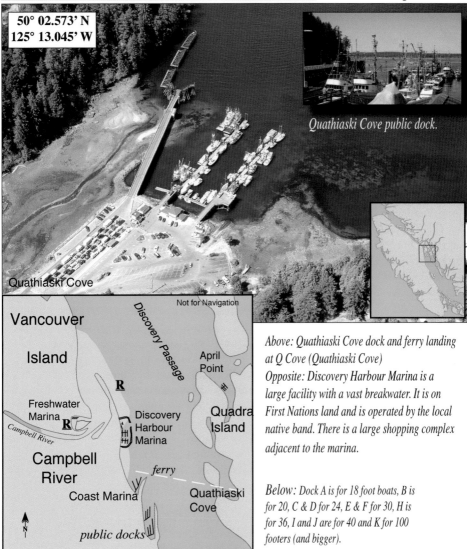

50° 02.573' N
125° 13.045' W

Quathiaski Cove public dock.

Quathiaski Cove

Not for Navigation

Vancouver

Island

Discovery Passage

April
Point

R

Freshwater
Marina **R**

Campbell River

Discovery
Harbour
Marina

Quadra
Island

Campbell
River

ferry

Coast Marina

Quathiaski
Cove

public docks

N

Above: *Quathiaski Cove dock and ferry landing at Q Cove (Quathiaski Cove)*
Opposite: *Discovery Harbour Marina is a large facility with a vast breakwater. It is on First Nations land and is operated by the local native band. There is a large shopping complex adjacent to the marina.*

Below: *Dock A is for 18 foot boats, B is for 20, C & D for 24, E & F for 30, H is for 36, I and J are for 40 and K for 100 footers (and bigger).*

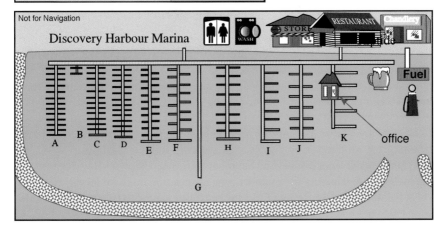

Not for Navigation

Discovery Harbour Marina

WASH

STORE

RESTAURANT

Chandlery

Fuel

A   B   C   D   E   F   H   I   J   K   office

G

Central East Vanc I

50° 08.104' N
125° 20.418' W

VHF 66A

Brown's Bay Marina
Brent Hollink and Mike Sparks
15021 Brown's Bay Rd
Campbell River BC V9W 7H6
Ph: 250-286-3135
Fax: 250-286-0951
www.brownsbayresort.com
Charts 3539, 3513, 3312
Marina services: Fishing resort.
Fuel: Gas, diesel, oils. Moorage.
Transient moorage available. Boats

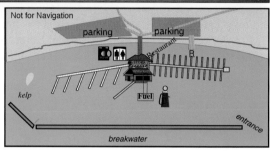

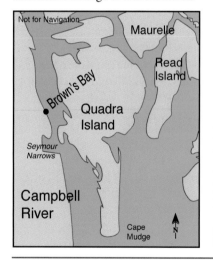

to 90 feet. **Power** at docks: 15, 30 amp. Water.
Garbage disposal.
Customer services:
Bed and breakfast accommodation. RV sites. Ripple Rock RV Park–many facilities.
Laundry, showers. Bait, public pay phone ashore. Store. Ice, foul weather gear, clothing, tide tables, tackle, fishing licences. Fish cleaning station.
Launch ramp. Seasonal restaurant–licensed.
Entertainment: Boat rentals. Fishing guides/charters. Wildlife charters. Guides available.
Walking: Unpaved road in fair condition. Walking or cycling. Cyclists beware of road traffic.
Fishing superior in general area near the harbour.
Note: Nearest golf course is 25 km by road.

Sequoia Springs Golf Course 250-287-4970

Campbell River is a busy place. There are resorts at this international sportfishing playground that cater to fishermen and eco-tourists, offering guided salmon fishing and tournaments and adventure tourism. Some lodges with marinas offer no transient moorage while others have an open door to overnight boating stops. The velocity of water surging through Seymour Narrows just north of the town is dangerous. Be mindful of tides and currents, especially when venturing through the narrows or around the bottom of Quadra Island and its infamous Cape Mudge during gusty winds and swift moving tidal waters.

Fuel up at Campbell River or just beyond Seymour Narrows at Brown's Bay, because you may not find fuel too conveniently for a while if you are heading north up Johnstone Strait. There is fuel at Blind Channel or Refuge Cove in Desolation Sound. It is available at Heriot Bay on the east side of Quadra Island as well as at Gorge Harbour on Cortes Island.

Desolation Sound
and the Discovery Islands

Section 5

Once in Desolation Sound you will not be stuck for fuel because there is a full service fuel stop at Refuge Cove. This facility is a centre for all boating needs to serve the cruising mariner. It has fresh produce, groceries, frozen foods, books, charts, liquor and more. The store and hamburger stand on the property above the marina makes an ideal place to wander or sit in the sun and enjoy the ambience of being out boating.

Desolation Sound is a popular place to anchor for days on end in the summertime. From the many coves and bays of Grace Harbour or Prideaux Haven to Pendrell Sound and Walsh Cove, or Roscoe Bay, Theodosia Inlet, Van Donop Inlet and Squirrel Cove to name a few, one can find the ideal place to set up home aboard for a few days or play musical moorages and move from one to the next as one spends a summer vacation in this warm water oasis in BC. Move early in the day to avoid difficulty in finding a place to drop anchor in some of the busier bays.

To the west is Heriot Bay for moorage and fuel and Drew Harbour with its anchorage behind Rebecca Spit. Kayaking is drawing increasing numbers to this area each year. Go to Surge Narrows from Heriot Bay, or cross over and spend the rest of your vacation at Gorge Harbour, one of the most sheltered large bays in the area, with a fine marina and restaurant to keep you in comfort for your stay. There is fuel at Gorge Harbour, a store, all facilities plus petroglyphs on the sheer rock face at the entrance. In the vicinity you may want to stop in for a stroll at nearby Whaletown. Dock space is limited. *See* **Anchorages and Marine Parks** *for more information on Desolation Sound.*

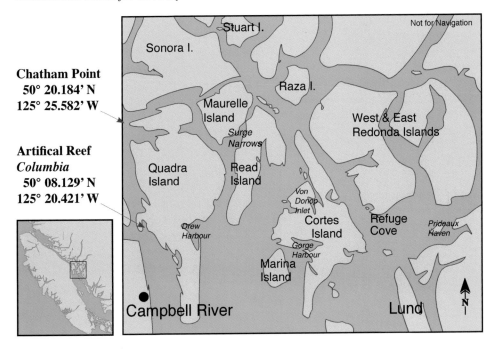

Chatham Point
50° 20.184' N
125° 25.582' W

Artifical Reef
Columbia
50° 08.129' N
125° 20.421' W

50° 05.419' N
125° 02.227' W

Gorge Harbour

Desolation Sound

Gorge Harbour Marina Resort

Bill Dougan
1374 Hunt Rd, PO Box 89
Whaletown, Cortes Island BC V0P 1Z0
Ph: 250-935-6433 Fax: 250-935-6402
info@gorgeharbour.com
www.gorgeharbour.com
Charts 3538, 3312, 3311   VHF 66A
Marina services: Fuel: Gas, diesel, oil.
Moorage: 2,300' of guest moorage.
Water. Power at docks: 30, 50 amp.
Customer services:
Grocery store. Coffee counter, pastries, fishing licences, tackle. ice, books, gifts, charts, propane, postage stamps. Internet access. **Laundry, showers, washrooms.** Pool and spa. Garbage drop. Kayak rentals. Private rooms with showers. Fish cleaning station on docks. Live music. jazz nights. Movie nights. Video and DVD rentals. Old Floathouse Restaurant.
Entertainment:
Adjoining campground with fa-

cilities. Trail to roadway. Walk to rustic Whaletown.
Adjacent facilities:
Licensed restaurant on property–The Floathouse Restaurant. All year weekends. July and August 10 am to 9 pm. Art and museum on island. RVs, Camping. Vehicle rentals. Small public dock (rafting)–no services, and launch ramp nearby.

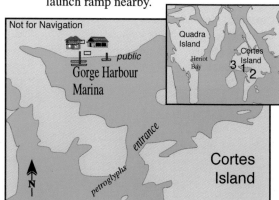

Not for Navigation

public

Gorge Harbour Marina

Quadra Island

Heriot Bay

Cortes Island

3

1

2

entrance

petroglyphs

N

Cortes Island

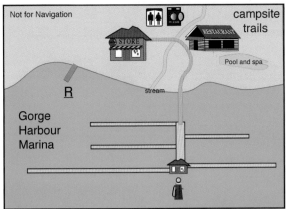

Not for Navigation

campsite
trails

STORE

RESTAURANT

Pool and spa

R

stream

Gorge
Harbour
Marina

Opposite: Gorge Harbour Marina docks and spa early and pre-season 2009.

Below: The entrance to Gorge Harbour is narrow and subject to current. There are petroglyphs on the west side rock face.

50° 04.306' N
124° 59.039' W

50° 06.479' N
125° 03.179' W

Manson's Landing
public dock and marine park

Siri Ellingsen

**PO Box 243, Manson's Landing
BC V0P 1K0   Ph: 250-935-0180
Charts 3311, 3538   VHF 66A**

Moorage: Limited moorage at small government dock–rafting.

Power 20 amps. No water.

Groceries nearby at Gorge Harbour.
Road to store and cafe.

Entertainment:
Walking on island roads.
Beaches. Lagoon.

Adjacent facilities:
Marine Park, toilets
Public pay phone.

Hazard: Exposed to westerly winds. Shallows on north approaches.

Above left and right: Manson's Landing and Whaletown.

Whaletown

Siri Ellingsen

**PO Box 243, Manson's Landing BC V0P 1K0
Phone: 250-935-0180**

No garbage disposal.

Power 20, 30 amps. Limited moorage at public dock–rafting. Float plane dock.

Services:
Post office (Mon, Wed, Fri) nearby.

Entertainment:
Walking on island roads, fishing, kayaking, bird watching. Library, Art gallery nearby. Easy walk to Gorge Harbour.

Adjacent facilities:
Ferry to Quadra.
Public pay phone.

Hazard: Rock near government dock. See chart 3538.

50° 06.159' N
125° 12.737' W

Heriot Bay

Desolation Sound

Heriot Bay Inn and Marina

Manager Lois Taylor
PO Box 100, Heriot Bay
Quadra Island BC V0P 1H0
Ph: 250-285-3322 Fax: 250-285-2708
Toll free 1-888-605-4545
Charts 3538/9, 3312   VHF 66A
info@heriotbayinn.com
www.heriotbayinn.com

Marina services:
Fuel: Gas, diesel, oil. Propane.
Moorage 1,800' of docks. Reservations recommended. **Power**: 15, 30 amps.
Fish cleaning station on dock.

Customer services:
Restaurant–patio service (seasonal), pub. Kayak rentals. Gift shop. Ice, books, gifts, charts. **Laundry, showers, washrooms.** Private rooms at Inn. Cottages. Water taxi. RV Park. Hook-ups, tents.

Heriot Bay Public dock

Quadra Island Harbour Authority
Dawn Ross manager Ph: 250-285-3555
qiha@island.net
Year round guest docks • Launch ramp • Garbage • Lights • Power: 15 amps
• wifi, water, outhouse, public phone.
Nearby: Plaza, pub, library, groceries.

Entertainment:
Historic Heriot Bay Inn and its classic pub. Wifi. Fishing, sight-seeing charters. Good scuba diving nearby. Bicycle rentals at marina. Walking–roadway and some beach access at nearby Rebecca Spit. Whale and bear watching. Kayaking, adventure packages. Guides fishing and kayak tours.

Adjacent and nearby facilities:
Repairs and marine service. Liquor store and mini shopping centre. Post office, grocery store at centre. Groceries delivery to boats–Ph: 250-285-3223. Popular anchorage in Drew Harbour at Rebecca Spit Marine Park. Public dock.

Taku Resort

PO Box 1, Heriot Bay
Quadra Island BC V0P 1H0
Ph: 250-285-3031 Fax: 250-285-3712
Toll free 1-877-285-8258
Charts 3538/9, 3312   VHF 66A
info@takuresort.com www.takuresort.com
Guest moorage 800'. **Washrooms, laundry, showers. Water. Power** at docks: 30, 50 amp. Luxury resort–accommodations by reservation. RV site. Easy walk to small shopping centre–groceries, coffee shop.

Cortes Island

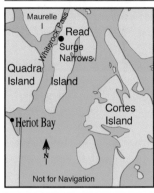

Maurelle I
Whiterock Pass
Read Island
Surge Narrows
Quadra Island
Cortes Island
Heriot Bay
N
Not for Navigation

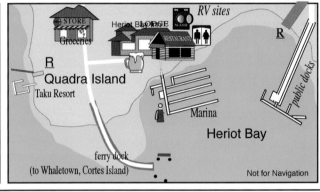

STORE
Groceries
Heriot BAY LODGE
RESTAURANT
WASH
RV sites
R
R
Quadra Island
Taku Resort
Marina
Heriot Bay
ferry dock
(to Whaletown, Cortes Island)
public docks
Not for Navigation

Surge Narrows
PO Box 31, Surge Narrows
Read Island BC V0P 1W0   VHF 12
Ph: 250-287-6962
Charts 3312, 3537, 3539

Small public dock and aircraft float with post office. Near south entrance to Whiterock Pass.

Whiterock Pass	
(north end)	**(south end)**
50° 15.055' N	**50° 14.561' N**
125° 06.061' W	**125° 06.877' W**

*Below: The former store and the post office on the wharf at
Surge Narrows. The post office opens 1 - 4 Mon, Wed, Fri.*

Surge Narrows

50° 13.629' N
125° 06.756' W

Passage through nearby Whiterock Pass to
the Rendezvous Islands is a good alternative
route to Big Bay. Check charts for depths.

*Top: The historic Heriot Bay Inn. Opposite page: The Heriot Bay Inn marina lies between the Cortes Island ferry
dock and the public marina. It is used also by families checked into the hotel's RV park. Inset: Inside the gift shop at
Heriot Bay Inn. Below: Taku Resort in Drew Harbour. The marina is opposite Rebecca Spit.*

Taku Resort

Taku Resort

Cortes Bay

Charts 3555, 3538, 3312

Cortes Bay public dock

Cortes Island
Harbourmaster Siri Ellingsen
PO Box 243
Manson's Landing BC V0P 1K0
Phone: 250-935-0180
www.haa.bc.ca
Hazard: Entering bay–keep rock and day marker at entrance to starboard (passage south of marker).

Moorage at government dock. About 200 feet of dock–rafting. Float plane dock. **Power** at dock: 20 amps. No water. Pay phone ashore. Good cell phone reception. Blind Creek Regional District launch ramp nearby.

Cortes Bay

The public dock is wide and sturdy although not anchored at the deep end. It is controlled by a wharfinger and shared with local residents owning pleasure and commercial craft. Space is limited. Many yachtsmen favour anchoring out in the bay.

Check with the wharfinger for island attractions such as the craft stores and the market. There are two yacht club out-stations in the bay, the Royal Vancouver and the Seattle yacht clubs. Neither of them permits non-member moorage.

Top: Cortes Bay with public dock to left, entrance to right. Note passage to south of the reef at the entrance.
Right top and bottom: Cortes Bay public dock.

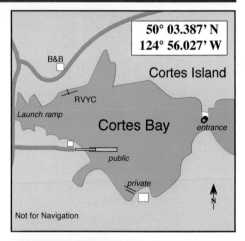

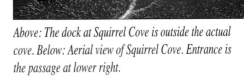

Garden shop at Squirrel Cove.

Squirrel Cove General Store

O'Byrne Taylor

1611 Forest, Cortes Island BC V0P 1T0
Ph: 250-935-6327 Fax: 250-935-6327
Charts 3555, 3538, 3312   VHF 66A
squirrelcovetrading@yahoo.ca
www.cortesisland.com/squirrelcove
Public dock (rafting). **Power** 20 amps.
Free high tide dinghy dock (west of main
dock–dries at low tide). Garbage drop.
Squirrel Cove Store Customer services:
Fuels on shore. Gas, diesel. Small launch
ramp. **Showers, laundry**. Groceries. Organic
foods. Fresh meat, prawns and salmon. Baked
goods and fresh produce, milk, frozen foods,
ice, water, tackle, bait, charts. Propane. Liquor. Gifts. Marine and hardware supplies.
Wireless internet. Post office. Dining at The
Cove Restaurant with a large patio overlooking Desolation Sound. Home baking, full
menu. Licensed. Ph: 250-935-6350. Hiking.
Island roads. Beaches. Tenting.

*Above: The dock at Squirrel Cove is outside the actual
cove. Below: Aerial view of Squirrel Cove. Entrance is
the passage at lower right.*

Adjacent/nearby facilities:
Squirrel Cove public docks, Squirrel Cove
Marine Park. Anchorage. Garden store.
Craft co-op open 7 days. Outdoor market
on Sundays.

Squirrel Cove
Marine Park

50° 07.436' N
124° 50.411' W

Refuge Cove

Charts 3555, 3538, 3312   VHF 66A

Refuge Cove

Colin and Lucy Robertson, Bill Shillito
Refuge Cove BC   V0P 1P0
Ph: 250-935-6659
refcov@twincomm.ca
Marina services:
Fuel: Gas, diesel, oil, propane. **Water** at dock.
Power: 15 amp. Garbage disposal.
Moorage: Overnight moorage. 1,100 feet of docks. Rafting permitted. Internet access.
Customer services:
Laundry, showers, washrooms.
Grocery store, post office. Liquor, ice, books, gifts, charts, Public pay phone.
Adjacent facilities:
Hamburger stand.

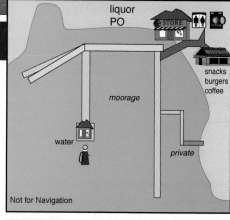

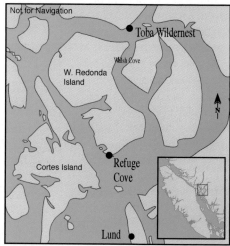

Above: Refuge Cove docks. Inset: Lucy Robertson (centre) and friends at the Refuge Cove General Store. Below: Tied up at the foot of the ramp to the store. Opposite page, top: A visiting boat slowly approaches the busy marina and fuel dock.

Desolation Sound

En route to all parts of Desolation Sound, Refuge Cove is a busy stop during the brief summer season. It affords replenishment of everything from fuels and fresh water to liquor, fresh produce, bread, meat and groceries. Charts, books and a limited selection of clothing are also sold at the store, as well as ice and fishing supplies. The store is positioned high and dry above the high-water mark. It and the fuel dock are run efficiently to accommodate the heavy traffic of the short summer season and survive for the remainder of the year.

50° 19.488' N
124° 47.742' W
Coordinates courtesy of Ken White 'Mr Buttercup.'

Toba Wildernest

Toba Wildernest
Kyle and Andrea Hunter
Mouth of Toba Inlet at
Double Island   VHF 66A
Desolation Sound Ph: 250-830-2269
Charts 3312, 3541
tobawildernest@lincsat.com
www.tobawildernest.com
Moorage 350 feet–for overnight or longer.
Facilities: **Shower** and **washroom**.
No power on dock. Ice. Fishing supplies.
Forest trails to nearby waterfall.
This is a nature resort offering rental cabins
for boaters and fly-in guests. It is located at
the mouth of Toba Inlet just north of Walsh
Cove in Desolation Sound.

Top: Dock at Toba Wildernest. Above: Falls in Toba Inlet. Below: Kyle Hunter at the resort and marina office. This is a nature resort for mariners and fly-in guests.

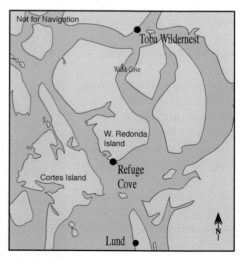

Johnstone Strait
To the Broughton Islands

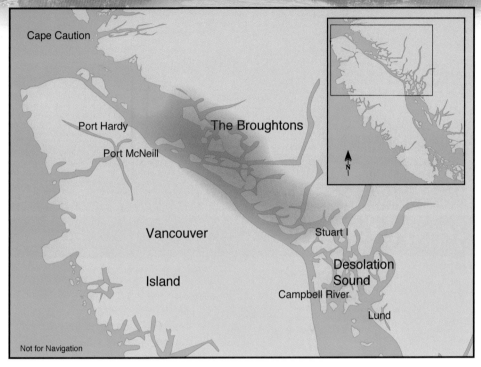

Cape Caution

Port Hardy

Port McNeill

The Broughtons

Vancouver

Stuart I

Desolation
Sound

Island

Campbell River

Lund

N

Not for Navigation

Travelling north of Desolation Sound the mariner must plan passage through the famous Yaculta Rapids, Dent Rapids, Green Point Rapids and Whirlpool Rapids. Or travel via Seymour Narrows and Kelsey Bay into Johnstone Strait. Slower boats would do well to plan stops through the waterways in which these rapids lie so as to take advantage of the best tidal currents. High water slack is usually best and it is particularly easier when the tidal changes are minimal. Stopping at places along the way rather than rushing through as many of the current-swept passages as possible in one leg allows for interesting meetings with local residents. Stop at the marinas along the Cordero Channel route to Port Neville in Johnstone Strait. Take advantage of the facilities provided at the various marinas and resorts and make that an integral part of your trip, if not your actual destination.

Churchhouse First Nations settlement just south of Stuart Island. It is slowly succumbing to nature.

On Sept 4, 2010 the largest recorded salmon was caught at Big Bay. It was estimated to be five years old and weighed in at 72 pounds.

Stuart Island

Charts 3543, 3312

Stuart Island Community Dock
Stuart Island BC V0P 1V0   VHF 66A
Managers: Roger & Cathy Minor
Phone: 250-202-3625
stuartislandca@aol.com
Watch for kelp and a reef near the dock.
Guest moorage: This is a community run facility. Stop here to wait for the tides. Boats to 150' welcome. **Water**, no power on docks, **washrooms, showers, laundry,** coffee shop, grocery store (look for local produce and crafts), liquor agency, post office, ice, fishing supplies. Summer shore facility for group events. Picnic tables on a covered deck. On Saturday of the August long weekend a charity event is held to support support local salmon enhancement.
Nearby facilities: Water taxi, float plane service, fishing (guides available) and adventure charters. Walk to Eagle Lake. There is good reception for cell phones.

Above: Big Bay, Stuart Island. Below: Arran Rapids and Big Bay. Work is constantly in progress at Big Bay.

Mariners are advised to enter and leave Big Bay with caution, noting the shallows near the shore facilities. Consult your chart and watch for kelp–a summertime marker for shallows and reefs.

Be mindful of the strong currents in the area. Use charts and tide and current tables to plan your passage.

Big Bay marks the beginning of the run through the rapids north to Cordero Channel, Johnstone Strait, the Broughton Islands and beyond. It is the passage of choice over Seymour Narrows for most small craft.

Below: From Big Bay, mariners travel north through Gillard Passage (to the left) or south through the Yuculta Rapids (right). Passage at centre not recommended. Avoiding the worst of the currents takes careful planning. Use the tide and current tables.

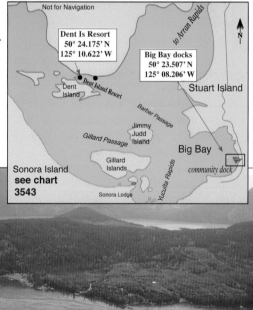

Not for Navigation

Dent Is Resort
50° 24.175' N
125° 10.622' W

Big Bay docks
50° 23.507' N
125° 08.206' W

to Arran Rapids

N

Dent Island

Dent Island Resort

Stuart Island

Barber Passage

Jimmy Judd Island

Gillard Passage

Big Bay

Gillard Islands

Yuculta Rapids

community dock

Sonora Island
see chart
3543

Sonora Lodge

Morgan's Landing Wilderness Retreat

Bob and Jodé Morgan
General Delivery Stuart Island BC V0P 1V0
Ph: 250-287-0237
Charts 3543, 3312   VHF 66A
jodemorgan@hotmail.com
Facebook: morganslanding

Marina services: Moorage, Open May to Sept 15. 375' dock space. **Water. Power** at docks: 30, 50 amp. Fish cleaning station. **Showers, Washrooms.** Weekend restaurant. Fishing licences, bait, ice. Rental rooms. Fishing charters. Guides. Scuba diving.

Dent Island Resort

Henry Moll, Denise Mitchell-Hills
Box 8, Stuart Island BC V0P 1V0
Ph: 250-203-2553 Fax: 250-203-1041
Charts 3312, 3543   VHF 66A
www.dentisland.com
info@dentisland.com
Moorage. Visitors dock–1,000 feet.
Facilities: Lodge with overnight accommodation, restaurant–seasonal. Wireless internet. **Power:** 30, 50, 100 amp. **Water. Washrooms. Showers.** Ice. Laundry. Hot tub and sauna. Fishing guides. Scheduled seaplane. Water taxi service.

Top: The way north along Cordero Channel. Seen in the photo is the exclusive Sonora Lodge, a well-known fishing resort. Its docks may accommodate a few visitors overnight. Check for available space at dock.

Hazards: Shoal in centre of Big Bay near the community dock. Strong currents in the area. Please slow to 5 kn on approach.

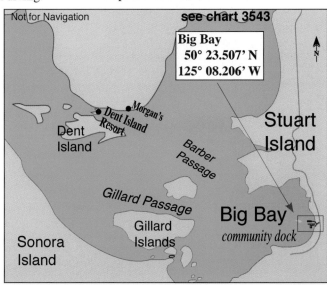

Top: Arriving at Dent Island Lodge docks. This is a luxury resort providing marine moorage and lodge facilities to overnight guests. Above: Staff are on hand to assist landing and to welcome visitors.

At Shoal Bay a public dock with fairly generous moorage provides overnight accommodation. Lodge & Marina owner Mark MacDonald offers fresh laid eggs and homegrown garden greens.
Shoal Bay Lodge is open May 1 to October 1. The facility offers outdoor adventure. It is a good overnight spot to tie up or anchor out in calm conditions. Usually it is only winter time when one has to be mindful of adverse winds coming out of Phillips Arm.

Cordero Channel
Charts 3543, 3312

**50° 27.751' N
125° 21.995' W**

Shoal Bay Lodge & Marina

Mark MacDonald   **VHF 66A**
**Shoal Bay,
East Thurlow Island
Ph: 250-287-6818**
shoalbay@mac.com
www.shoalbay.ca

Public dock managed by Shoal Bay Pub. Rafting when busy. Float length: 300 feet. **Laundry, washrooms, showers.** Fully licenced pub. Liquor/pub. U-pick fresh vegetables. Eggs. Hiking trails. Logging roads. View points along a network of paths. Fishing can be arranged. View animals, marine life and eagles.
Nearby: Canoeing and kayaking day trips in the adjacent waterways, including Thurston Bay.

Charts 3538, 3539, 3312
Owen Bay
Read Island public dock
• Float length 9 metres •

Evans Bay
Read Island public dock
• Float length 18 metres •

Slow down when passing. The floating lodge pictured above, in Cordero Channel, is known internationally for fine dining and successful fishing charters. Inset: Doris Kuppers.

| 50° 26.717' N |
| 125° 26.906' W |

Cordero Lodge   VHF 66A

Reinhardt and Doris Kuppers
G D Blind Channel BC V0P 1B0
Ph: 250-287-0917
info@corderolodge.com
www.corderolodge.com
Charts 3543, 3312
Marina services: 500' guest moorage. No power. **Water** on the main dock.
Customer services: Lodging–up to eight guests. Restaurant–fine dining.
Fishing: Boats–guided. Mariners are requested to slow down when passing by.
Entertainment:
Sunsets and views. Animal and marine life. Bears and eagles.
Adjacent facilities:
Cordero Islands anchoring. *Use caution as strong currents sweep through the area.*

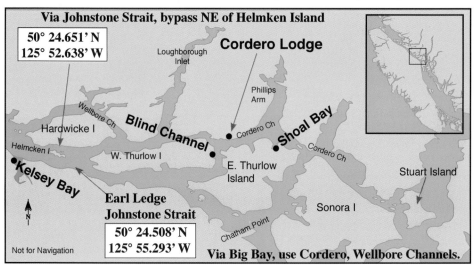

Via Johnstone Strait, bypass NE of Helmken Island

50° 24.651' N
125° 52.638' W

Loughborough Inlet

Cordero Lodge

Phillips Arm

Wellbore Ch

Blind Channel

Cordero Ch

Shoal Bay

Cordero Ch

Hardwicke I

Helmcken I

W. Thurlow I

E. Thurlow Island

Stuart Island

Kelsey Bay

Earl Ledge
Johnstone Strait

50° 24.508' N
125° 55.293' W

Chatham Point

Sonora I

Not for Navigation

Via Big Bay, use Cordero, Wellbore Channels.

50° 24.797' N
125° 29.984' W

Blind Channel

Blind Channel Resort

The Richter family
Blind Channel BC V0P 1B0
Ph: 250-949-1420
Toll free: 1-888-329-0475
Charts 3544, 3543   VHF 66A
info@blindchannel.com
www:blindchannel.com

Marina services:
Moorage: Transient moorage.
Fuel: Gas, diesel, propane.
Spring drinking water at dock. Ice.
Power at docks: 15, 30, 50 amps.
Wireless internet access.

Customer services:
Laundry, showers, washrooms.
Restaurant open June—Labour Day.
Fine dining-excellent cuisine. Patio.
Post office. Public pay phone.
Groceries. Baked goods, bread, fresh
produce, milk, frozen foods, ice,
tackle, bait, charts. Excellent fishing
and prawning nearby.
Rental cottage available. Liquor. Art,
crafts, gifts. Scheduled flights. Water
taxi service.

The marina lies in a sheltered nook in Mayne Passage.

Entertainment:
Hiking trails. Logging roads. Several view
points along a network of paths. See the huge
"Thurlow" cedar tree. Incredible sunsets and
views. Animal, eagles and marine life. Docks
are wide with tasteful embellishments.

Adjacent facilities:
Picnic area.

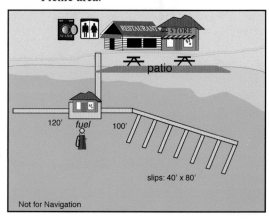

Blind Channel
Fine Dining and good facilities

This long-established marina in one of the coast's busy waterways has evolved over the years to become a very well maintained and contemporary facility for cruising yachtsmen. Three generations of Richters are busy around Blind Channel when guests are moored at their docks. Philip Richter's parents established the marina. Founder Edgar Richter still lives at the property and continues to be involved with planning and preparing further additions. Assisted by son Eliot and daughter-in-law Laura, Philip manages the store while his wife, Jennifer, can be found preparing bread and other baked delectables for the store and restaurant. They also attend a productive vegetable garden and maintain creative landscaping of the property. The marina offers moorage, fuel, water, propane and shore power at the dock. Services include showers, laundry, ice, liquor agency, store and post office.

Nature lovers and hikers will be kept busy for days hiking trails that have been established by a large logging and sawmill company on West Thurlow Island. These trails, which begin about 300 meters from Blind Channel Marina, are designed to show the features of a second growth forest. There are three different trails, one to a spectacular viewpoint overlooking Mayne Passage and East Thurlow Island, a second to the "Big Cedar", a tree with a diameter of 16 feet, via a forest of 80-year old second growth, and the third through a thinned western hemlock stand that was naturally established in 1964.

Years ago the Richters lobbied to have the first growth Thurlow cedar preserved when the logging company intended to log the hillside. The family persuaded them it would be advantageous to establish interpretive trails. The final segment of the second trail descends through 100-year old second growth.

Blind Channel waterfront restaurant.

The stop at Blind Channel Resort has been a favourite among mariners for many decades and the Richter family (top) continues to cater to their needs with fresh produce, baked goods and gourmet cuisine in a fine waterfront restaurant. Laura and Eliot presented the family with a new member, Jonah Edgar in 2009.

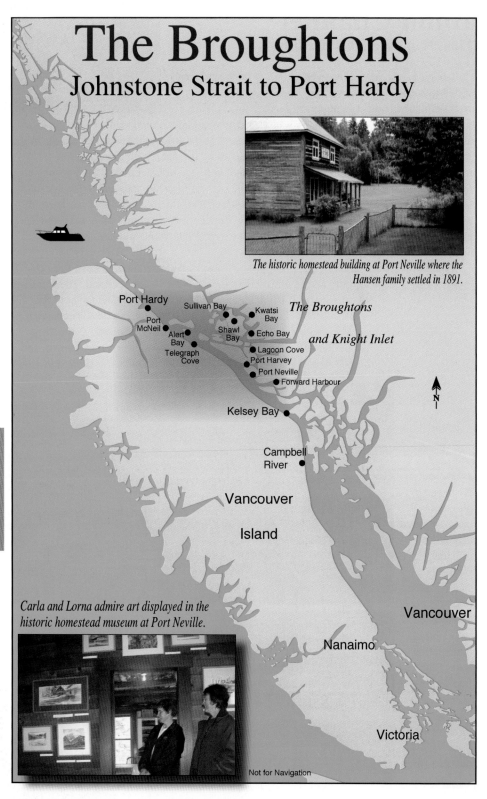

The Broughtons
Johnstone Strait to Port Hardy

The historic homestead building at Port Neville where the Hansen family settled in 1891.

Port Hardy

Sullivan Bay

Kwatsi Bay

The Broughtons

Port McNeil

Shawl Bay

Echo Bay

Alert Bay

and Knight Inlet

Telegraph Cove

Lagoon Cove

Port Harvey

Port Neville

Forward Harbour

N

Kelsey Bay

Campbell River

Vancouver

Island

Carla and Lorna admire art displayed in the historic homestead museum at Port Neville.

Vancouver

Nanaimo

Victoria

Not for Navigation

Enter Kelsey Bay harbour at slack tide and find a slip, perhaps raft alongside a working boat.

Kelsey Bay

Public dock, Vancouver Island
Sayward Harbour Authority
Maurice Croteau
Ph: 250-282-3623   Chart 3544
Float length 185 metre. Floating breakwater • Garbage • Water • Lights • Electric winch at loading bay (220 volt) • Power: 20, 30 amp •. Shower and facilities to come. Groceries are available–call from pay phone on the dock–check with locals at the harbour. Gift shop on the wharf.

Deep Sea Port of Kelsey Bay
Sayward Futures Society dock
Wharfinger Ph: 250-282-0018
sfs@saywardvalley.net
www.portofkelseybay.com
• Float length 31 m • Water • Lights
Deep water moorage for larger vessels. Gift shop, information adjacent.

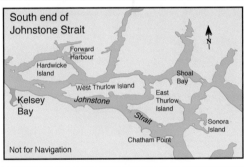

South end of Johnstone Strait

Forward Harbour
Hardwicke Island
West Thurlow Island
Kelsey Bay
Johnstone
Shoal Bay
East Thurlow Island
Strait
Sonora Island
Chatham Point
Not for Navigation

North via Johnstone Strait

Baker I
Echo Bay
Bonwick I
Gilford I
Knight Inlet
Village I
Malcolm Island
Farewell Harbour
Turnour I
Port McNeill
Harbledown I
R
Alert Bay
Hanson I
Telegraph Cove
R
W Cracroft I
Not for Navigation
Johnstone Strait

Sayward Futures Society dock behind wharf

Public dock

The dock and historic store at Port Neville.

At Port Neville there is a post office and an art gallery and gift shop in the renovated historic family building.

Port Neville

	50° 28.646' N
	125° 05.595' W

Historic settlement.
Johnstone Strait
Transport Canada dock
Port Neville BC V0P 1M0
Lorna Chesluk Hansen
Ph: 250-287-2844
Charts 3564, 3545
Float length 34 m.
Seasonal antique display, art gallery and gift store in historic family building. Open subject to the caretaker being available on the property.

The dock at Port Neville.

Minstrel Island
Public dock
Charts 3564, 3545, 3515
Float length 135 m • Aircraft float • Lights
Privately owned property. Stopping at dock is allowed. No marina facilities ashore.

50° 36.868' N
126° 18.148' W

The public dock at Minstrel Island is adjacent to the private, historic property. This is located beyond Port Harvey en route to the Broughton Islands.

Port Neville.

Port Harvey

50° 32.285' N
126° 17.274' W

Not for Navigation

Port Harvey Marine Resort

George and Gailanne Cambridge
PO Box 40 Minstrel Island BC V0P 1L0
Ph: 250-902-9003
Charts 3564, 3545   VHF 66A
cambridge@xplornet.com
portharvey.blogspot.com
Marina services:
Moorage: Transient moorage.
Water. Power. Laundry, showers.
Customer services:
Store–groceries, baked goods, hardware.
Pub/restaurant. Fresh cinnamon buns made on
site, coffee, ice cream. Gift shop. Free wireless
internet. Good cellphone coverage.
Walking trails, fire pit and outdoor game
areas. Cabins and camping sites.
This marinia was established in 2009 and has
been visited by numerous boats in season. The
owners are present year round to welcome
guests. There is a post office located nearby
in Chatham Channel.

*Top: The Port Harvey Marina Resort is shown in the
upper right side of the photograph. It can handle large
pleasure craft and offers transient moorage, restaurant
and other mariner services.*

On the dock at Port Harvey Marina.

Photo: Sharon Allman

GPS South end of Chatham channel:
50° 34.786' N   126° 12.646' W
GPS North end of Chatham channel:
50° 34.781' N   126° 14.244" W

The **Post Office** is located near the north end
of Chatham Channel, close to Minstrel Island.
Mail is picked up Wednesdays. Gallery, gift
shop, rental cabins. Jen Rueker delivers
baked goods to **Lagoon Cove Marina**
three times a week in July and August
and picks up outgoing mail.

Charts 3564, 3545, 3515

*Use Chatham Channel via Havanah Channel and Port
Harvey entrance to reach Knight Inlet, Minstrel Island
and Lagoon Cove from Johnstone Strait.*

Lagoon Cove

50° 36.061' N
126° 19.065' W

Lagoon Cove Marina

Bill and Jean Barber
Minstrel Island PO BC V0P 1L0
Charts 3564, 3545
VHF 66A
Post office is located in Chatham Channel
Marina services:
Moorage: Transient moorage. Open year round. Rafting allowed.
Fuel: Gas, diesel, propane. Oils.
Some repairs subject to available help.
Haulouts to 40'. **Water** at dock. **Showers, washrooms. Power:** 30, 50 amps in summer. Edgewater Emporium store with selection of clothing. Charts, books.
Customer services:
Pot luck appetisers. Fishing licences, ice, tackle, bait, sodas, candies. Crab and prawn traps. Float plane service. Floating cabins and house for rent. Excellent fishing and prawning nearby.
Entertainment:
Hiking trails. Sunsets and views. Animal and marine life. Bears and eagles.

Some people choose to anchor in Lagoon Cove, but with secure docking when the wind is up it is worth stopping at the marina.

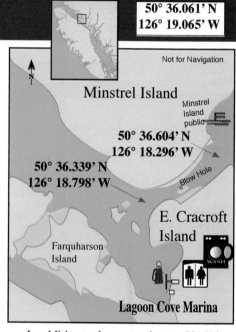

Not for Navigation

Minstrel Island

Minstrel Island public

50° 36.604' N
126° 18.296' W

50° 36.339' N
126° 18.798' W

Blow Hole

E. Cracroft Island

Farquharson Island

WASH

Lagoon Cove Marina

In addition to the convenience of facilties, there is the friendly greeting from owners Bill and Jean Barber. An incredible collection of marine and other hardware, enough for a museum were left by former owners. Some items have been discarded but many remain in a workshed display area. There is an "Appy Hour" at 5 pm. Prawns are served. Bring an appetizer and join the social on the deck at the top of the dock.

Above left: The marina at Lagoon Cove is a popular stop for big boats heading to Alaska in the spring. Above: Fuel dock at Lagoon Cove. Left: Bill Barber with freshly caught prawns for his famous afternoon "Appy hour." Below: Lagoon Cove showing the marina and shallow navigable passage beyond, leading to Chatham Channel or Knight Inlet and Tribune Channel to Kwatsi Bay.

Kwatsi Bay Marina lies beneath towering coastal mountains off Tribune Channel.

50° 50.622' N
126° 16.932' W

Kwatsi Bay

Kwatsi Bay

Anca Fraser and Max Knierim
c/o Simoom Sound BC V0P 1S0
Cell Ph: 250-949-1384
Chart 3515   VHF 66A
kwatsibay@hughes.net www.kwatsibay.com
This is a small marina at remote Kwatsi Bay off Tribune Channel. Cruise from Echo Bay or from Minstrel Island via beautiful scenery in the Tribune Channel area.

Shawl Bay

Kingcome Inlet

Kwatsi Bay

Broughton Island

Tribune Channel

Gilford Island

Knight Inlet

Minsrtel I

Lagoon Cove

Not for Navigation

Guest moorage. open year round. Water (good and plentiful), showers. Nearest fuel at Lagoon Cove, Echo Bay or Sullivan Bay. Gift store, evening pot luck appetizers. Wilderness facilities. Peaceful and quiet. Anchorage at the head of the bay in 30 ft.

The Kwatsi Bay dock gets busy in season. It has space for large and small boats.

Kwatsi Bay is a small inlet off Tribune Channel about midway between Knight Inlet and Echo Bay. It is one of the loveliest spots on the coast, so remote that the less said about it here the more it will be enjoyed.

From Knight Inlet follow the east side of Gilford Island, bypassing Thompson Sound and Bond Sound. Enter Kwatsi Bay beyond Irvine Point and Miller Point.

From Echo Bay turn east after Viner Sound and follow Tribune Channel east to Kwatsi Bay just beyond Watson Cove.

Top: The marina in Kwatsi Bay continues to grow and attract more visitors. Centre: Regular visitor and friend Linda Lewis arrives at Kwatsi Bay. Above: Anca Fraser shares a light moment with the crew on a BC Forest Service boat.

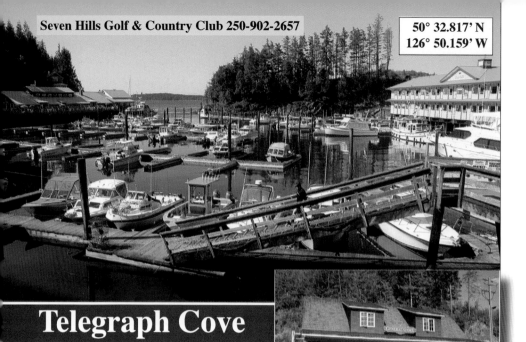

Seven Hills Golf & Country Club 250-902-2657

Telegraph Cove

North of Desolation

Telegraph Cove Marina
Travis Meinhold
1642 B Telegraph Cove Rd   VHF 66A
Telegraph Cove BC V0N 3J0
Ph: 250-928-3163 Fax: 250-928-3162
reservations@telegraphcove.ca
www.telegraphcove.ca   **Chart 3546**
Moorage: 130 small lips. Also commercial dock for loading. **Power, water.** Hotel accommodations. **Laundry, washrooms, showers. 50' wide launch ramp. Fuel**: Available at entrance to cove. Gas, oil (no diesel), restaurant, pub, general store. Coffee shops, cafe. Whale watching and scuba diving–contact **Stubbs Island Charters** on the boardwalk via the fuel dock ramp at the entrance to Telegraph Cove. RV park.

The store at Telegraph Cove Resorts.

Small launch ramp at Telegraph Cove

Telegraph Cove Resorts
Moorage reserved for resort clients with slips to 25'. Telegraph Cove **Marina** offers

Telegraph Cove

Right: Tied up at the whale watching boat dock. Opposite page top and bottom: Telegraph Cove Marina and entrance, showing the fuel dock and whale interpretive centre (museum). Below: 2009 off-season aerial view shows Telegraph Cove dock layout.

overnight visitor moorage. General store on the property. Small launch ramp. Stop briefly at the fuel dock at the entrance and visit the craft shop on the wharf. The gas dock is operated by Telegraph Cove Resorts– **Phone: 250-928-3131.** There is fuel, diesel and gas available at Port McNeill.

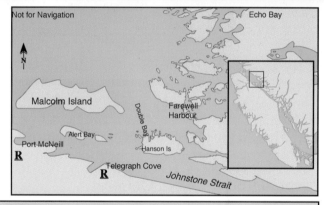

Not for Navigation

Echo Bay

Malcolm Island

Farewell Harbour

Double Bay

Alert Bay
Port McNeill R

Hanson Is

Telegraph Cove
R

Johnstone Strait

Stubbs Island Charters

Jim and Mary Borrowman
PO Box 7   Chart 3546   VHF 10
Telegraph Cove BC V0N 3J0
Ph: 250-928-3185 Fax: 250-928-3102
stubbs@island.net
www.stubbs-island.com

Customer Services:
Whale watching day trips. Store with gifts, fine art, books.
Nearby: On boardwalk: Whale Interpretive Centre, cabin accommodations, dining, snacks. Also–resort, marina, campground and general store.

Note the tidal habitat lagoon

Photo: Courtesy Steve Jackman

Port McNeill

Port McNeill Fuel Dock & Marina

Steve Jackman
PO Box 488. 1488 Beach, PO Box 488
Port McNeill BC V0N 2R0   VHF 66A
Ph: 250-902-8128 or 250-956-4044
Fax: 250-956-3922
sjackman@portmcneill.com
www.portmcneill.com
Fuel: Gas, diesel, avgas, propane. **Water**.
Power: 20, 30, 50 (120/208v), 100 amps.
Moorage: Docks available for all sizes of
vessels. Boat storage and detailing. Boat
sitting. Year round dry storage for boats.
On staff scuba diver– hull inspections,
diesel and gas mechanics.Adventure enter-
tainment packages, marine charts, ice, bait.
Wireless internet. Private theatre rentals.
Adjacent and nearby facilities:
C.A.B. Industrial Automotive Supply–auto
and marine parts, Grizzly Helicopters,
laundromat, groceries, hospital, taxi,
banks. **Launch Ramp.**

Alert Bay

A ferry ride to Alert Bay and Sointula makes a good
alternative way to visit those places from Port McNeill.

   Alert Bay attracts mariners as a stop for replenishment and an opportunity to go ashore for some
exercise as they travel en route to points north or home again. Among the reasons for stopping at Alert
Bay is to visit to the Ecological Park. It is more like something you would expect to stumble across on
a tour of Florida. The park is a marshy, swampy glade complete with large still pools of water afloat
with the massive leaves of various forms of vegetation and sprouting large sprays of skunk cabbage.
Wooden boardwalks have been constructed to allow access for easy walking and viewing. The most
prominent feature is the incredible trees which appear to have been struck by lightning at one time.
From the marinas of Alert Bay to the Ecological Park is a good uphill walk to the back of the residential
area overlooking the bay. The route is marked by signs that end up near the transmitter station and

Seven Hills Golf & Country Club 250-902-2657

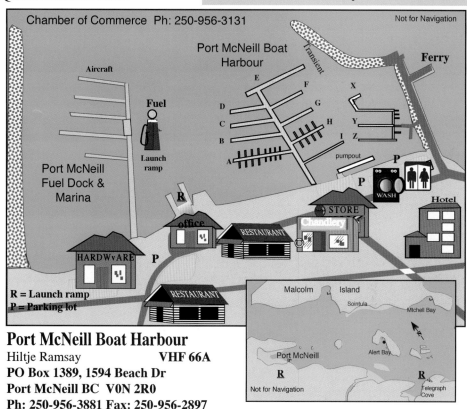

Chamber of Commerce Ph: 250-956-3131

Port McNeill Boat Harbour

Not for Navigation

Ferry

Aircraft

Fuel

Port McNeill Fuel Dock & Marina

Launch ramp

pumpout

WASH

Hotel

STORE

Chandlery

office

RESTAURANT

HARDWvARE P

R = Launch ramp
P = Parking lot

RESTAURANT

Malcolm   Island
Sointula
Mtchell Bay

Port McNeill
Alert Bay

R   R
Not for Navigation
Telegraph Cove

Port McNeill Boat Harbour

Hiltje Ramsay   **VHF 66A**
PO Box 1389, 1594 Beach Dr
Port McNeill BC V0N 2R0
Ph: 250-956-3881 Fax: 250-956-2897
pmharbour@telus.net
www.portmcneillharbour.ca

Moorage: Extensive sheltered docks to 5,000'. Outer floats D-G are reserved for transient moorage. Limited guest reservations, call ahead. Oil disposal. Water. **Power**: 15, 20, 30, 50, 100 amps. **Launch Ramp** adjacent. New docks due in 2011. **Services:** Garbage disposal. Fish cleaning station. Oil disposal, washrooms, showers, laundry. Pumpout. Free wireless internet access. Free loading dock while shopping.

Opposite, top: Port McNeill is a gateway to the Broughtons. The fuel dock is usually busy with commercial and pleasure boats as well as float planes.

Entertainment: Walk along shore and sea wall. Uptown facilities–hotels, restaurants, shops. Museum. Scenic flights.
Adjacent and nearby facilities:
Ferry to Sointula and Alert Bay. Marine repairs–fuel barge. Ice, laundry, showers, groceries. Marine store and service. Hospital nearby.

entrance to the park and will eventually lead you to the wooden planked walk through the glades.

Alert Bay boasts the once tallest totem in the world. It is located a short walk up the hill next to the Big House behind the U' mista Native Cultural Centre which is on the shore adjacent to the docks north of town. The cultural centre is well worth a visit. Among other interesting items, it has on display segments of exhibits that were shown at Expo 86 in Vancouver.

You may be lucky when visiting Alert Bay and experience some rare calm, sunny weather. If not, watch the currents that sweep around the northern channel en route to Port Hardy or the open northern reaches of Johnstone Strait. In windy conditions it is usually possible to sneak around the south end of Malcolm Island and through the rocky channels and islets in the area. We once took shelter for two days in the Plumper Islets while the wind raged. It is not really a suitable anchorage for more than a temporary stop because the current rips through quite fast especially at high tides.

Left: Sointula has protected docks with lots of room. It is a long established fishing village settled by Fins early in the last century. The settlement has many artists, a fine museum and lots of history. There is a restaurant, grocery store, museum and a liquor agency near the ferry dock. Opposite: Alert Bay. There is a public dock at the centre and another at the north end of the village and the small, exposed Town Dock at the south end.

Above: Courtesy Christine Cornelia and Harbour Authority

Sointula

*** 50° 37.733' N
127° 02.640' W**

Sointula Boat Harbour

Malcolm Island Lions Club Harbour Authority
Manager Lorraine Williams
710 First St, Sointula BC V0N 3E0
Ph: 250-973-6544   **Chart 3546**
milha@island,net   www.dfo-mpo.gc.ca

Docks totalling 865 metres. Washrooms, laundry, showers. Power 20, 30 amp. Hardware store, snacks, restaurant at ferry dock (to Port McNeill). No dock space can be specifically reserved. **Mitchell Bay** dock has no amenities.

Caution: Enter public docks past the floating breakwater (added since the photo at top of page).

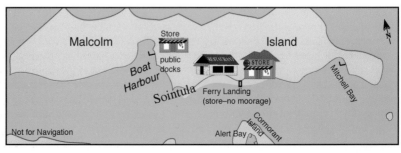

North of Desolation

Queen Charlotte Strait

Left: The public dock lies in the centre of Alert Bay. The ferry lands at the fingers alongside the breakwater.

Alert Bay

Chart 3546
VHF 66A

**50° 34.957' N
126° 56.151' W**

Alert Bay Boat Harbour
Corporation of Village of Alert Bay
Bag Service 2800, Alert Bay BC V0N 1A0
Eric Gregory
Ph: 250-974-8255

boatharbour@alertbay.ca   www.alertbay.ca
Marina services: Transient moorage. Float length 533 metres. **Power:** 20, 30 amp. **Water.** Breakwater. Aircraft float. Washrooms, garbage disposal. Internet access.
Laundry is still being planned.
Note: Fuel is available at Port McNeill.

Nearby: ATM. Restaurants. Groceries. Tackle, bait, charts. All services at village of Alert Bay. Nimpkish Inn and other accommodations. Liquor, drug store. Library. Hospital. Dental, medical services.
Entertainment:
Walking–hiking trails and roads. Visit the **Ecological Park** on the hill above the town. Animal and marine life. Prime whale watching and scuba diving nearby.

U'mista Cultural Centre.
Visit this outstanding display of native history. World's once-tallest totem and Big House at the north end of the bay.
Nearby facilities: Paved airstrip (2,800').

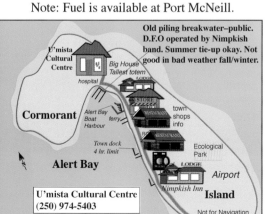

Old piling breakwater–public. D.F.O operated by Nimpkish band. Summer tie-up okay. Not good in bad weather fall/winter.

U'mista Cultural Centre
Big House
Tallest totem
hospital
LODGE
STORE
RESTAURANT
Cormorant
Alert Bay Boat Harbour
ferry
town shops info
Town dock 4 hr. limit
Ecological Park
Alert Bay
LODGE
WAG HOUSE
Airport
Nimpkish Inn **Island**
Not for Navigation

**U'mista Cultural Centre
(250) 974-5403**

Municipal (Town) dock
Chart 3546 • Manager Eric Gregory
Ph: 250-974-8255 • Free launch ramp
• Float length 61 metres • Garbage •
Water (on wharf only) • Lights.

Alert Bay Information Centre
Travel Info Centre Ph: 250-974-5024.
info@village.alertbay.bc.ca   www.alertbay.ca

Pierre's Echo Bay.
Right: Pierre working at a prime rib roast.

Echo Bay

50° 45.326' N
125° 29.952' W
Chart 3515   VHF 66A

Pierre's Echo Bay

Jerome and Lucy Rose, Pierre & Tove Landry
Box 257, Gabriola Island BC V0R 1X0
or: **Simoom Sound PO BC V0P 1S0**
Phone: 250-713-6415 or: 250-663-8905
info@pierresbay.com
www.pierresatechobay.com

Marina services:
Transient moorage over 1,850'. Reserve in peak season–July, August. Open seven days a week all year round. Additional moorage opposite at Cliffside. Covered picnic float. **Fuel**: Gas, diesel, propane. **Water** at dock. **Power:** 15, 30, 50 amps. **Laundry, showers, washrooms.**
The main dock is a part of the former Lake Washington floating bridge.

Customer services:
Wireless internet. Cellular phone service. Post office. Store–groceries, supplies. Block and party ice. Fresh produce, milk, frozen foods, tackle, books, charts and gifts. Boat sitting. Rental suites–contact for availability.

Entertainment:
Happy Hour every evening under the tent. Dinners during the season include Wednesday night prime rib, Thursday night Italian and Saturday night themed pig roast (requires a Friday/Saturday stay). Call ahead for reservations. Various airlines make scheduled flights in and out of Pierre's. There is plenty of area to get out and stretch, walk the dog and take the trail to Billy Proctor's Museum. Fishing, prawning & crabbing are readily available.

Adjacent facilities:
Local crafts and artists. Billy Proctor's Museum. Nearby anchorage and public float at marine park. Dog-walk. Playground. Walk-in campsites.
Nikki's Echo Bay EcoVentures offers some exclusive adventure tours–contact her through Pierre, Billy Proctor or by email at *theforestdweller@gmail.com.*

Left: The author's wife, Carla (centre) with Pierre and Tove Landry at Pierre's Echo Bay.

Above and bottom: Pierre's Echo Bay Marina. The lodge to the right of the docked boats has overnight accommodations, well-appointed self-contained rental suites and a spacious lounge for relaxing.

Opposite: The marina. Note the barge at the entrance to the bay that houses the post office, the store and the barbeque area. Inset: Pierre at the barbecue.

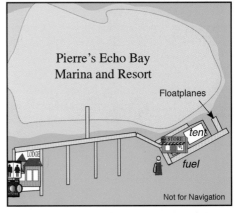

Pierre's Echo Bay
Marina and Resort

Floatplanes

tent

LODGE

STORE

fuel

Not for Navigation

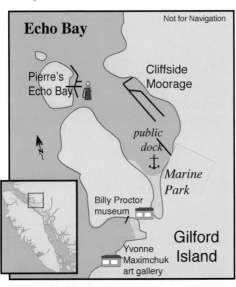

Echo Bay

Not for Navigation

Pierre's
Echo Bay

Cliffside
Moorage

*public
dock*

*Marine
Park*

Billy Proctor
museum

**Gilford
Island**

Yvonne
Maximchuk
art gallery

*Marine park, dock
and anchorage.*

*Head of Echo Bay and
the Proctor homestead.*

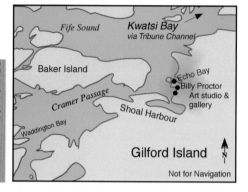

Top and right: Billy Proctor alongside his boat Ocean Dawn *and at the entrance to his museum.*

History and commerce converge at Echo Bay. It is a hub of activity drawing summertime travelling boaters, whale watching tourists out of Telegraph Cove, sportfishing groups from near and far and a constant flow of local people from neighbouring logging camps and fish farms to pick up fuel, supplies and mail. Or to replenish some of their grocery needs. The resort caters to a steady flow of visitors in for a few days of fishing or stopping by in their boats for a spell in the area. Fuel and moorage with power and water are available from Pierre's Echo Bay marina which also serves as post office and store.

The marina on the opposite shore, Cliffside Moorage, previously Windsong Sea Village, has large floats that will accommodate an overflow of Pierre's Echo Bay

Gilford Island
Gilford Village • Chart 3515 • Float length 60 m • Aircraft float.

Kingcome
Transport Canada • Chart 3515 • Float length 55 m • Windy and exposed.

boats. This marina is mostly occupied by private tenants.

Artist Yvonne Maximchuk has a studio just outside the entrance to Shoal Harbour and provides an opportunity for artists or tyros to brush up on their skills. Here, in her gallery studio, she conducts instruction and classes in art, water colour, acrylics and oils, available to people on visiting boats.

She also has a fine selection of works for sale and can be reached by calling her at *Sea Rose* on channel 16.

Billy Proctor, a long-time resident of Echo Bay, has co-authored two books about the area, with Yvonne Maximchuk and Alexandra Morton. His museum is worth a visit.

Echo Bay Marine Park. All weather anchorage. Small, 70' boat dock. Camping sites, water, toilets. Waddington Bay, not far from Echo Bay, part of Broughton Archipelago (Park), offers additional anchorage. See *Anchorages and Marine Parks.*

Shawl Bay

Shawl Bay Marina

Lorne, Shawn and Rob Brown
c/o Simoom Sound PO BC V0P 1S0
Ph: 250-483-4169
Chart 3515   VHF 66A
shawlbaymarina@shawlbaymarina.com-
www.shawlbaymarina.com

Marina services:

Moorage: Transient 1,000' and floathouse moorage. **Power** 15, 30 amps.

Water. Showers. Store–Carol the Bead Lady. Home baked bread, cinnamon rolls and pies can be ordered day before. Ice. Rental cabins. Wireless internet access.

Entertainment: Pancake breakfast included with moorage. Starting July 1st seafood chowder nights every two weeks during the summer. Starting July 7th deep fried turkey every two weeks, alternating with seafood chowder event.

Above: Boats in the marina, seen from under the shelter on the marina's entertainment deck.

Adjacent facilities:

Daily scheduled flights to Seattle, Port McNeill and Campbell River. Kenmore Air and Northwest Air.

Shawl Bay is a busy place during the summer season. Many regular boating friends and customers of the family that owns and operates the cosy marina at the far corner of the bay, return each year to tie up at the spacious docks. These docks and the structures on them comprise Shawl Bay Marina, operated until the mid 1900s by the late Edna Brown and her sister Johanne along with Edna's son Gary.

Brother Alf Didriksen ran a logging camp in the bay for many years and the family's hospitality is legendary among fishermen, loggers and pleasure boaters alike. It is now being run by Lorne and Shawn Brown, their son Rob. Aunty Jo, who collected moorage fees for many years, passed away in August 2010.

Kingcome Inlet

entrance

yacht club

marina

Note: Look for the turquoise docks to identify the marina in the bay.

Aerial photo shows the location of Shawl Bay Marina in a corner of the bay. Buildings along the dock include the store, laundry and washrooms. Rob Brown in foreground. Inset: Visit the Bead Lady, Carol Ellison at her store.

Nearby destination alternatives

Turn off at Tribune Channel after Echo Bay for a visit to Kwatsi Bay, or continue to Shawl Bay and Sullivan Bay with a stop at Greenway Sound.

Kwatsi Bay is delightful, tranquil and majestic with tall mountains rising steeply around it. Greenway has been a busy stop since it was opened in 1985 by Tom and Ann Taylor. Moorage is typically busy with large visiting yachts, some of which remain during summer. Walk the length of the floats at Greenway twice and you have walked a mile. Another favoured walk in Greenway Sound is to the lake up the mountainside. A dinghy float and ramp provide access to the path that leads to the lake.

Tom and Ann Taylor

>Check your notes for Whaler Bay Galiano Is

Greenway Sound

Greenway Sound
Marine Resort

Tom and Ann Taylor
PO Box 759, Port McNeill BC V0N 2R0
Ph: 604-629-9838
Ph: 360-466-4751 (winter)
Charts 3547, 3515   VHF 66A

tomnann@ncia.com
www.greenwaysound.com

Marina services:

Moorage: Large destination marina with plenty of transient moorage with up to 2,200 feet of red carpeted docks. Good for power walking. Reserve dock space in peak season.

Laundry, showers, washrooms.

Garbage accepted. **Water** at dock is good and abundant. **Shore Power**: 15 and 30 amp/120 volt and 50 amp/208 volt. Free W-Fi to all locations on dock. Uses 802.11.

Restaurant. Reservations essential for dinner 6:30-8 pm. Licenced. Menu on website. Steak, prawns, chicken, pastas, awesome desserts. Groceries. Milk, produce, frozen foods, bread, deli, sticky buns, ice, bait, tackle, books, charts, film, and gifts, great clothing, hardware, sundries.

Postal service, telephone, fax.
Conscientious boat sitting.
Excellent fishing and prawning nearby.
Ice cream and espresso.
Free video and pocketbook exchange.
Flown-in fresh dairy and produce.

Entertainment:

Adjacent park for hiking, walking, swimming, exploring. Incredible sunsets and views. Animal and marine life.

Customer services:

Regular scheduled flights to Port Hardy, Port McNeill, Campbell River, Vancouver, Kenmore and Renton (Seattle). See website. Assistance with travel arrangements or customs as needed. Local cruising and exploring advice. Reasonably current newspapers to borrow. VISA, Mastercard, Discover. (No Amex.)

Broughton Island

Greenway Sound/Sullivan Bay

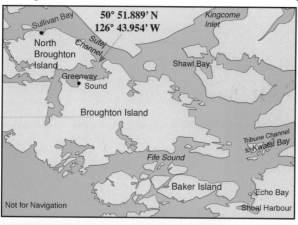

50° 51.889' N
126° 43.954' W

Sullivan Bay
Kingcome Inlet
North Broughton Island
Sutlej Channel
Shawl Bay
Greenway Sound
Broughton Island
Tribune Channel to Kwatsi Bay
Fife Sound
Baker Island
Echo Bay
Shoal Harbour

Not for Navigation

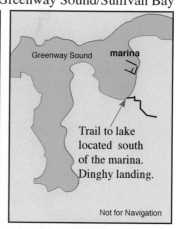

Greenway Sound   **marina**

Trail to lake located south of the marina. Dinghy landing.

Not for Navigation

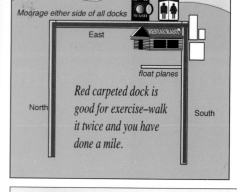

Moorage either side of all docks

WASH

East

RESTAURANT

float planes

North

Red carpeted dock is good for exercise–walk it twice and you have done a mile.

South

Not for Navigation

The restaurant at Greenway Sound is on a float alongside the dock. It also houses a small store as well as the marina office. The aircraft float is reserved for floatplanes arriving regularly in summer.

Above: Taking on fuel at Sullivan Bay. Above left: Views of Greenway Sound Marine Resort. Nearby, there is a hiking trail from a dinghy dock leading to Broughton Lake Park. Access off Sutlej Channel to the marina at Greenway Sound is very easy.

Left: Ahead of the busy dinnertime in the restaurant at Sullivan Bay.

50° 53.381' N
126° 49.676' W

Sullivan Bay

Sullivan Bay   Chart 3547 VHF 66A
Marine Resort

Chris Scheevers & Debbie Holt
Box 6000, Port McNeill, BC V0N 2R0
Phone: 250-629-9900
sullivanbaymarina@gmail.com
www.sullivanbay.com

Marina services: Fuel: Gas, diesel, pro-pane, oil, ice, bait. Mechanic and services at Vancouver Island towns and ports. Some repairs possible. Internet access.

Moorage: Large permanent marina with plenty of guest moorage up to 2,500 feet of dock. Reserve in peak season. Open year round. **Water** at dock. **Laundry, showers, washrooms. Power** at docks: 15, 30, 50, 100 amp (240V).

Customer services: Licensed restaurant. Liquor store. Groceries. Mail drop. Fresh produce, dairy products, frozen foods, ice, tackle and souvenirs. Video movie rentals. Scheduled floatplane service. Private floating homes village. Specialized boat sitting.

Entertainment:
Library. Novel building structures, street

Not for Navigation

Restaurant open in summer

Guests

names on docks. Happy hour. Fishing, crab-bing and prawning locally. July 4th party, parade, barbecue, dance (by reservation). This facility was a major coastal seaplane refuelling stop but no longer. It has an inter-esting aviation history. Read Jack Schofield's books on local aviation history.

Right: The fuel dock and store in Sullivan Bay.

Jennis Bay

Jennis Bay Extreme Expeditions, Ltd.

Owner/Manager: Allyson Major

PO Box 456   VHF 66A   Chart: 3547
Port McNeill BC V0N 2R0
Phone: 403-987-9410

jennisbay@hughes.net
www.jennisbay.com

Location: Jennis Bay, Drury Inlet.

Marina services: Guest moorage, gift shop, eco-tourism, Geo-cache "treasure" hunting, hiking/biking trails, bike & sit-atop kayak rentals, guided trail & lake excursions, Cajun cookouts Tuesday nights, washroom, shower, campfire get-togethers, pets and children are welcome. Self-contained cabin rentals.

Above and below: Jennis Bay in Drury Inlet.
Inset: A view of the marina, always improving.

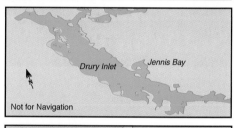

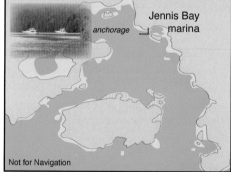

Port Hardy

Quarterdeck Inn & Marina Resort

Owner/manager: Karl Thomas
6555 Hardy Bay Rd
PO Box 910
Port Hardy BC V0N 2P0
Ph: 250-949-6551 Fax: 250-949-7777
marina@quarterdeckresort.net
www.quarterdeckresort.net
VHF 16, (66A also used)
Marina: Fuel: Gas, diesel, propane.

Showers, laundry. **Launch ramp**.
Moorage: 100 slips to 100' boats. Reservations suggested. **Power** 15, 30, 50 amp.
Water. 60 ton travel lift. Some repairs. Pressure wash. Marine store. Charts, ice, dry ice, fishing tackle. Internet access. 40 room Motor Inn Hotel. Courtesy Car.
Nearby: Flights, bus service. Pub restaurant, wine and beer store, hotels nearby. Taxis. BC Ferries and shopping. Adventure charters.

Top and inset: The docks at Fisherman's Wharf and a view of the Quarterdeck Inn and Marina Resort overlooking the launch ramp.

Port Hardy outer dock

Hurst Island

Port Hardy Inner Dock
Fisherman's Wharf (Inside breakwater)
Port Hardy Harbour Authority
6600 Hardy Bay Rd. PO Box 68,
Port Hardy BC V0N 2P0
Ph: 250-949-6332 Fax: 250-949-6037
Managed by Pacificus Biological Services
phfloats@cablerocket.com
www.district.porthardy.bc.ca
Charts 3548, 3605
• Float length 574 m • **Launch ramp** •
Breakwater • Grid • Garbage • **Water**
• Lights • **Power**: 15, 30 amp • Public
pay phone • **Washrooms** • **Fuel** nearby
• Pumpout.
Close to town with all services and
facilities. Fuel available at Quarterdeck
Inn & Marina and at Petro-Canada
Marine located at Bear Cove near the
ferry terminal.

Port Hardy Outer dock
Seagate Marina (Outside breakwater)
Ph: 250-949-6332 Fax: 250-949-6037
Managed by Pacificus Biological Services.
• Float length 250 m • **Garbage** • **Water** • **Moorage**: Commercial but some
transient when space available. Floats
in place May to September only. Coast
Guard station adjacent. Downtown Port
Hardy location with access to shops and
services.

50° 50.394' N **127° 35.694' W**	

God's Pocket
Bill Weeks & Annie Ceschi
PO Box 130, Port Hardy BC V0N 2P0
Ph: 250-949-1755
Charts 3921, 3549, 3605   VHF 66A
info@godspocket.com
www.godspocket.com
Moorage and facilities: Limited, sheltered docks. Washrooms.
Some accommodation available. Cabins.
Entertainment:
Walking trails on island. Hiking. Scuba
diving. Kayaking charters.

Bull Harbour
Hope Island Government dock
Charts 3921, 3549 Float length 35 m
Anchor in bay. Dinghy to dock.

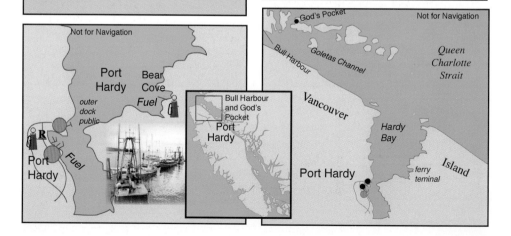

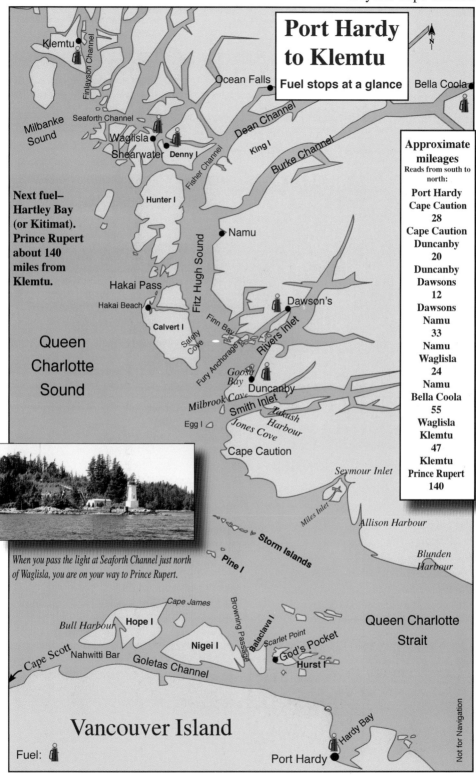

Port Hardy to Klemtu

Fuel stops at a glance

N

Klemtu

Finlayson Channel

Ocean Falls

Bella Coola

Milbanke Sound

Seaforth Channel

Waglisla

Shearwater

Denny I

Dean Channel

King I

Burke Channel

Next fuel–Hartley Bay (or Kitimat). Prince Rupert about 140 miles from Klemtu.

Hunter I

Fisher Channel

Namu

Fitz Hugh Sound

Hakai Pass

Hakai Beach

Calvert I

Finn Bay

Dawson's

Queen Charlotte Sound

Safety Cove

Fury Anchorage

Rivers Inlet

Goose Bay

Duncanby

Milbrook Cove

Smith Inlet

Zakush Harbour

Egg I

Jones Cove

Cape Caution

Seymour Inlet

Miles Inlet

Allison Harbour

Approximate mileages
Reads from south to north:
Port Hardy Cape Caution 28
Cape Caution Duncanby 20
Duncanby Dawsons 12
Dawsons Namu 33
Namu Waglisla 24
Namu Bella Coola 55
Waglisla Klemtu 47
Klemtu Prince Rupert 140

Blunden Harbour

When you pass the light at Seaforth Channel just north of Waglisla, you are on your way to Prince Rupert.

Storm Islands

Pine I

Queen Charlotte Strait

Cape James

Browning Passage

Bull Harbour

Hope I

Balaclava I

Scarlet Point

God's Pocket

Nigei I

Hurst I

Cape Scott

Nahwitti Bar

Goletas Channel

Vancouver Island

Hardy Bay

Fuel:

Port Hardy

North Coast

Not for Navigation

The North Coast
Beyond Cape Caution

Section 6

Duncanby Landing

51° 23.450' N
127° 42.400' W

Photo: Norman Elliot

Rivers Inlet

Chart 3934

Duncanby Landing

Lodge Cory Gordon
Rivers Inlet PO BC V0N 1M0
Ph: 1-877-846-6548   VHF 06
reservations@duncanby.com
www.duncanby.com
Moorage. Water, power: 30 amp.
Fuel: Gas diesel, propane, lubricants.
Showers, laundry, washrooms.
Bait, charters, boat rentals.

Ice, telephone, internet service. Limited accommodations. Lounge. Restaurant–breakfast, lunch, dinner. Located at Goose Bay at the entrance to Rivers Inlet.

Photos: Norman Elliot

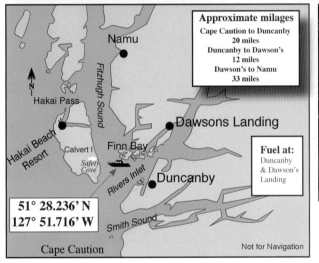

Approximate milages
Cape Caution to Duncanby
20 miles
Duncanby to Dawson's
12 miles
Dawson's to Namu
33 miles

Namu

Fitzhugh Sound

Hakai Pass

Hakai Beach Resort

Calvert I

Finn Bay

Safety Cove

Dawsons Landing

Fuel at:
Duncanby
& Dawson's
Landing

Rivers Inlet

Duncanby

51° 28.236' N
127° 51.716' W

Smith Sound

Cape Caution

Not for Navigation

Photos: Norman Elliot

Top and opposite: The dock at Duncanby Landing. Above: Fish cleaning station.

To reach Rivers Inlet from Port Hardy it is necessary to round Cape Caution and pass the entrance to Smith Inlet. There are no facilities between God's Pocket just out of Port Hardy, and Rivers Inlet. If weather is a deterrent temporary anchorage is possible off Hurst Island or moorage at God's Pocket dock if space is available. Bull Harbour, slightly out of the way for a passage around Cape Caution is a good anchorage. It is shallow off Cape Caution and many yachtsmen round the Cape about five miles off. Local mariners cut close to the Cape and take passage behind the islands, rocks and islets off Smith Inlet to slide around into Rivers Inlet off Goose Bay. Choose to round Cape Caution in gentle wind and sea conditions and be wary of fog. On the passage around Cape Caution one can find temporary and some good protected overnight anchorages at places such as Blunden Harbour, Allison Harbour, Skull Cove, Miles Inlet, Seymour Inlet, Jones Cove and Milbrook Cove. Please refer to **Anchorages and Marine Parks**.

The first fuel stops are at Duncanby Landing in Goose Bay, or farther up Rivers Inlet at Dawson's Landing. Some mariners travel past Rivers Inlet, stopping, if necessary for overnight anchorage, at Safety Cove on Calvert Island, or at Fury Anchorage at the entrance to Rivers Inlet.

51° 34.476' N
127° 35.514' W

Photo: Sharon Allman

Dawsons Landing

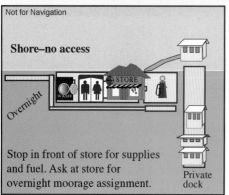

Not for Navigation

Shore–no access

Overnight

STORE

WASH

Stop in front of store for supplies and fuel. Ask at store for overnight moorage assignment.

Private dock

Photo: Norman Elliot

Top and above: Tied up to the fuel and store dock at Dawsons Landing. Inside the store there is always a warm welcome. Below: An aerial view with dock layout (photo courtesy of Dawsons Landing).

Dawsons Landing
General Store
Robert and Nola Bachen
Dawsons Landing BC V0N 1M0
Ph: 604-629-9897 Fax: 250-949-2111
dawsons@dawsonslanding.ca
www.dawsonslanding.ca
Charts 3934, 3932   VHF 66A
Marina services: Moorage. Water.
Washrooms. Fuel: Gas, diesel, stove oil.
Customer Services: Showers, laundry.
Accommodations. General store: tackle, fishing licences, bait, groceries, block and cube ice, fish freezing, liquor agency.

Photo courtesy Dawson's Landing

Scheduled air service to Port Hardy. Post office, gifts, toys, souvenirs, books, charts, supplies for marine maintenance and repairs.
Anchorage among nearby islands.

Photo: Sharon Allman

Fitzhugh Sound

Hakai Beach Institute

Dock manager
Pruth Harbour, Calvert Island
PO Box 309, Heriot Bay BC V0P 1H0
Charts 3935, 3727
contact@hakai.org
www.hakai.org

Anchor in bay. This is not a public dock or
marina. Shore access–tie up small dinghies
under ramp inside marina. Walk to white,
sandy beach on open Pacific.

Anchorage–Pruth Bay. Hakai Beach
Institute is funded by the Tula Foundation,
a privately endowed family foundation
located on Quadra Island.
See *www.tula.org www.tula.org*
Note: Visiting mariners may go ashore.

North Coast

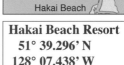

Hakai Beach Resort	Namu to
51° 39.296' N	**Bella Coola**
128° 07.438' W	**55 miles**
	Waglisla to
*Mid channel (Namu)	**Ocean Falls**
Fitzhugh Sound	**30 miles**
51° 52.044' N	**Waglisla**
127° 57.841' W	**to Klemtu**
	47 miles

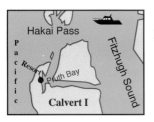

*Above and right:
The resort at Hakai
Pass. Anchor off,
row ashore and
walk to beach on
the west side.*

Photo: Sharon Allman

Namu to Bella Coola	55 miles
Namu to Waglisla	24 miles
Waglisla to Ocean Falls	30 miles
Waglisla to Klemtu	47 miles
Ocean Falls to Bella Coola	50 miles
Namu to Kitimat	181 miles

51° 51.597' N
127° 52.116' W

Photos: Sharon Allman

Top and bottom: The docks and buildings at Namu.
Above: The fuel dock at Namu sells gas and diesel.
There is a small gift shop at the landing.

Namu

Namu BC V0T 1Z0
Caretakers Pete and Rene Darwin
General Delivery Waglisla BC V0T 1Z0
Ph: 250-949-4090 Fax: 250-624-8984
VHF 10 monitored at times.
Charts 3936, 3727
namuharbour@hotmail.com
Moorage. Water at main dock.
Washroom. Barbecue area.
Customer services: Constant changes are in place. Buildings and docks are in a mixed state of repair but the operators are redeveloping some facilities for visitors. Namu is an interesting historic and archaeological site. This is a popular area for kayaking, with many kayakers making nearby Hakai Pass a destination of choice. There are anchorages nearby, such as Codville Lagoon and Fougner Bay. No garbage disposal. Fuel at Bella Bella or Shearwater.

Caution: Beware of unmarked rocks in the bay. See chart 3785 for Loo Rock.

52° 09.706' N
128° 08.457' W

Waglisla

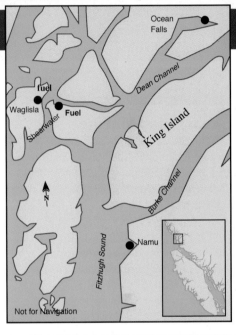

Waglisla (Bella Bella)

226 Waglisla, Waglisla BC V0T 1Z0
Campbell Island
Ph: 250-957-2440 Charts 3938, 3939
Fuel dock: Gas, diesel, stove oil. **Water.**
Moorage: Visitors may stay at fuel dock
overnight at no charge. General store with
groceries and public phone, bar, restaurant.
BC Ferries stop weekly.
RCMP station. Hospital. ATM. Liquor
store. Corner store. Repairs. Taxis. Air-
port. Short distance to Shearwater Marine.
Waglisla is a First Nations village.

Top and below: Visitors to Waglisla may tie up at the
fuel dock overnight if space is available. The large
building, shown below, is the general store.

North Coast

52° 08.869' N
128° 05.218' W

Photo: Sharon Allman

Shearwater

Shearwater Marine
PO Box 68
Denny Island BC V0T 1B0   VHF 66A
Ph: 250-957-2305   Fax: 250-957-2422
Toll free: 1-800-663-2370 (Vancouver office)
Charts 3938, 3939
www.shearwater.ca

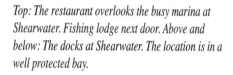

Sharon Allman

Top: The restaurant overlooks the busy marina at Shearwater. Fishing lodge next door. Above and below: The docks at Shearwater. The location is in a well protected bay.

Marina services: Fuel: Gas, diesel. Propane. Marine service. Lubricants.
Moorage. 1,600 feet of docks (mostly concrete) **Water. Power** 15, 30, 50 amps.
Laundry, showers, washrooms. Public pay phones. Pub. Liquor. Off-sales. Boat and engine repairs. 70 tonne travel lift.

Boat launch. Grocery/hardware store. Post Office. Wireless internet access.
Customer services:
Electronics shop. Store: tackle, fishing licences, bait, gifts. Charts, marine supplies. ATM.

Photo: Sharon Allman

Restaurant
Ph: 250-957-2366.
40 room hotel.
3,000 foot airstrip.
Yacht charters.
Fishing charters,
boat rentals.
Scuba air station.
Daily plane service
nearby. BC Ferries
terminal. Floating
breakwater.
Launch ramp.
Seabus to Waglisla.

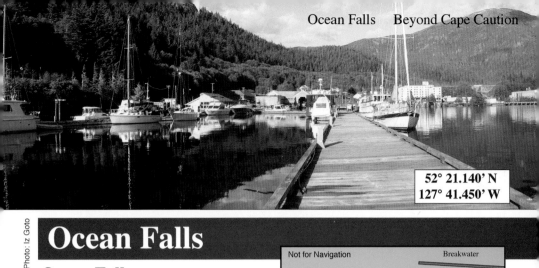

52° 21.140' N
127° 41.450' W

Photo: Iz Goto

Ocean Falls

Ocean Falls Harbour Authority

Manager Herb Carpenter
Neil McLachlan–wharfinger
GD, Ocean Falls BC V0T 1C0
Ph: 250-289-3859/3352
Fax: 250-289-3859   VHF 09
Charts 3939, 3729
Marina: Moorage. Power: 20, 30 amps.
Water. Fish cleaning station. The docks are in good shape, unlike the decaying town of Ocean Falls. Between the remnants of Ocean Falls and the nearby community at Martin Valley there are accommodations and amenities. These include medical services, a saloon, gift shop, groceries at local store, a post office, liquor store, laundry, showers, and a marine ways. Coast Lodge and Cafe for meals.

Walk the roadway to Link Lake and the dam. There is a hatchery for fish farming. The old powerhouse provides power to Bella Bella and Shearwater. Tours are available during ferry stopovers. Boats and aircraft check in at dock.

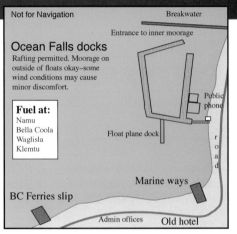

Not for Navigation   Breakwater

Entrance to inner moorage

Ocean Falls docks
Rafting permitted. Moorage on outside of floats okay–some wind conditions may cause minor discomfort.

Fuel at:
Namu
Bella Coola
Waglisla
Klemtu

Float plane dock

Public phone

road

Marine ways

BC Ferries slip

Admin offices   Old hotel

Top and below: Ocean Falls docks. The floats include a small shack that serves as the office. There is a recreation room with two computers for visitors.

Ocean Falls

Photo: Iz Goto

Bella Coola

Chart 3730

52° 19.319' N
126° 45.840' W

Bella Coola Harbour Authority

Manager: Thomas Carney
PO Box 751, Bella Coola BC V0T 1C0
Ph: 250-799-5633
Fax: 250-799-5632   VHF 16
bcha@belco.bc.ca

Marina: Rafting necessary at pleasure boat moorage near shore on east side of marina. Larger vessels easy access guest moorage. **Power:** 20, 30 amps. **Water.** Pumpout. Garbage disposal. **Showers, laundry, washrooms. Fuel dock** 250-799-5580: Gas, diesel. One and a half miles to uptown stores, restaurants, museum, motel, car rentals. Post office, credit union, hospital. Store: Tackle, fishing licences, bait, groceries, liquor, gifts. Charts, marine supplies. No food services at marina. Poor VHF radio reception. Broadband internet service is available. Wharfinger office open 8.30 - 4.30 pm (weekdays). BC Ferries.

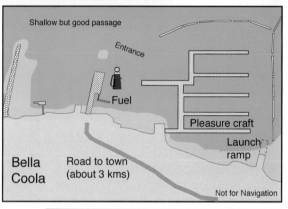

Shallow but good passage
Entrance
Fuel
Pleasure craft
Launch ramp
Bella Coola
Road to town (about 3 kms)
Not for Navigation

If you ask the townsfolk at Bella Coola where their favourite hot springs is located, they may tell you. Just down North Bentinck Arm to South Bentinck Arm and turn south. Several miles down the arm just beyond Bensins Island and on the opposite shore is Talheo hot springs at the mouth of Hotsprings Creek. Anchor off and row ashore for a hot soak in the sulphur waters of this delightful pool. It has been improved by the local people of Bella Coola so respect it and leave it clean.

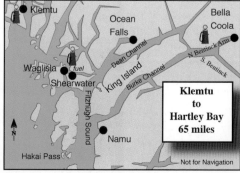

Klemtu
Ocean Falls
Bella Coola
Waglisla *fuel*
Shearwater
Dean Channel
King Island
Burke Channel
N Bentinck Arm
S Bentinck
Fitzhugh Sound
Namu
Hakai Pass

Klemtu to Hartley Bay 65 miles

Not for Navigation

Aerial photo courtesy DFO/Small Craft Harbours

52° 35.577' N
128° 31.297' W

Photo: Sharon Allman

Klemtu–Hartley Bay

Charts 3941, 3742,
3941/2/3, 3902

Klemtu Tourism Dock

Wharfinger. **Ph: 250-839-3246** **VHF 06**
PO Box 401, Klemtu BC V0T 1L0
Ph: 1-877-644-2346 Charts 3941, 3711
info@spiritbearadventures.com
www.spiritbear.com

Moorage: Mooring float for guests at
nearby band operated dock. Washrooms,
showers, laundry. Two stores. Tourism
dock at fuel dock. **Fuel:** Gas, diesel, stove
oil, propane, water. Store at fuel dock.
Groceries, ice, marine and fishing supplies,
ATM. Hiking trail to water tower lookout.
Medical services, Post Office. Guided
tours, kayak rentals. Floathouse Inn, Spirit
Bear Lodge, Klemtu Lodge. Cabin rentals etc. Up town Robinson-Mason general
store (near the church): groceries. Visit the
Big House. Ask at fuel dock for directions.

Above: The village dock and the Lodge at Klemtu.

> Klemtu Band membership, reception at
> Kitasoo-Xai'xais Government House:
> Warren Edgar Ph: 250-839-1255
> Klemtu and Hartley Bay are the last fuel stops
> before Prince Rupert or Kitimat.
> Distance Klemtu to Prince Rupert 150 miles.

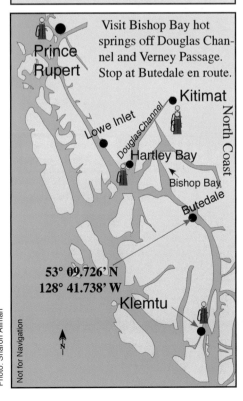

Visit Bishop Bay hot springs off Douglas Channel and Verney Passage. Stop at Butedale en route.

53° 09.726' N
128° 41.738' W

Prince Rupert
Lowe Inlet
Douglas Channel
Kitimat
Hartley Bay
Bishop Bay
Butedale
Klemtu

North Coast

N

Not for Navigation

Photo: Sharon Allman

Butedale

Hartley Bay
53° 25.265' N
129° 15.015' W

Photo: Sharon Allman

Hartley Bay (Txal giu)

Fuel dock manager: Marshall Reece
GD, Hartley Bay BC V0V 1A0
hbvc@gitgaat.net
Ph: 250-841-2626
Fax: 250-841-2679
Marina: Moorage at public docks behind the breakwater.
Fuel: Gas, diesel. Credit cards accepted.
Power: 20 amps. **Water**.
Groceries. Post office. General store. Garbage drop. Emergency helipad. Nearby mooring buoys in Stewart Channel. This is a government dock run by the local band–office at 445 Hayimiisaxaa Way, a short walk into the village.

Above: The docks and fuel dock at Hartley Bay. Below: M.K. Bay Marina in Kitimat. It is located on the east side of Douglas Channel adjacent to the Haisla First Nations Kitimaat village. Bottom and below: M.K. Bay Marina.

M.K. Bay Marina

Kitimat
53° 59.200' N
128° 40.572 ' W

M.K. Bay Marina

M.K. Bay Marina   VHF 68

Manager: Richard Smeal
Kitamaat Village Rd, PO Box 220
Kitimat BC V8C 2G7
Ph: 250-632-6401 Fax: 250-632-6889
www. mkbaymarina.com
Chart 3743, 3736   Launch ramp.
Fuel: Gas, diesel, oils. **Water. Moorage:**
150 slips. **Power** 15, 20, 30, 50 amps.
Laundry, showers, washrooms.
Haulouts to 20 tons. ATM. Charts, fishing supplies, licences, bait. Deli, campground. Playground. Taxi to stores–7 miles (11 km) to town on Minette Bay Rd. Liquor store, post office, hospital. Marine stores.

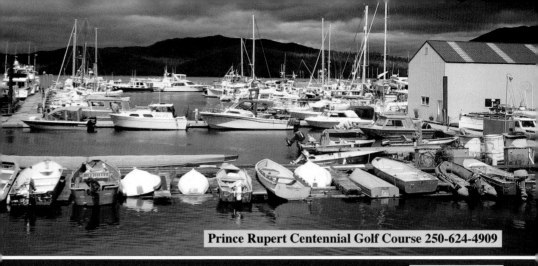

Prince Rupert Centennial Golf Course 250-624-4909

Prince Rupert

North Coast

Prince Rupert Rowing & Yacht Club

Nicole Boulton
299 George Hills Way
Prince Rupert BC
Ph/Fax: 250-624-4317
Charts 3964, 3958, 3955, 3957   VHF 73
info@prryc.com
www.prryc.com

Marina services: Customs station.
Moorage: Boats to 150'. **Power:** 30 amps.
Water. Shower, ice, bait. No reciprocal club moorage.
Adjacent facilities:
Fuel: Esso 250-624-5000.
Up town Prince Rupert is five minutes walk. Also restaurants (Smiles, Breakers Pub, Crest Hotel).
Anchorages at Pilsbury Cove and Tuck Inlet.
Public docks nearby–busy during fishing season: rafting. Fishing openings usually begin 6pm Sundays. BC Ferries, Alaska Ferries.

The Prince Rupert Yacht Club. It is located on the east shore of the harbour, seen also in the photo on the following page. Call on channel 73 for moorage. Note: Fairview welcomes visitors.

Prince Rupert   Chart 3958

Fairview Harbour
South end of Prince Rupert Harbour
Dwayne Nielsen
PO Box 1820
Port Edward BC V0V 1G0
Chart 3958, 3957
Ph: 250-624-3127   Fax: 250-624-9430
Marina Services: Power: 15, 30 amps, water, washrooms, garbage disposal. Fishing harbour. 300 vessel capacity.
Pleasure boats welcome at Fairview.

Rushbrooke Harbour
Bonnie Klassen
288 George Hills Way
Port Edward, BC V0V 1G0
Ph: 250-624-9400 Fax: 250-624-9460
Marina services: This is a rafting marina with 400 boat capacity. Power: 15 amps.
Water, washrooms, showers, public pay phone, public launch ramp adjacent. Garbage disposal. 20 minutes walk to town.

Cow Bay Floats
Bonnie Klassen
Next to Prince Rupert Yacht Club
Ph: 250-624-9400 Chart 3958, 3957
Primarily day use dock. No water. No power available.

Prince Rupert Harbour.

Prince Rupert Yacht Club.

Prince Rupert, BC, is a fishing town. Its docks in season are brimming with commercial vessels rafted as many as six deep at the town's two major public docks. Moorage overnight for pleasure craft is best at the Prince Rupert Yacht Club or nearby at Port Edward. Yacht Club spaces are tight and subject to being available only if members are away temporarily. It is necessary to call ahead to reserve space, although frequently boats arriving early in the day will be allocated a slip immediately or later in the day.

Directly above the marina there are friendly services for the transient mariner, from laundry and showers to nearby restaurants, pubs, shopping and marine repairs. Arts of local people can be found in stores up town. A good hotel with restaurant and pub sits atop the cliff overlooking the harbour. And there are more near the club.

Fuel is available at a fuel dock on the waterfront. Prince Rupert is the final major stop before continuing to Alaska. Mariners learn while talking to other yachtsmen during stops along the British Columbia coast that entering Alaska may not always be straight forward.

Wind can prevent vessels, especially slow cruising yachts, from making the Rupert to Ketchikan run all in one stretch. The reason most skippers plan it in one step is the belief that one has to do so as a Customs clearing requirement. What one learns is that it is possible to stop en route, either on the Canadian side at Dundas Island or on the Alaskan side several miles up channel from Cape Fox at Foggy Bay. If there is any doubt that you can make the run in one leg, it is best to call Alaska Customs and ask for permission to stop at a specific place en route. Remember also that Alaska, unlike BC, remains on Standard Time all year.

Once in Ketchikan there is much to do and see, from a visit to the Totem Heritage Center to walking the old town with its infamous Creek Street, once the place of bawdy houses and frontier life at its most colourful.

It's a tourist town with several large cruise ships at a time lining the docks right alongside the downtown main streets. And it's a town which will prompt you to stay a while, test the delights of fine cuisine and then go on deeper into the Alaskan Southeast or Panhandle, whichever you prefer to call it. There are several books and guides on cruising to and in Alaska. Once in the waters of the State you will find easy access to lots of cruising options with easy availability of fuel and services along the way.

Prince Rupert to Alaska charts: 3909
3955, 3957, 3959, 3960, 3963, 3964.
Also (small scale) :
3000, 3001, 3002, 3802.

Port Edward

Prince Rupert alternative moorage

Porpoise Harbour
Marina Complex

Port Edward Harbour Authority

General manager–Rick Hill
200 Bayview Dr, PO Box 1820
Port Edward BC V0V 1G0
Ph: 250-628-9220 Fax: 250-628-9233
rhill@peharbor.ca
www.peharbour.ca
Charts 3955, 3957, 3958
Marina services: Fishing harbour–public moorage. **Power:** 20, 30 amp.
Water, laundry, washrooms, public pay phone. **Adjacent facilities:** Travel lift. Cab service to Prince Rupert–Skeena Taxi Ph: 250-624-2185. Convenience store. North Pacific Cannery Museum. Bus service.

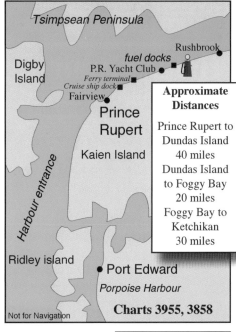

Tsimpsean Peninsula

Digby Island

Rushbrook

fuel docks
P.R. Yacht Club
Ferry terminal
Cruise ship dock
Fairview

Prince Rupert

Kaien Island

Harbour entrance

Ridley island

Port Edward
Porpoise Harbour

Not for Navigation

Charts 3955, 3858

Approximate Distances
Prince Rupert to Dundas Island 40 miles
Dundas Island to Foggy Bay 20 miles
Foggy Bay to Ketchikan 30 miles

Top: Port Edward Harbour. An alternative to moorage at Prince Rupert. Historic cannery museum nearby (inset).

Opposite page top to bottom: Prince Rupert cruise ship terminal and views of the Yacht Club docks adjacent to it.

Note: Five knots speed limit strictly enforced in Prince Rupert Harbour. Vessel speeds are monitored by radar. Leave no wash in your wake.

Photos courtesy Harbour Authority.

Haida Gwaii
Charts 3890, 3894, 3853, 3854, 3892

North Coast

Sandspit Harbour Society

Kathy Goalder
PO Box 477, Sandspit BC V0T 1T0
Ph/Fax: 250-637-5700
Charts 3890, 3894   VHF 73
mimc@qcislands.net
www.sandspitharbour.com
Marina services: Fuel: Gas, diesel.
Moorage up to 100'. Power: 15, 30, 50, 100 amp. Pumpout. Garbage disposal. Water, **showers, washrooms**. Launch ramp.

Adjacent facilities: Car rentals, shops and city services and amenities. Public phone. For those visiting Haida Gwaii there are a few marinas available for transient moorage. There is a large, well-protected marina at Sandspit, a downtown public dock at nearby Charlotte and a busy community dock in Masset and one at Port Clements. While some sail directly from Port Hardy to Rose Harbour via Cape St James, the more timid use the crossing of Hecate Strait from Prince Rupert to Sandspit. Great care should be taken crossing Hecate Strait, especially in changing weather. It is a shallow body of water and winds are frequent. Make sure you have enough fuel for the crossing. Visitors to Gwaii Haanas must register. Phone 250-559-8818 or see www.pc.gc.ca/gwaiihaanas

Photos courtesy Harbour Authority.

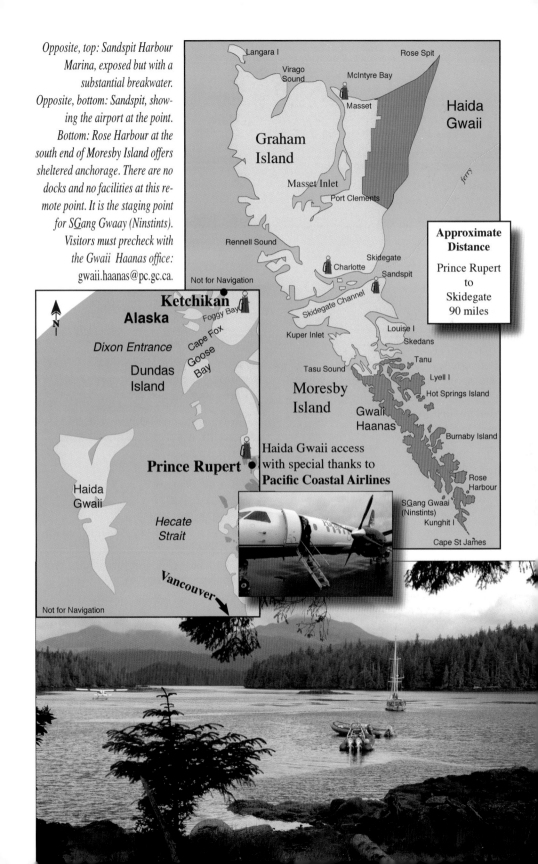

Opposite, top: Sandspit Harbour Marina, exposed but with a substantial breakwater. Opposite, bottom: Sandspit, showing the airport at the point. Bottom: Rose Harbour at the south end of Moresby Island offers sheltered anchorage. There are no docks and no facilities at this remote point. It is the staging point for SGang Gwaay (Ninstints). Visitors must precheck with the Gwaii Haanas office: gwaii.haanas@pc.gc.ca.

Langara I

Virago Sound

Rose Spit

McIntyre Bay

Masset

Haida Gwaii

Graham Island

Masset Inlet

Port Clements

Rennell Sound

Charlotte

Skidegate

Sandspit

Not for Navigation

ferry

Approximate Distance

Prince Rupert
to
Skidegate
90 miles

Skidegate Channel

Kuper Inlet

Louise I

Skedans

Tasu Sound

Tanu

Lyell I

Hot Springs Island

Moresby Island

Gwaii Haanas

Burnaby Island

Rose Harbour

SGang Gwaii (Ninstints)

Kunghit I

Cape St James

Ketchikan
Alaska

Foggy Bay

Cape Fox

Goose Bay

Dixon Entrance

Dundas Island

Prince Rupert

Haida Gwaii

Hecate Strait

Haida Gwaii access with special thanks to **Pacific Coastal Airlines**

Vancouver

Not for Navigation

Queen Charlotte
Small Craft Harbour

Steve Collinson

PO Box 68   VHF 06
Queen Charlotte BC V0T 1S0
Ph/Fax: 250-559-4650
Charts 3890, 3894
harbour@qcislands.net
Marina services: Public dock. Water,
garbage drop. **Power:** 15, 30 amp.
Nearby fuel: gas, diesel, propane. Marine
store, mechanic. City has all amenities.

*Top: The harbour at Charlotte. Below: Fuel dock at
Masset. Bottom: Delkatla Slough at Masset.*

Port Clements Small Craft
Harbour

Chris Marrs

PO Box 126
Port Clements BC V0T 1R0
Ph: 250-557-4295
Fax: 250-557-4568
marrs@islands.net
Power: 20 amp. Water. Garbage disposal.
Launch ramp. Chart 3893
Caution: shallow at low tide.

Delkatla Slough

Harbour Authority
Harbourmaster–Al Ward
PO Box 68, Masset BC V0T 1M0
Ph: 250-262-5487
Charts 3892, 3895 VHF 66A
Moorage: Rafting dock. **Power:** 20 amps.
Water. Tidal grid, garbage disposal.
Nearby: Masset Village: restaurants, gro-
ceries, shower, laundry, shops. Airport.
Fuel nearby at city wharf–North Arm
Transportation 250-626-3328.
Day use float adjacent. Art, crafts also at
Old Masset nearby.

Top: The harbour in Delkatla Slough at Masset. It lies a short way down Masset Inlet, beyond Old Masset (Haida) at the north end of Graham Island.
Right: Port Clements.
Bottom: Charlotte is a busy centre for marine activity. The harbour offeres protection and easy access to all services in the adjacent town.
Inset: The harbourmaster at Charlotte, Steve Collinson.

Photos courtesy Noreen Rudd

Ketchikan–first stop in Alaska–
northernmost point in this guide.

Above: Creek Street, Ketchikan recalls its past with
former bawdy houses as souvenir and gift stores.
Above, centre: Ketchikan Harbor.

Next stop—Alaska

Proceeding to Alaska, your fist stop may be Ketchikan, via a short stay at Foggy Bay. This protected bay is a short distance beyond Cape Fox which you pass as you cross Dixon Entrance. If you are planning to stop in American territory before reaching Ketchikan, an official Customs port of entry, you must obtain permission from Customs in Ketchikan first. This can be done by calling 907-225-2254 and advising them that you will need to stop at Foggy Bay. Ask for permission to do so rather than telling the Customs officer that you are going to stop there. If the weather permits a straight, uninterrupted run into Ketchikan simply dock at a convenient slip and call Customs. They may ask you to walk up town to their offices to clear. Note: It is important to read the Customs document you are issued, as it instructs you to notify Customs at certain other Alaskan points as you proceed farther along the coast even though you have cleared at Ketchikan (or elsewhere in Alaska). Customs hours are office hours, week-days only.

A safe harbour to spend time waiting for suitable wind and sea conditions to cross Dixon Entrance is Goose Bay on Dundas Island. Travel when conditions improve. At Dundas you are about 20 miles from Foggy Bay or about 70 from Ketchikan. Rupert to Ketchikan is 90 miles. This is the farthest north this guide takes you.

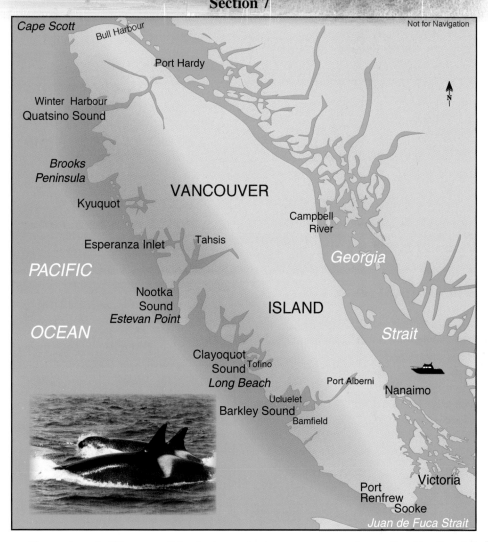

Cape Scott
Bull Harbour
Port Hardy
Winter Harbour
Quatsino Sound
Brooks
Peninsula
Kyuquot
VANCOUVER
Campbell
River
Esperanza Inlet
Tahsis
Georgia
PACIFIC
Nootka
Sound
ISLAND
Estevan Point
OCEAN
Strait
Clayoquot
Sound
Tofino
Long Beach
Port Alberni
Nanaimo
Ucluelet
Barkley Sound
Bamfield
Victoria
Port
Renfrew
Sooke
Juan de Fuca Strait

Not for Navigation

The west coast of Vancouver Island enjoys a short summer season of recreational boating. All year around, however, there is maritime activity catered to by a small number of marine facilities. These are scattered among the inlets and coves that indent the rugged coast and serve as a home away from home to those out working the coast. They serve also as havens of safety and replenishment for those seeking to extend their pleasure boating experiences in British Columbia. It is possible to travel along the Pacific west coast of Vancouver Island yet remain in sheltered waters a good deal of the time.

The open coast is broken up by numerous islands, large and small, forming inlets and protected waterways. One can travel along these waterways, poking out into the open Pacific during calm conditions and moving along to the next inlet which in some cases is no more than about 25 miles distant. The longest stretches of open water are between Juan de Fuca Strait and Barkley Sound in the south and between Quatsino Sound and Bull Harbour in the north.

West Coast Vanc I

Photo courtesy The Outpost

50° 30.784' N
128° 01.729' W

Winter Harbour

West Coast Vanc I

The Outpost (Former BC Packers dock)

Ron Lust
GD, Winter Harbour BC V0N 3L0
Ph: 250-969-4333 Fax: 250-969-4334   VHF 19
winterharbour@telus.net
www.winterharbour.ca

Moorage. Over 900'. The marina does not have power. Water is available. **Fuel:** gas, diesel, filters, oils.

There is a coin operated **laundry** and **showers**. A general store: fresh produce, groceries, ice, fishing tackle, and liquor agency are on site. The marina serves 35 RV campsites which are fully serviced. Guided fishing charters available.

Above and opposite bottom: The Outpost at Winter Harbour.

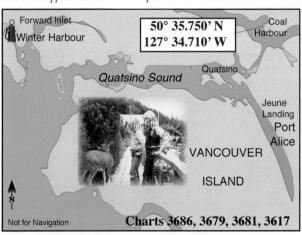

Forward Inlet
Winter Harbour
Coal Harbour

50° 35.750' N
127° 34.710' W

Quatsino Sound

Quatsino

Jeune Landing
Port Alice

VANCOUVER

ISLAND

N

Not for Navigation   **Charts 3686, 3679, 3681, 3617**

Winter Harbour

Winter Harbour Authority GD, Winter Harbour BC V0N 3L0. • Float length 171 metres • Garbage disposal • Derrick • Water • General store nearby. Washrooms, library, public pay phones at community building. 250-969-4284.

Coal Harbour

Transport Canada dock Charts 3681, 3617 Large dock for public use • Garbage-waste oil disposal • Derrick • Lights • Power • The Coal Harbour public port facility is located on Holberg Inlet on Vancouver Island and includes a wharf, on approach, and two floats.

Quatsino

Transport Canada dock. Charts 3681, 3679 Loading dock. Museum.

50° 23.008' N 127° 27.312' W

Port Alice

Quatsino Bergh Cove

Port Alice Jeune Landing

Port Alice Yacht Club

Regan Hickling

Ph: 250-284-6204   **Charts 3681, 3679**

Power, water. Fuel can be delivered by truck to marina or government wharf. Some moorage available. Launch ramp adjacent to club. It's a pleasant cruise down the inlet. The marina, which is a four minute walk from the nearby settlement, provides shelter from windy conditions. Check for space also at Jeune Landing.

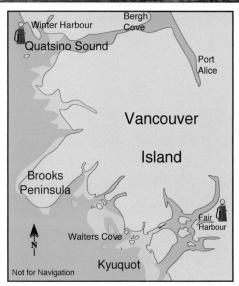

Top: Port Alice yacht club. Centre: The dock at Bergh Cove serving the Quatsino community (left) and Jeune Landing. Opposite and left: The Outpost at Winter Harbour. The photograph on the map, opposite bottom, was taken some years ago. Wildlife presence and the "main road" walkway have not changed much in recent years.

Photo courtesy The Outpost

247

Walters Cove Kyuquot.

Photo: Robin Battley

Photo: James Cameron

Kyuquot

Charts 3651, 3677, 3683, 3623

50° 23.008' N
127° 27.312' W

Walters Cove
Kyuquot Transport Canada dock
Susan Bostrom
PO Kyuquot BC Ph: 250-332-5209
Moorage–public dock. Float length 103 metres. Post office and store at head of dock (see photo above). Several fishing lodges in the cove. Welcome at Houpsitas. **Water** available–funded by donation. No power. **Fuel: Not available at Walters Cove. Gas is available at Fair Harbour.**

Kyuquot (Houpsitas)
Fisheries & Oceans dock
Float length 82 m
Charts 3651, 3677, 3683, 3623

Swan Song at Fair Harbour (Fuel)
Owner: Peter Hanson & Daisy Hanson
217-1434 Island Hwy   VHF 14
Campbell River BC V9W 8C9
Store phone: 250-830-2230
E-mail: swansong@crcn.net
Fuel: Gas, diesel, propane. **Chart: 3682**
Marina services: Guest moorage for about eight boats. Water, outhouse, internet access, launch ramp, marine/fishing supplies, ice, groceries, 10 campsites, credit cards accepted. Reservations suggested.

Walters Cove Kyuquot.

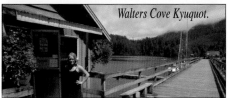

Walters Cove Kyuquot.

Fair Harbour, Kyuquot.

Top and centre: The visitor dock at Walters Cove, Kyuqout.
Above: The post office and store is at the head of the dock.
*Right: The landing and **fuel dock** at Fair Harbour.*

Zeballos

Zeballos

**49° 58.685' N
126° 50.771' W**

Zeballos

Village dock

Small craft

Zeballos Fuels

Keith Fraser
PO Box 100, Zeballos BC V0P 2A0
Ph: 250-761-4201 Fax: 250-761-4618
Charts 3676, 3664   VHF 68
Fuel: Gas, diesel, propane. Store, marine supplies, fishing tackle. Seaplane landing.
Nearby: Moorage at nearby public docks.**Water, garbage** drop, public pay phone. General store, liquor agency, ice at adjacent ice plant, museum, medical clinic, laundromat, restaurants, post office. Washrooms, showers. Walking trails. New Zeballos Hotel opens Spring 2011.

Zeballos

Zeballos Harbour Authority
Arlene Coburn   **VHF 66A**
PO Box 99, Zeballos BC V0P 2A0
Ph/Fax: 250-761-4333   250-761-4238
Guest moorage. Float length 400 metres. Garbage/oil disposal. **Water. Power:** 15 amp. **Nearby:** Grocery store. Launch ramp. Showers, washrooms. **Fuel** at Zeballos Fuels. **Charts 3676, 3604**

Zeballos Village Dock
Ph: 250-761-4229
For commercial vessels.

Esperanza

PO Box 398, Tahsis BC V0P 1X0
Charts 3676, 3604 **VHF 66A**
Float length 42 metres • Water • Lights • Summer–transient moorage available.
Esperanza public dock/fuel dock.
Washrooms. Float length 15 m • Wharf 29 m • Derrick • Lights. Fuel: Gas, diesel, stove oil, • Water. Mini store • Showers. Laundry. Phone ashore (emergency use only). Meals available at Mission camp McLean Centre.

Below: Esperanza has a small dock with snacks and fuel –available most times–in summer. The adjacent mission camp offers lunches as space permits.

Esperanza

49° 54.683' N
126° 39.676' W

Westview Marina, Tahsis.

Tahsis–Nootka Sound

Westview Marina & Lodge

Cathy Daynes
PO Box 248, Tahsis BC V0P 1X0
Ph: 250-934-7672 Fax: 250-934-6445
Toll free 1-800-992-3252   Chart 3676
info@westviewmarina.com   **VHF 06**
www.westviewmarina.com

Moorage–year round. Summer transient. Reservations recommended.
Fuel: Gas, diesel, ice. **Power:** 15, 30 amp.
Launch ramp. Water. Accommodations. Store–groceries. Garbage disposal. **Laundry, showers, washrooms.** Marina Grillhouse licenced restaurant/patio. Wifi. Pool, restaurants, supermarket, Friday fruit stand. Post office nearby. RCMP. Info Centre and Museum–quarter mile to Tahsis. Annual fishing derby from Westview takes place mid-August.

Critter Cove Marina

Cameron Forbes
PO Box 1118
Gold River BC
V0P 1G0

49° 42.536' N
126° 30.340' W

Ph/fax: 250-283-7364
Charts 3675, 3603   **VHF 07**
info@crittercove.com
www.crittercove.com

Moorage: 1,000 feet of dock space as available in summer June 18 to September 6. Call

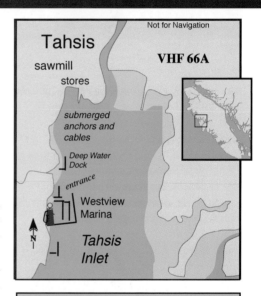

Tahsis

sawmill
stores

VHF 66A

Not for Navigation

submerged anchors and cables

Deep Water Dock

entrance

Westview Marina

Tahsis Inlet

N

Tahsis

Public (Deep Water) dock and wharf
Float length 30 metres • Garbage disposal • Water • Launch ramp • Post office • Hotel with Off-sales. Shops and accommodations nearby.
Charts 3676, 3604

for reservations. Anchoring nearby. Rental cabins and suites available. Licensed restaurant, snack bar. **Fuel:** Gas. Store, licences, bait. **Showers, washrooms, water.** Launch ramp at Gold River.

Friendly Cove, Nootka Sound.

Gold River

**49° 40.614' N
126° 07.419' W**

The town of Gold River is about eight miles inland. The harbour is subject to wind and tidal conditions making it not suitable for moorage. A ramp adjacent to the breakwater serves small boat launching. Overnight at Critter Cove Marina, in Hannah Channel off Mutchatlat Inlet. Vessels stopping at **Friendly Cove** will find a dock where the supply ship lands at the lighthouse. Good anchorage. **Fuel is available at times at Friendly Cove.**

Gold River

Public dock. Charts 3675, 3603
Manager • Float length 47 metres •
Wharf • Aircraft float • Garbage
disposal • Water • Lights • Power •
Telephone • Sheds • Launch ramp

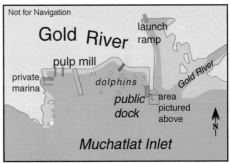

Gold River

Critter Cove

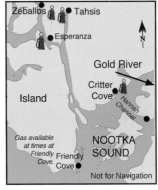

Hot Springs Cove

West Coast Vanc I

Hot Springs Cove
Parks Canada (Refuge Cove)
Charts 3674, 3603   VHF 66A

Maquinna Marine Provincial Park. 60 m visitors dock. Outside of floats used by water taxis, tour boats and float planes. Inside for day use and overnight. There is a weight/length restriction to minimize damage to floats. No services at the dock. Private campground north of dock operated by First Nations. Toilets, 2 km boardwalk to 50° C Hot Springs–change house at the pools., $3/person/day fee. Across the bay: **Fuel**, accommodations and groceries.

The hot springs at Hot Springs Cove is still enjoyable in its natural state, located in Maquinna Provincial Park in the remote northern end of Clayoquot Sound. The boiling spring water bubbles up from deep in the earth and cascades down a small cliff into a series of natural layered rock pools, cooled by the incoming Pacific Ocean, each pool slightly cooler than the one above it. At high tide the surf surges into the two lower pools creating a unique blend of hot and cool water. This tidal action also flushes the pools twice daily, so they are always noticeably clean. The spring water is very hot (47 degrees Celcius, 117 degrees Fahrenheit), and is clear with just a faint smell and taste of sulphur.

The Hesquiaht First Nations village on the opposite side of Refuge Cove (HSC) has a lodge, small store with snacks and sells diesel fuel at the dock–Ph: Toll Free: 877-232-1100 (credit cards used, but it is advisable to have cash).

Top: Hot Springs Cove dock and anchorage in Refuge Cove. Inset: The path to the springs is paved with boards left by visiting mariners. Opposite: Ahousat store (inset) is on the approaches to the landing for the First Nations village in Matilda Inlet.

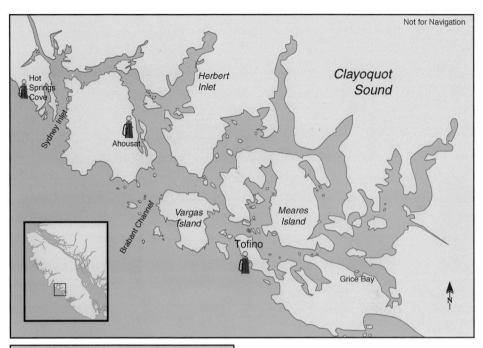

Hot Springs Cove

Ahousat

Herbert Inlet

Clayoquot Sound

Brabant Channel

Sydney Inlet

Vargas Island

Meares Island

Tofino

Grice Bay

N

49° 16.939' N   126° 04.277' W

Ahousat, Matilda Inlet

Ph: 250-670-9575

Charts 3673, 3674, 3603

Moorage: 400' transient dock • Derrick • Lights • Public phone. Cell reception.

Fuel: Gas, diesel, stove oil. Lodge.

Attractions and amenities:
General store. Restaurant. Post office. Marine Ways. Water. Nearby is the Gibson Marine Park and warm Springs. Beware of rock at entrance to village.

Ahousat docks

Located on the opposite shore to the commercial side of Matilda Inlet on Flores Island is the First Nations village of Ahousat. Vera's B&B, Cathy's Cafe. Several artists, carvers and weavers and a 12' Welcome Figure. Walk the Wild Side–11 km trail through Gibson Marine Provincial Park from the village. Sandy beaches and part boardwalk trail. Fee of $25 per person at the Band Office. Warm springs–25° C.

Tofino

Charts 3685, 3673, 3603, 3674

Fourth Street Harbour

Vince Payette (also Armitage Point)
Tofino Harbour Authority
PO Box 826, Tofino BC V0R 2Z0
Ph: 250-725-4441 Fax: 250-725-4461
tofhar@island.net   **VHF 66A**
• Float length 444 metres • Breakwater
• Grid • Garbage/oil disposal • Pumpout
• Water by pay per minute. (water shortage) • Power: 20 amp • Sheds • Launch
ramp • Public phone ashore. Showers,
laundry, regular and handicapped washrooms. Internet access. General stores,
liquor agency, post office, shops and
accommodations nearby.

Armitage Point (Crab Dock)
• Float length 121 metres • Crane •
Lights. Public pay phone ashore. General stores, liquor agency, Post office,
shops, laundry and accommodations in
town nearby. It is recommended that
mariners looking for moorage try the
public docks. Water pay per minute

First Street Dock
Day use by First Nations, ferries water
taxis and float planes.

Method Marine

Method Marine Supply

Steve Bernard
380 Main St., PO Box 219,
Tofino BC V0R 2Z0   VHF 6
Ph: 250-725-3251 Fax: 250-725-2111
Fuel: Gas, diesel. **Water**, ice, propane,
laundry, toilets for fuel dock customers.
Chandlery, marine service station–parts
and accessories. Tackle shop, coffee. Scuba
air fills. Charts, bait. Clothing.
Note: **No transient moorage.**

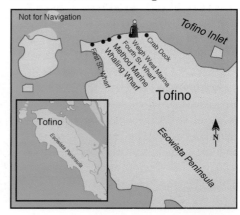

Top: Armitage Point public docks. Note navigational aid markers and buoys Right: Method Marine docks in Tofino. Fog is common in the summer months.

Entrance from west Templar Channel
49° 09.038' N   125° 55.021' W

Pass the first two fingers, reserved for tour and commercial vessels, and find a slip beyond for overnight stays.

Tofino Harbour Authority Fourth St.

Tofino Harbour Fourth Street docks from the land approaches.

Weigh West Marine Resort

Weigh West

385 Campbell St, PO Box 69
Tofino BC V0R 3Z0
Ph: 250-725-3277 Fax: 250-725-3234
Guest moorage, Power, water, garbage disposal. Restaurant and pub. This is a marine resort with accommodation and a marine adventure centre for fishing enthusiasts. Reservations. Whale watching, hot springs, bear watching, scuba diving and snorkeling tours. Kayaking available.

Charts 3646, 3671, 3603

West Coast Vanc I

Ucluelet

> **Ucluelet Entrance**
> 48° 55.290' N　　125° 30.9951' W

Ucluelet public docks
Boat Basin (inner and outer harbour)
Hemlock Street
PO Box 910, Ucluelet BC V0R 3A0
Ph/fax: 250-726-4241 or 250-266-0354
Manager Steve Bird. • Float length 820 metres • Garbage/oil disposal • Water • Lights • Power: 30, 50 amp • Phone • Toilets • Near general stores, restaurants, Post office, shops, pool, laundry, accommodations, showers. There are additional public docks in the outer harbour:
Otter Street–(52 Steps) *Clear customs here.* One km away from Boat Basin. District of Ucluelet dock No customs available at Bamfield.
There is no power at this dock. Manager Steve Bird. • Float length 150 m • Garbage disposal • Lights • Public pay phone • Water •
CANPASS: Ph: 1-888-CANPASS

Main Street (Whiskey Dock)–public dock. Manager Steve Bird • Float length 36 m • Wharf • Garbage disposal • Derrick • Lights • Seaplane float. Commercial boats.
Port Albion facility dock (not managed) Float length 49 metres. No amenities.

> **"52 Steps" Otter Street dock**
> 48° 56.474' N 125° 32.482' W

Island West Fishing Resort
PO Box 879, Ucluelet BC V0R 3A0
Ph: 250-726-7515 Fax: 250-726-4414
Charts 3646, 3671, 3603　VHF 66A
fish@islandwestresort.com
www.islandwestresort.com
Marina services:
Moorage–Summer transient available at times. **Power**: 15 amp. **Launch ramp.** Water, ice, tackle shop, **laundry, showers, washrooms**. Pub/Restaurant. Marine supplies, accommodations. Charters. Fish freezing. RV park, **Nearby:** Stores, restaurants, bakery.
Fuel dock: Eagle Marine Limited.
Gas, diesel, stove oil. Ph: 250-726-4262.

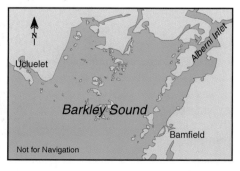

Not for Navigation

Opposite page: The docks at Islands West Fishing Resort early in the year await arrival of many small boats.
Top: Ucluelet Boat Harbour docks–the entrance is off to the right. The Canadian Princess has a dock for its charter fishing vessels.
Right: Pub at Islands West.
Diagrams show: Ucluelet and Ucluth Peninsula–note approximate location of primary marinas; Barkley Sound (opposite) with Ucluelet and Bamfield locations. Use a large scale chart for safe navigation.

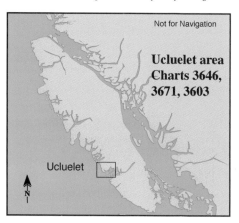

Not for Navigation

Ucluelet area Charts 3646, 3671, 3603

Ucluelet

N

Vancouver Island

Boat Basin

Outer public dock
Island West Resort
Outer public dock
Port Albion

52 Steps public dock

Ucluelet

Ucluelet Harbour

fuel dock

N

Pacific

Ocean

Ucluth Peninsula

light-house

Not for Navigation

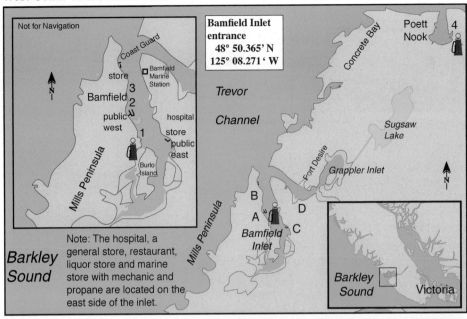

Not for Navigation

Coast Guard

store

Bamfield Marine Station

Bamfield 3

2

public west

hospital

store public east

1

Burlo Island

Mills Peninsula

Bamfield Inlet entrance 48° 50.365' N 125° 08.271 ' W

Trevor

Channel

Concrete Bay

Poett Nook 4

Sugsaw Lake

Port Desire

Grappler Inlet

N

B

A

D

C

Mills Peninsula

Bamfield Inlet

Barkley Sound

Victoria

Note: The hospital, a general store, restaurant, liquor store and marine store with mechanic and propane are located on the east side of the inlet.

Barkley Sound

Bamfield

Charts 3646, 3671, 3602, 3688   VHF 06/66A

"Music By The Sea" in July. www.musicbythesea.ca

1. McKay Bay Lodge
Brian and Cheryl McKay
PO Box 116, Bamfield BC V0R 1B0
Ph: 250-728-3323 Fax: 250-728-3255
Charts 3646, 3671, 3602
mckaybay@island.net
www.mckaybaylodge.ca
Moorage: 400' of dock space reserved for overnight guests. **Fuel:** gas, diesel. Ice, **washrooms**. Complete fishing tackle and bait. Accommodations (resort). Dinner at restaurant by reservation.

Marine service at Breakers Marine, Bamfield east side. Ph 250-728-3281.

3. Harbourside Lodge
Bamfield BC V0R 1B0
Ph: 250-728-3330
john@harboursidelodge.com
www.harboursidelodge.com
Boat and seaplane **moorage**. **Power** 30, 50 amp 110v, **Water**. **Showers**. Store. Ice, cubed drinking ice, bait, fishing tackle, salt, charts. **Gas and diesel** arranged.

Fishing charters-accommodation packages.

Left: The docks at Port Desire.

*Barkley Sound is known for its fishing and scuba diving.
The town of Bamfield is a good base for reaching some of the beautiful waters and beaches strewn throughout the Sound, especially in the islands of the Broken Group.*

With special thanks to John and Sheryl Mass.

Bamfield Docks

A. West–Bamfield Harbour Authority. Float length 154 m • Rick McLeod–wharfinger. Ph: **250-728-34540**. Check for availability of moorage.
B. West–Transport Canada dock CCG. Richard Zoet–manager for Transport Canada docks. Float length 24 m • Derrick • Store nearby. Garbage disposal.
C. East–Transport Canada dock. Float length 128 metres–transient–reserve. Garbage disposal • Derrick • Lights • General store, restaurant, mechanic.
D. Port Désiré. Ph: 250-728-3006 • Float length 22 m • Launch ramp (and Bamfield Centennial Park campground).
Services at Bamfield: Post office, grocery, bakery, liquor store, restaurant, marine store and medical services.

4. Poett Nook Marina
Dave Dillon
Saritra Road, Poett's Nook
Ph: 250-758-4440
poettnookmarina@shaw.ca
www.poettnook.com
Moorage: Boats to 26 feet. No power. Campground. **Fuel**: Gas. **Water. Washrooms, showers.** Small general store: Snacks, ice, fishing licences, tackle.

5. Green Cove Store
Uchuklesit Inlet (near Kildonan)
Ph: 250-724-1832.
Gas. Supplies. (Diesel in Ucluelet.)

Top: The public dock at Bamfield, west side. In the background is the entrance to the inlet.

Broken Island Adventures
John and Sheryl Mass
Box 3500, Bamfield BC V0R 1B0
Ph: 1-888-728-6200 Local: 250-728-3500
Charts 3646, 3671, 3602
broken@island.net
www.brokenislandadventures.com
Moorage–at public dock.
Whale watching, bear watching, nature tours. Scuba tours in winter. Kayak rentals. Shuttle to Broken Group.

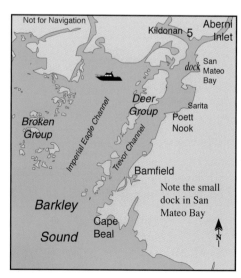

Clutesi Haven

Harbour Quay Marina

Chart 3668

Port Alberni

Clutesi Haven Marina

Marina Manager Mike Carter   **VHF 66A**
Port Alberni Port Authority
5104 River Rd, Port Alberni BC V9Y 6Z1
Ph: 250-724-6837 Fax: 250-723-1114
clutesihaven@portalberni.ca
www.portalberniportauthority.ca
Moorage: Fresh water tidal moorage up
Somass River. Summer transient available
at times. **Water. Power** 20, 30 amp.
Fuel: Gas. Picnic tables. 4-lane launch
ramp. Ice. **Washrooms.** Cleaning station.
Fishing gear and charters.
Nearby: Port Alberni: Port Boathouse.
Groceries, hardware, propane, restaurants,
laundry, liquor store and other facilities.

China Creek Marina

Marina Manager Mike Carter   **VHF 16**
Port Alberni Port Authority
2750 Harbour Rd, Port Alberni BC V9Y 7X2
Ph: 250-723-9812 Fax: 250-723-9842
chinacreek@portalberni.ca
www.portalberniportauthority.ca
Moorage: summer transient moorage if
space available. Reservations suggested.
Fuel: Gas, diesel, propane.
Water. Power: 15, 20, 30 amps. Ice.
Laundry. Showers. Washrooms.
Four-lane launch ramp at marina.
Mini-store–fishing gear, supplies, cafe.
Campground, playground. Nine miles to
Port Alberni.

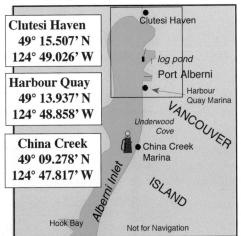

Clutesi Haven
49° 15.507' N
124° 49.026' W

Clutesi Haven

log pond
Port Alberni

Harbour Quay
49° 13.937' N
124° 48.858' W

Harbour
Quay Marina

Underwood
Cove

VANCOUVER

China Creek
49° 09.278' N
124° 47.817' W

China Creek
Marina

Alberni Inlet

ISLAND

Hook Bay

Not for Navigation

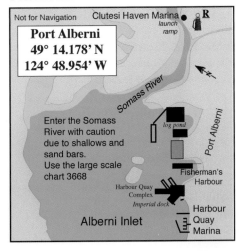

Not for Navigation   Clutesi Haven Marina   **R**
launch
ramp

Port Alberni
49° 14.178' N
124° 48.954' W

Somass River

Enter the Somass
River with caution
due to shallows and
sand bars.
Use the large scale
chart 3668

log pond

Port Alberni

Fisherman's
Harbour

Harbour Quay
Complex

Imperial dock

Harbour
Quay
Marina

Alberni Inlet

West Coast Vanc I

Harbour Quay Marina

Marina Manager Mike Carter
2900 Harbour Rd   **VHF 06**
Port Alberni BC V9Y 7X2
Ph/fax: 250-723-1413
harbourquay@portalberni.ca
www.portalberiportauthority.ca

Port Alberni Yacht Club

48° 53.554' N
125° 07.091' W

Moorage: Subject to available slips. This harbour is located behind the breakwater at the south end of town.

Power: 20, 30 amps, **water** and nearby shore facilities. **Washrooms, showers, laundry.** Visit the quay at nearby Fisherman's Harbour for **visitor moorage,** restaurants, gift and craft shops and The Boathouse chandlery nearby.

Clutesi Haven

Port Alberni Yacht Club

PO Box 37, Port Alberni BC V9Y 7M6
Located in Robber's Passage at Fleming Island in the Deer Group of Barkley Sound. It has sheltered guest moorage of about 240' dock space. Power available in emergency. Water, washrooms and showers, fish cleaning and picnic tables. Ashore there are trails, caves, viewpoints, outhouses and a beach for swimming. There is a store and **gas available at Green Cove** near Kildonan in Uchuklesit Inlet. Diesel fuel is available at China Creek and in the harbours of Bamfield and Ucluelet.

Port Alberni Harbour Authority

Right, top to bottom: Port Alberni Yacht Club in Barkley Sound; Fuel dock at Clutesi Haven on the Somass River; The launch ramp at Clutesi Haven; Right–clockwise: Clutesi Haven Marina, Port Alberni Harbour, China Creek. Bottom: China Creek entrance. Opposite: Clutesi Haven and Harbour Quay Marina.

Fisherman's Harbour

Port Alberni Port Authority
Manager Jayne Braithwaite
3140 Harbour Rd, Port Alberni
V9Y 4B9 Ph/Fax: 250-723-2533
fishermansharbour@portalberni.ca
Garbage disposal • Sani-pumpout • Derrick
• Showers • Water • Power: 20, 30, 50 amp

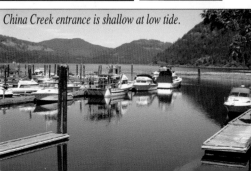

China Creek entrance is shallow at low tide.

Port Renfrew

48° 34.461' N
124° 25.052' W
Gordon River   Chart 3647

West Coast Vanc I

Port Renfrew Marina

Rex Colburn, Budd Watt
Gordon River Rd, Port Renfrew BC
Ph: 250-473-1878
Marina 250-647-0002
Fax: 250-478-3696
info@portrenfrewmarina.com
www.portrenfrewmarina.com
Charts 3647, 3606   **VHF 06, 68**
Marina: 140 small boat slips. Maximum
size 32'. Access requires 3' tide. Bait, ice,
tackle and fishing licences.
Fuel: Gas, oil. RV park. Campground.
Cook Shack restaurant. **Launch ramp**.
Open May through mid October.
Nearby: At Port Renfrew–restaurant,
motels, general store, laundry.

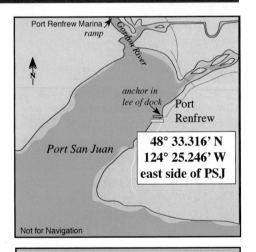

Port Renfrew Marina
ramp
N
anchor in
lee of dock   Port
Renfrew
Port San Juan

48° 33.316' N
124° 25.246' W
east side of PSJ

Not for Navigation

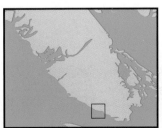

*Photo top: The
Port Renfrew
Marina is
located on the
Gordon River.*

Port Renfrew docks

On east side of Port San Juan
This dock is operated by the local community and does not offer overnight
moorage. It is possible to anchor off the
docks, behind the breakwater.
• Pub. Restaurants nearby.

*Enter up Gordon River on instructions from
marina. Larger boats require high tide.*

Sunny Shores Marina

Sooke

Sooke Basin

N

Sooke public docks
Sooke Harbour Marina

Vancouver
Island

Becher
Bay

Not for Navigation

Sooke

Sooke Government Wharf
Foot of Maple Rd. Ph: 250-642-4431
Chart 3411, 3410 • Harbour Manager
Linda Young • 2 floats of 300' each •
Pay phone • Garbage disposal • Derrick
• Water • Lights • Power: 20, 30 amps •
Security gate, surveillance camera. Easy
walk to town for all shops and services.

*Above: The public docks at Sooke are located on the
west shore of the harbour just after passing Whiffen
Spit. Exercise great caution entering Sooke, using the
channel markers to avoid hazards at the entrance.
Below: Sooke public docks.*

**Entering Sooke, beware of sand bank in
the channel. Follow markers and use the
large scale marine chart 3411.**

48° 22.167' N
123° 43.557' W

Sooke public dock

Sooke Harbour Resort & Marina

Rick Horn
6971 West Coast Rd, Sooke BC V9Z 0A1
Ph: 250-642-3236
Chart 3410
info@sookeharbourmarina.ca
www.sookeharbourmarina.ca
Moorage–limited summer transient.
Power: 15 amp. Water. Showers. Washrooms.
Launch ramp. Snacks. Garbage disposal.
Nearby: Town Restaurants, shops.

Charts 3410, 3411, 3461, 3606
(Approach from Whiffin Spit following the markers–red right returning)

Top: Sooke Harbour Resort and Marina docks are seen beyond the ramp. It lies to the left of the wharf in the photograph below of the Crab Shack recreational fish boat dock. The Crab Shack office and tackle shop is shown in the photograph at right.

Sunny Shores Marina

Andrew Planeta
5621 Sooke Rd, Sooke BC V9Z 0C6
Ph: 250-642-5731 Fax: 250-642-5731
info@sunnyshoresresort.com
www.sunnyshoresresort.com
Fuel: Gas, diesel, oil. **Power** 15 amp.
Water. Launch Ramp. Moorage Some summer transient slips. **Showers. Washrooms. Laundry.**
Ministore–groceries. Pool.
Nearby: Restaurants and bus service to Sooke and Victoria. This is mostly an RV and fishing facility.

The Crab Shack
Elden Smith
6947 West Coast Rd, Sooke V9Z 0N4
duck5@telus.net
Ph: 250-893-2722 Fax: 250-642-5346
Seafood. Fishing Tackle.
Fishing Charters available complete with use of boat launch.

Becher Bay

Cheanuh Marina

Mike Chipps

4901 East Sooke Rd, Sooke BC V9V 1B6
Ph: 250-478-4880 Fax: 250-478-5800
Charts 3410, 3461. VHF 16 switch to 68
Fuel: Gas only. **Water. Moorage**–some summer transient–call for reservations. Ice. Washrooms. Pumpout. Garbage disposal.
Launch ramp. The marina is located behind Fraser Island in Becher Bay.

48° 20.108' N
123° 36.147' W
Caffery Point

Top: Cheanuh Marina is tucked away at the head of Becher Bay.

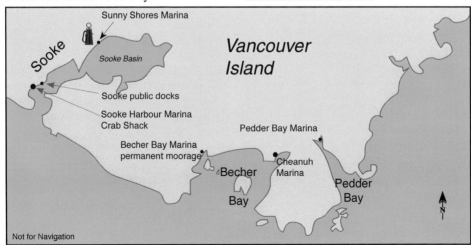

265

Metchosin Golf Course 250-478-3266

Pedder Bay Marina.

48° 20.833' N
123° 34.103' W
Ash Point

Pedder Bay

West Coast Vanc I

Pedder Bay RV Resort and Marina
Richard Taggart
**925 Pedder Bay Dr,
Victoria BC V9C 4H1
Ph: 250-478-1771 Fax: 250-478-0285**
pbm@obmg.com
www.pedderbay.com
**Charts 3410, 3461, 3606   VHF 66A
Fuel:** Gas. **Moorage**–some summer transient. Fishing licences. **Power:** 30 amp,
washrooms, showers, laundry. Wifi.

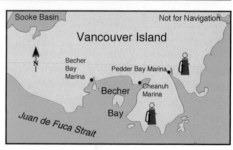

Launch Ramp. Rental boats and fishing guides available. RV resort, mini chandlery. Small coffee shop.
Beware of the reef at entrance to marina.

Pedder Bay Marina.

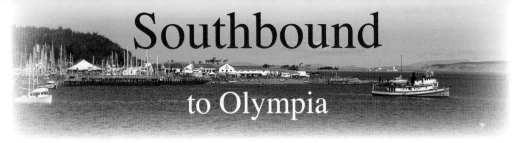

Southbound

to Olympia

Section 8

Most vessels returning from a cruise in British Columbia or the San Juans to their home ports in Puget Sound are probably familiar with much of the following information.

Hopefully there are some docks in this section that you have not yet discovered and will experience pleasure in visiting them. The information relating to the marinas is intended to provide input for the mariner to check into the most suitable overnight facilities.

For those mariners who have spent all or most of their boating years in British Columbia waters, a pleasant surprise is in store for you when you travel south. There are destination marinas that are well equipped to cater to visiting boats. And there are surroundings that will make you want to stay longer than intended and return again soon.

Many Canadians are inclined to think of Puget Sound as a busy, commercial and built-up residential-lined waterway. But there are passages, bays and coves that compare with some of the most remote wilderness areas of northern British Columbia. In the following pages I have included those marinas which offer overnight moorage. Most have special visitor moorage, some have visitor docks and additional space available for guests while others offer space as available. Whether returning home from northern destinations or just going south for a change, plan a visit to Admiralty Inlet, Puget Sound or Hood Canal and check out some of the outstanding facilities for yourself.

Right: Popular boating in Lake Washington, with access from Lake Union via the canal.
Below: Skyline Marina at Anacortes, where resident boats occupy hundreds of slips and special docks are set aside for visitors.

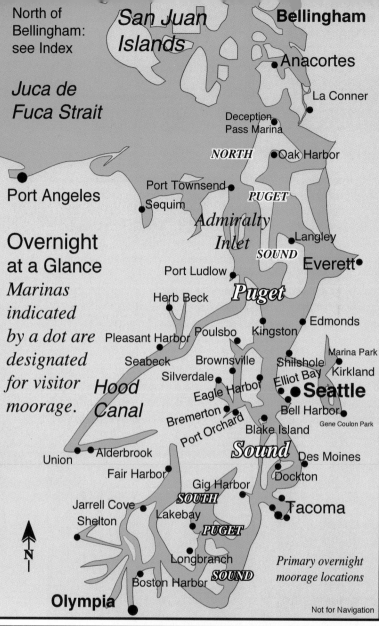

San Juan Islands

Bellingham

Juca de Fuca Strait

Anacortes

La Conner

Deception Pass Marina

NORTH

Oak Harbor

Port Angeles

Port Townsend

Sequim

PUGET

Overnight at a Glance

Marinas indicated by a dot are designated for visitor moorage.

Admiralty Inlet

Langley

Everett

SOUND

Port Ludlow

Herb Beck

Puget

Edmonds

Pleasant Harbor

Poulsbo

Kingston

Marina Park

Seabeck

Brownsville

Shilshole

Kirkland

Silverdale

Elliot Bay

Eagle Harbor

Seattle

Hood Canal

Bremerton

Bell Harbor

Port Orchard

Gene Coulon Park

Blake Island

Union

Alderbrook

Sound

Des Moines

Fair Harbor

Dockton

Gig Harbor

Jarrell Cove

SOUTH

Shelton

Lakebay

Tacoma

PUGET

Longbranch

Primary overnight moorage locations

SOUND

Boston Harbor

N

Olympia

Not for Navigation

Top and left: One of the newest and most exemplary marinas on the coast. This is Bremerton Marina and its adjacent, newly developed business center in Puget Sound. The view in the photograph on the left shows its scenic location with the snow-capped range of the Olympic Peninsula beyond.

Right: Shopping at the farmers market at Anacortes on Saturdays. Relaxing at Coupeville. Docking at La Conner.

Juan de Fuca Strait

48° 29.387' N
124° 43.676' W
Juan de Fuca
Strait (Racon)

NEAH BAY Charts 18485, 18484
Makah Marina
Port director: Bob Buckingham
Port of Neah Bay
PO Box 137, Neah Bay WA 98357
Ph: 360-645-3015 Fax: 360-645-3016
portofneahbay@centurytel.net
VHF 16 and 66A
Moorage. Commercial boats to 100 ft.
Pleasure boats check in with Big Salmon
Resort. **Launch ramp. Water.**
Power: 30, 50 amps. **Fuel:** Gas, diesel.
Showers, washrooms. Pumpout. Wifi.
Nearby: Accommodations, shops, museum, culture center.

Big Salmon Resort
PO Box 140, Neah Bay WA 98357
Ph: 360-645-2374 Fax: 360-645-0722
Toll free 1-866-787-1900   VHF 68
bigsalmon@centurytel.net

www.bigsalmonresort.net
Moorage at Makah Marina. Seasonal April
to September–boats to 70 feet.
Water. Power: 30, 50 amps. **Fuel:** Gas,
diesel. **Washrooms.** Pumpout. Ice.
Launch ramp. General store with all fishing supplies. Boat rentals, charters. Boat
rentals, charters. Delicatessen.
Nearby: Groceries. Big Salmon Resort
manages the moorage for recreational customers at Makah Marina, open from April
through September.

Launch ramp (off to left) at Makah Marina
and Big Salmon moorage.

Neah Bay's Makah Marina

Juan de Fuca Strait

Snow Creek Resort

PO Box 248, Neah Bay WA 98357
Ph: 360-645-2284 Fax: 360-374-8861
Toll free 1-800-833-1464
snowcreek@centurytel.net
www.snowcreekwa.com

48° 21.442' N
124° 33.225' W

Charts 18460, 18484 VHF 16, 17
Moorage to 24' mooring buoys to 30'. **Water.**
Showers. Washrooms. Portadump.
Launch ramp, scuba air fills, camping, RV
park, haulout, rail launch to 30 feet. Cabins.
Nearby: Charters.

SEKIU Chart 18460

Olson's Resort

Donalynn & Arlen Olson **CB 21**
444 Front St, PO Box 216, Sekiu WA 98381
Ph: 360-963-2311 Fax: 360-963-2928
info@olsonsresort.com
www.olsonsresort.com
Fuel: Gas, diesel, oil. **Moorage. Water.**
Washrooms, laundry, showers. Camping.
Convenience store. Motel accommoda-
tions. Fishing charters. Launch ramp.
Nearby: Air strip.

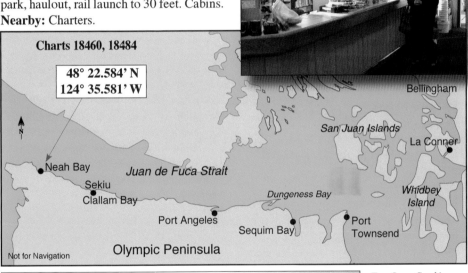

Charts 18460, 18484

48° 22.584' N
124° 35.581' W

Bellingham

San Juan Islands

La Conner

Neah Bay Juan de Fuca Strait

Sekiu

Clallam Bay

Dungeness Bay

Whidbey Island

Port Angeles

Sequim Bay

Port Townsend

Not for Navigation Olympic Peninsula

Olson's Resort Marina

48° 15.501' N
124° 17.526' W

*Top: Snow Creek's
small dock for
launched boats.
Inset above: Olson's
well-stocked store.
Left: Olson's Resort
marina dock.
Opposite, top: Olson's
Resort and adjacent
Van Riper's marina
docks at Sekiu.*

271

View along the beach towards Sekiu.

48° 15.273' N
124° 16.515' W

SEKIU Chart 18460

Van Riper's Resort

Valerie & Chris Mohr
280 Front St
PO Box 246
Sekiu WA 98381
48° 15.486' N
124° 17.515' W

CB 14

Ph: 360-963-2334 Toll free 1-888-462-0803

www.vanripersresort.com

Moorage: 3000' dock. **Water.**
Showers, Washrooms. Portadump. Rental boats. Groceries, books, ice. Motel. Campground. Launch ramp.
Nearby: Restaurant. Marine store–5 miles.

Curley's Resort and Dive Center

48° 15.466' N
124° 17.518' W

Jim and Virginia Bartz
291 Front St, Box 265, Sekiu WA 98381
Ph: 360-963-2281 Fax: 360-963-2291
Toll free: 1-800-542-9680

www.curleysresort.com

Moorage: Open May–Sept 30.
Boats to 30 feet.
Motel. Rooms and cabins to rent.
Dive shop. Air fills.

Sequim Bay State Marine Park

Sequim Bay
Ph: 360-902-8844
Charts 18460, 18484
424 foot dock, floats and buoys.
Washrooms. Picnic sites, scuba diving, launch ramp. Shallow at low tide.

Sequim Bay Marine Park dock

Juan de Fuca Strait

SEQUIM Chart 18471
John Wayne Marina
Ron Amundson
2577 W Sequim Bay Rd, Sequim WA 98382
Ph: 360-417-3440 Fax: 360-417-3442
www.portofpa.com
Fuel: Gas, diesel. **Moorage**: Visitor dock at marina inside breakwater. **Power:** 30 amp. **Washrooms, laundry, showers.** Pumpout. Restaurant: Dockside Grill **Adjacent:** Store–Bosun's Locker, books, marine supplies. Launch ramp. **Nearby:** Beach, picnic area, grocery store. *Follow channel to the marina.*

John Wayne Marina. Top photo shows its entrance. Right: The fuel and guest dock. Bottom left: The ramp at John Wayne Marina. Bottom, right: A bronze of the famous actor in the office lobby.

John Wayne Marina

48° 04.906' N
123° 02.444' W

John Wayne Marina

48° 07.271' N
123° 25.353 ' W

Harbour: 48° 07.733' N 123° 24.030' W

Launch ramp on Marine Drive alongside the Coast Guard station.

48° 08.362' N
123° 27.271 ' W

Launch ramp at Boat Haven

Port Angeles

Chart 18468

Juan de Fuca Strait

City of Port Angeles City Pier

312 E Fifth St, Port Angeles WA 98362
Ph: 360-417-4550 (Port Angeles Parks)
Moorage: Visitor dock, seasonal.
Washrooms. Public aquatic centre (showers), nearby stores, restaurants. Customs. Visit the Marine Science Center.

City of Port Angeles Boat Haven

Chuck Faires
832 Boat Haven Dr, Port Angeles WA 98363
Ph: 360-457-4505 Fax: 360-457-4921
pamarina@olypen.com www.portofpa.com
Fuel: Gas, diesel. **Moorage**: Visitor dock, boats to 150 feet. **Power:** 20, 30, 50 amp.
Washrooms, showers. Customs. Pumpout. Portadump. **Adjacent: Launch ramp.** Haulouts to 70 tons, 200 ton railway, repairs, service, marine supplies, charts, stove oil, kerosene. Cafe. Laundry nearby. Customs port 360-457-4311.

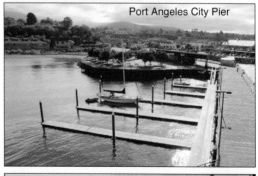

Port Angeles City Pier

Port Angeles Boat Haven

Right: Boat Haven visitors dock at Port Angeles. This page, centre: The docks at Port Angeles City Pier and a mural on the Marine Science Center. Opposite page: Boat Haven. Centre: The launch ramps at Boat Haven and across the harbour. Bottom: The City Pier and a beach alongside.

Port Angeles City Pier

48° 07.146' N
123° 25.397' W

After Juan de Fuca Strait, Port Angeles or the San Juan Islands, going south, your choices are Hood Canal, Admiralty Inlet or Puget Sound. If you are in the vicinity of Crescent Beach or Point Roberts and intend to travel south down Puget Sound you may find a visit to Blaine worthwhile. The town has been embellished with paving and landscaping. The marina has many facilities and a warm welcome for visitors. The same can be said for Semiahmoo Marina on the opposite side of Drayton Harbor. This modern marina loves to have visitors. Call ahead to reserve moorage and look forward to a pleasant stay with options of golf or time in the spa. If you stay there and want to visit Blaine you can use the ferry in summer.

In the Puget Sound area most mariners are familiar with destinations such as Port Townsend known for its historic buildings and holiday atmosphere, or Anacortes for its bustling activity as a port for larger vessels,

ferry traffic and business community. Check out such places for their large, accommodating marinas. And visit other ports such as Poulsbo for its colorful Scandinavian village, Silverdale, Port Ludlow or Jarrell's Cove for remoteness from anywhere. These and other marinas and towns in the Sound and Hood Canal can provide lots of entertainment, new experiences and friendships, and a joyful boating experience. Moreover, getting to some of these places can be a lot of fun.

State marine parks which provide substantial or adequate visitor moorage and other facilities have been included in the following pages.

48° 59.654' N
122° 47.026' W

Semiahmoo Marina

Blaine

Semiahmoo Marina

Ron France
9540 Semiahmoo Pkwy
Blaine WA 98230
Ph: 360-371-0440 Fax: 360-371-0200
VHF 68   Chart 18421, 18423
semimarina@comcast.net
www.semiahmoomarina.com
Moorage: 500 feet, plus slips.
Fuel: Gas, diesel, propane. **Power:** 30, 50
amp. Coffee and gift shop. **Washrooms,
showers, laundry,** portadump, **pumpout.**
Adjacent: Resort accommodations, golf
course, pool, health spa, restaurants.
Access to Blaine by ferry throughout summer, on weekends.

Semiahmoo Marina

Semiahmoo Marina

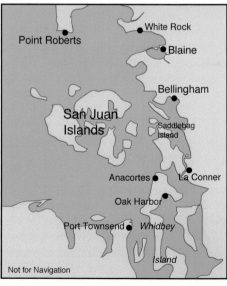

Semiahmoo Marina

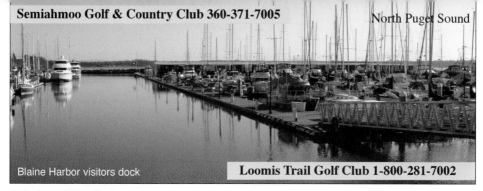

Blaine Harbor visitors dock   **Loomis Trail Golf Club 1-800-281-7002**

Blaine Harbor

Operated by Port of Bellingham
Pam Taft
235 Marine Dr, Blaine WA 98231
Ph: 360-647-6176 Fax: 360-332-1043
VHF 16 switch to 68   Chart 18423
blaineharbor@portofbellingham.com
www.portofbellingham.com
Moorage: 850 feet guest moorage plus
slips. **Fuel:** Gas, diesel, propane, at Blaine
Marina Fuel dock.
Power: 30, 50 amp. **Washrooms,
showers,** portadump, pumpout, **laundry.**

*Photos above and opposite show the two marinas at
Blaine. Note their juxtaposition (below, right).*
*Just across the border, is the seaside British Columbia
town of White Rock (yacht club docks bottom left) with
many restaurants and shops. Minimal dock facilities.
Use small east side dock, also used by Canada Customs.*

Customs: phone in for NEXUS only.
Adjacent: Haulouts, repairs, supplies,
restaurants. Launch ramp. Landscaped
parkland. Short walk to uptown Blaine.
Blaine Marina Fuel dock– 360-332-8425.

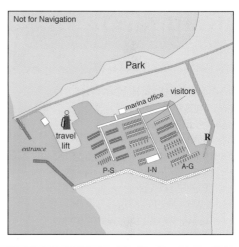

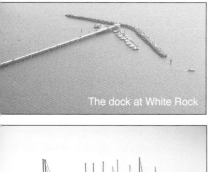

The dock at White Rock

The dock at White Rock

Blaine Harbor Marina

Squalicum Harbor

Shulsan Golf Course 360-293-3444

Bellingham

North Puget Sound

Squalicum Harbor
Port of Bellingham

Harbourmaster Mike Endsley
722 Coho Way WA 98225
Ph: 360-676-2542 Fax: 360-671-6149
squalicum@portofbellingham.com
www.portofbellingham.com   **VHF 16**
Chart 18424, 18423
Moorage: Visitor's dock 1,500 feet.
Fuel: Gas, diesel, propane. **Power:**
30 amp**. Water. Showers, laundry,
washrooms.** Garbage disposal. Portadump. **Pumpout.**
Adjacent: Marine supplies, service,
150 ton travel lift. Restaurant, groceries, stores, **4-lane launch ramp.**
Seasonal free shuttle to town.

48° 15.101' N
122° 30.563' W

Squalicum Harbor

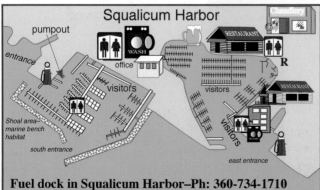

Squalicum Harbor

pumpout
entrance
office
visitors
visitors
Shoal area-
marine bench
habitat
south entrance
east entrance
WASH
RESTAURANT
RESTAURANT
Chandlery
R
VISITORS

Fuel dock in Squalicum Harbor–Ph: 360-734-1710

Not for Navigation

*Top: Bellingham Bay's Squalicum
Harbor. Above: Inside the Squalicum Harbor marina entranceway
and near the launch ramp area and
harbor offices.*

*NOTE: Fairhaven–vessels
need clearance for access
to facilities due to security
regulations.*

Squalicum Harbor

Squalicum Harbor

Saddlebag Island Marine State Park
East of Guemes Island, Padilla Bay.
Chart 18423 30' dock, trails, picnic,
vault toilet. Watch depths on all sides.

*Top and above left: East entrance and waterway in
Squalicum Harbor's recreational yacht basin. Visitor docks
parallel the shore. Above right: Sand castle competition at
Bellingham annual Sand-in-the-City event. Bottom: Fairhaven's launch ramp and linear moorage for visitors.*

Fairhaven. Numerous mooring
buoys and a linear floating dock for visitors
(dinghy to shore) during boating season.
Park, scenic and historic area and ferry
terminal with services adjacent. **Water.**
Launch ramp. Garbage disposal.

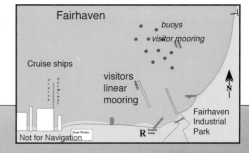

Fairhaven

buoys
visitor mooring
Cruise ships
visitors
linear
mooring
Fairhaven
Industrial
Park
N
R
Boat Works
launch
ramp
Not for Navigation

Fairhaven

48° 43.415' N
122° 30.761' W

La Conner

48° 23.930' N   122° 29.837' W

La Conner Marina   VHF 66A

Harbormaster Paul Mattos

613 N Second St
PO Box 1120, La Conner WA 98257
Ph: 360-466-3118 Fax: 360-466-3119
paulm@portofskagit.com
www.laconnermarina.com

Moorage: 2,400 foot guest dock plus slips. Closed Sundays & holidays in winter.
Power: 30, 50 amps. **Water.**
Showers, washrooms, laundry. Pumpout. Swinomish Yacht Club adjacent south.
Fuel nearby: Gas, diesel, propane, ice.
Nearby: Stores, marine supplies, service, light boat launcher to 7,500 lbs (roller equipped trailers), 100 ton travel lift.

Boat storage. Historic town of La Conner. Stores, gifts, artisans, restaurants. Moorage available at several La Conner business and public docks.

1. La Conner Landing Marine

PO Box 1020, La Conner WA, 98257
Ph: 360-466-4478 **Services.** Fuel dock: Gas, diesel, oils. Store: Groceries, beer and wine, fishing equipment, bait, ice. Open 7 days a week in late spring and summer.

2. Twin Bridges Marina under Hwy 20 on Swinomish Channel–indoor boat storage, limited marine store. No visitor docks.

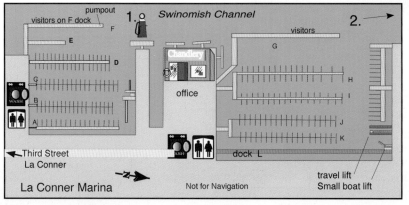

La Conner Marina

Top: Some docks in Swinomish Channel offer day or overnight moorage. La Conner Marina has transient moorage.

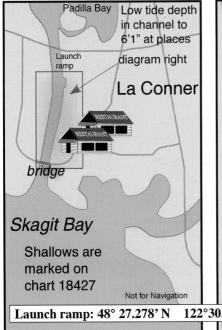

Padilla Bay

Low tide depth
in channel to
6'1" at places
diagram right

Launch
ramp

La Conner

RESTAURANT

RESTAURANT

bridge

Skagit Bay

Shallows are
marked on
chart 18427

Not for Navigation

Launch ramp: 48° 27.278' N   122°30.876' W

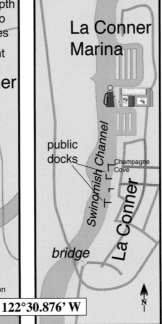

**La Conner
Marina**

public
docks

Champagne
Cove

Swinomish Channel

La Conner

bridge

N

*Top: La Conner and the
channel looking north from
the bridge. Center: The
Swinomish Channel looking
north from Champagne
Cove. Insets and above:
The Champagne Cove store
inside and out. Tourism
thrives at La Conner with
art galleries and stores
sharing space with restaurants on the waterfront.*

Cap Sante Boat Haven–entrance

48° 30.682' N   122° 35.670' W

Anacortes

Cap Sante Boat Have

Cap Sante Boat Haven

Harbourmaster/manager: Dale Fowler
PO Box 297   VHF 66A
1019 Q Ave, Anacortes WA 98221
Ph: 360-293-0694 Fax: 360-299-0998
marina@portofanacortes.com
www.portofanacortes.com
Charts 18423, 18427, 18421
Moorage: Guest docks. 150-200 slips.
Reservations recommended.
Power: 20, 30, 50 amp. **Showers, laundry, washrooms.** Pumpout. Portadump.
Internet access. Two hoist launch ramps–
35,000 lbs and 3,500 lbs. Small boats
self operated. **Fuel nearby at Cap Sante Marine:** Gas, diesel.
Nearby: Restaurant, stores, **Marine Supply and Harware**, service, historic town

Top and above: Cap Sante Boat Haven has guest moorage and facilities for visitors and is adjacent to restaurants and stores in the historic town of Anacortes.
Below: Farmers Market held at Anacortes on Saturdays.

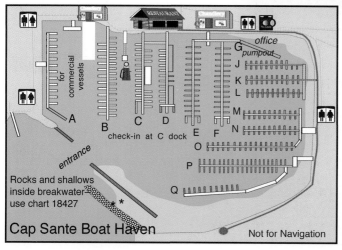

office
pumpout
for commercial vessels
check-in at C dock
entrance
Rocks and shallows
inside breakwater
use chart 18427
Cap Sante Boat Haven
Not for Navigation

of Anacortes–stores,
gifts, galleries, restaurants, summer events.
Adjacent: Launching
and service center located at Cap Sante Boat
Haven. **Marine Service
Center Ph: 360-293-8200**–free pumpout,
some moorage–in Fidalgo Bay. **Fuel, Power,**
showers, washrooms
Haulout facility and
repair yards.

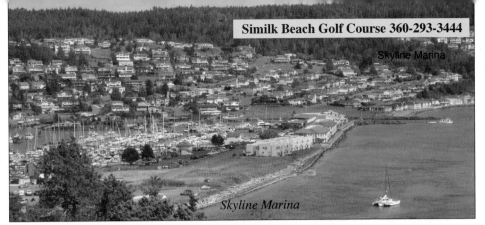

Similk Beach Golf Course 360-293-3444

Skyline Marina

Skyline Marina

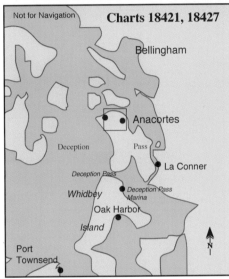

Not for Navigation

Charts 18421, 18427

Bellingham

Anacortes

Deception   Pass

La Conner

Deception Pass

Whidbey   Deception Pass
                Marina

Oak Harbor

Island

Port
Townsend

N

Skyline Marina

48° 29.306' N
122° 40.619' W

Manager: Kelly Larkin

2011 Skyline Way (Flounder Bay)
Anacortes WA 98221
Ph: 360-293-5134 Fax: 360-293-7557
info@skylinemarinecenter.com
www.skylinemarinecenter.com

Moorage: 25 slips. Internet access. **Power:** 15, 20, 30 amps. Garbage disposal. **Showers, laundry, washrooms.** Pumpout. Mechanic. **Fuel docks:** Gas, diesel, propane.

Adjacent: Stores, marine supplies, fishing tackle, bait, charts, books, service, repairs. Sling launch. Travel lift to 55 tons. Restaurants and groceries. Four miles to town. Washington Park with beaches, trails and camping. *Another view of marina next page.*

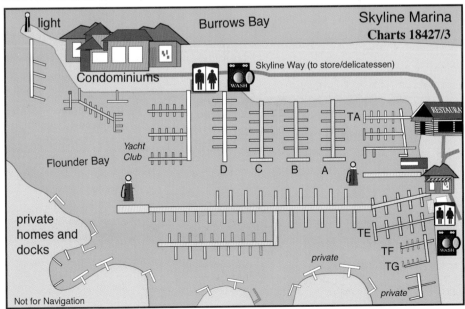

light   Burrows Bay   Skyline Marina
                                          Charts 18427/3

Condominiums   Skyline Way (to store/delicatessen)

WASH

Yacht   TA
Club
Flounder Bay   RESTAURA

                D   C   B   A

private
homes and
docks   TE
                                                   TF
                        private
                                                   TG   WASH

                                          private

Not for Navigation

283

Skyline Marina looking west.

Deception Pass

Deception Pass Marina

Dundee Woods
200 W Cornet Bay Rd
Oak Harbor WA 98277
Ph: 360-675-5411
VHF 16, 68 Charts 18423, 18427
Moorage: Guest dock plus slips. **Fuel
dock:** Gas, diesel, kerosene, stove oil,
propane. **Power:** 30 amps. **Water.**
Garbage disposal, washrooms. Dock
carts. fish cleaning area.
Adjacent: Haulouts, pumpout. General
store, bait, fishing tackle, charts, books,
ice, fishing supplies, groceries, beer and
wine store. Located next to State Park.

> **Deception Pass Marine State Park
> (Sharpes Cove, Bowman Bay)**
> **Ph: 360-902-8844.**
> 1,980' dock space. Launch ramps. Pic-
> nic sites, campground, portable toilets,
> pumpout. Mooring buoys at Skagit
> Island and Hope Island. Public dock at
> Cornet Bay Road and Bayview Lane.

48° 24.055' N   122° 37.633' W

Deception Pass Marina

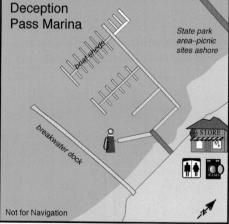

Deception
Pass Marina

boat sheds

breakwater dock

State park
area–picnic
sites ashore

STORE
WASH

Not for Navigation

*Public dock at Cornet Bay, opposite Deception Pass Marina.
Nearby Deception Pass can be tricky in strong currents.*

Oak Harbor Marina on Whidbey Island.

Whidbey Island

48° 17.051' N   122° 38.411' W

Whidbey Golf and Country Club, Oak Harbor Ph: 360-675-5490
Useless Bay Country Club, Langley Ph: 360-321-5960 (private club).

Oak Harbor Marina

Harbourmaster Mack Funk
1401 SE Catalina Dr, Oak Harbor WA 98277
Ph: 360-279-4575 Fax: 360-240-0603
Fuel Dock: 360-279-4575
Charts 18428, 18423, 18441
ohmarina@whidbey.net
www.whidbey.com/ohmarina   **VHF 16**
Visitor moorage 52 40' slips. Internet access.
Power: 30 amp. **Water. Showers, laundry, washrooms.** Pumpout. Nearby stores, service, haulouts. **Fuel:** Gas, diesel, propane.
Launch ramp, 6,500lb sling hoist, marine mechanic. Adjacent to Yacht Club.
Easy access to Oak Harbour. There are shops, stores and restaurants within walking distance of the marina. Playground.

Note: Rocks between R2 channel marker and Maylor/Forbes Point; deepest water is on red buoy side of channel; shoals on green buoy side.

Above: The main guest dock adjacent the manager's office. Oak Harbor Marina is a large facility, as shown in the photo at the top of the page.

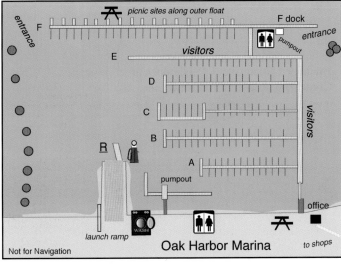

48° 13.381' N   122° 41.061' W

Coupeville dock

Port of Coupeville

Harbormaster Long Bechard
Port of Coupeville, PO Box 577
Coupeville WA 98239-0577
Ph: 360-678-5020 Fax: 360-678-7424
execjim@verizon.net   **Chart 18441**
Moorage. Seven feet at low tide. Two floats providing a total of 400 feet of moorage. **Fuel:** Gas, diesel. **Water. Showers, washrooms.** Cafe, coffee shop.
Adjacent: Gifts. Store, ice, charts, books, art gallery. Gray whale exhibit. Whale watching, kayak tours. **Nearby: Launch ramp**–parks, beach access, restaurants, stores, post office, public transit. Dine and lunch at a wide varied of restaurants nearby.

Shops at Coupeville

Top: Coupeville dock. Above and right: Uptown Coupeville is along the waterfront. Visit other parts of Whidbey Island by free bus service.

Coupeville Auto Repair. Marine service available Ph: 360-678-1746

48° 02.897' N   122° 25.806' W

Port of South Whidbey

Harbourmaster Rick Brewer
Langley Harbor.
PO Box 872, Freeland, WA 98249
Phone: 360-221-1120 Cell: 360-914-1739
Fax: 360-221-4265
harbormaster@portofsouthwhidbey.com
www.portofsouthwhidbey.com
Moorage: Reservations recommended.
24 slips. **Power:** 20, 30 amps**, water,**
washrooms, showers, pumpout.
Launch ramp. Internet access.
Nearby: Five-minute walk to Langley
Post office, restaurants,
liquor store, groceries.
Art galleries, gift shops,
bookstores, pharmacy. Ac-
commodations. Scuba diving
on artificial reef. Marine
mechanic. ATM. Medical
services.

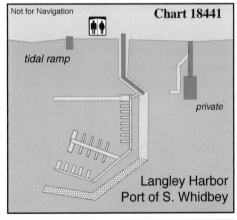

Not for Navigation   **Chart 18441**

tidal ramp

private

Langley Harbor
Port of S. Whidbey

Top: Port of South Whidbey in
Langley Harbor. Right: Uptown
Langley has bakeries, coffee shops,
restaurants and alleys with art,
crafts and souvenir shops.

Top: Good weather anchorage off South Whidbey Island, near the harbor. Below: The launch ramp at Keystone, alongside the ferry landing. Above: Free bus service on Whidbey Island, available Monday through Saturday.

12th Street Harbor

Run by Port of Everett
Marina Director: Cindy Olson
PO Box 538, Everett WA 98206
Ph: 425-259-6001
Fax: 425-259-0860
Toll Free: 1-800-729-7678
marina@portofeverett.com
www.portofeverett.com
VHF 16, switch to 69
Charts 18444, 18443
Moorage: 'A' Dock 1,000',
'J' Dock groups & clubs
Power: 30, 50 amps. Water, pumpout,
Showers, laundry, washrooms.
Nearby: Port of Everett with all
facilities and services.
See Port of Everett Marina.

Photo courtesy of Port of Everett

Port of Everett

47° 59.790' N   122° 13.516' W

Port of Everett Marina

Cindy Olson
1720 W Marine View Dr, Everett WA 98201t
Ph: 425-259-6001 Fax: 425-259-0860
marina@portofeverett.com
www.portofeverett.com
VHF 16 switch to **69 Charts 18444, 18443**
Moorage: 4,173' guest dock plus slips.
Fuel dock: Gas, diesel. **Power:** 20, 30, 50 amp. Snack bar. Garbage disposal. 25 ton travel lift. Recycling. **Showers, laundry, washrooms.** 3 pumpouts. Internet access. **Adjacent:** Village restaurants and shops. Marine stores, propane, fishing tackle, bait, charts, books. Wheelchair access float. Haulouts, storage, repairs, service. Launch ramp. Be aware of the 500' Naval Station boundary.
Nearby: Restaurants, grocery stores, chandlery, playground, hiking trails, medical services, post office, banks.

Top: The marina at Everett is one of the biggest in Puget Sound. The 13-lane launch ramp is impressive with multiple lanes and spacious parking facilities.

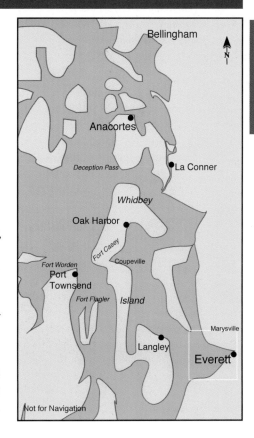

Bellingham

N

Anacortes

Deception Pass

La Conner

Whidbey

Oak Harbor

Fort Casey

Coupeville

Fort Worden

Port Townsend

Fort Flagler   Island

Marysville

Langley

Everett

Not for Navigation

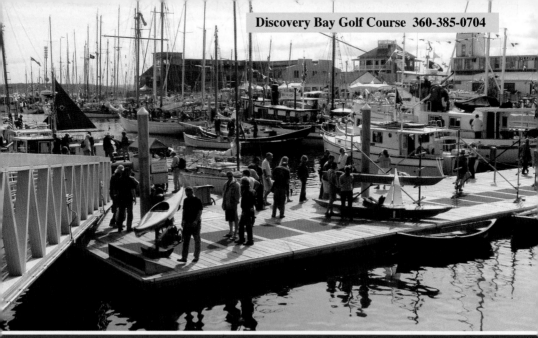

Port Townsend

Charts 18464, 18471, 18441

North Puget Sound

Point Hudson Marina & RV Park

Tami Ruby
103 Hudson St, PO Box 1180
Port Townsend WA 98368   VHF 09
Ph: 360-385-2828 Fax: 360-385-7331
Toll Free Phone: 1-800-228-2803
phudson@portofpt.com www.portofpt.com
Moorage: Slips to 40', lineal slips to 65'. Check in at the marina office on the northeast side of the marina. **Water. Power:** 30 amps. Internet access. Propane, **Fuel:** available at Port Townsend Boat Haven, one mile south of city public dock, opposite Safeway. **Laundry, showers, washrooms.** Pump-out. Garbage disposal. The Northwest Maritime Center is adjacent. **Sea Marine Chandlery** adjacent to harbor–travel lift, mechanical service and repairs. Bank, post office. **Nearby:** Restaurants, stores, groceries, medical services, Port Townsend is a quaint, historic town with many antique stores, galleries, classic restaurants and specialty stores.

Top: Point Hudson Marina's annual Wooden Boat Festival held every September.

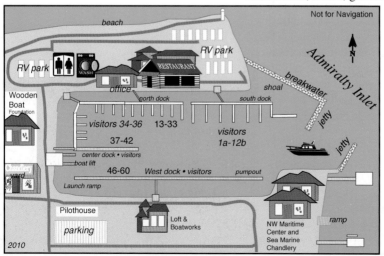

Above: Approaching Point Hudson Marina.
Right, top to bottom: docks and Wooden
Boat Foundation at Point Hudson.

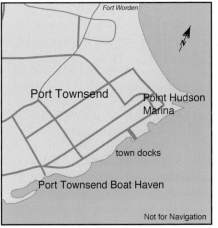

Fort Worden

Port Townsend

Point Hudson
Marina

town docks

Port Townsend Boat Haven

Not for Navigation

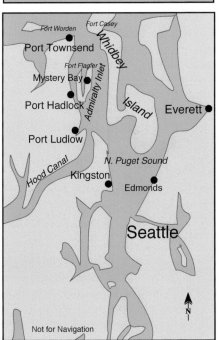

Fort Worden   Fort Casey

Port Townsend

Whidbey

Fort Flagler

Mystery Bay

Port Hadlock

Admiralty Inlet

Island

Everett

Port Ludlow

N. Puget Sound

Hood Canal

Kingston

Edmonds

Seattle

Not for Navigation

48° 06.875' N   122° 44.964' W

Point Hudson Marina

Wooden Boat Foundation at Point Hudson.

Point Hudson Marina

Port Townsend Boat Haven

48° 06.411' N   122° 46.223' W

North Puget Sound

Port Townsend Boat Haven

Tami Ruby

2601 Washington St, PO Box 1180
Port Townsend WA 98368
Ph: 360-385-2355 Fax: 360-379-8205
info@portofpt.com
www.portofpt.com
Charts 18464, 18441 VHF 66A
Moorage: Transient slips available.
Power: 30, 50 amps.
Fuel: Gas, diesel. **Laundry, showers, washrooms.** Pump-out.
Garbage disposal. **Launch ramp**.
Haul outs to 300 tons.
Nearby: This marina lies one mile south of the town. Restaurants. Stores, groceries, marine store, service and repairs adjacent.
Customs: 360-385-3777.

Launch ramp and a town dock south of Point Hudson. First come basis. Open to wash and weather.

Top: The large public dock at Port Townsend has overnight moorage for visitors. Several exposed docks along the waterfront take recreational vessels on a first come basis. Below: Anchorage is possible off the Port Townsend waterfront in calm conditions.

Port Townsend waterfront.

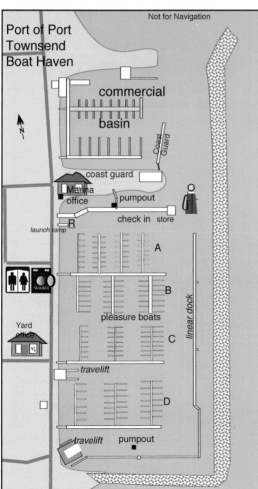

Port of Port
Townsend
Boat Haven

commercial

basin

Coast Guard

coast guard

Marina office

pumpout

check in   store

launch ramp

R

WASH

A

B

pleasure boats

linear dock

C

Yard office

travelift

D

travelift   pumpout

Historic Port Townsend and a section of its commercial docks adjacent to Boat Haven.

Fort Worden Marine State Park   Port Townsend

Ph: 360-344-4400   360-385-4730
reservations: www.Parks.wa.gov
Charts 18441, 18464
Moorage. 235' docks. **Washrooms, showers, laundry. 2 boat ramps.** kayak/bike rentals, tennis, golf, hiking trails, picnic, camping, historic town. Marine Science Center.

Port Ludlow Golf Course 360-437-8272

Port Hadlock

Welcome to PORT HADLOCK MARINA

48° 01.877' N   122° 44.725' W

Anchorage near Port Hadlock marina

Admiralty Inlet

Admiralty Inlet

Port Hadlock Marina

Jerry Spencer   Charts 18464, 18441
310 Hadlock Bay Rd
PO Box 14342, Port Hadlock WA 98339
Ph: 360-385-6368 Fax: 360-385-3067
VHF call on 16 switch to 66
porthadlockmarina@hotmail.com

Moorage: Some transient moorage. **Power**: 30, 50 amps. **Showers, washrooms.** Pumpout. Laundry. Internet access.
Nearby: Inn at Port Hadlock with restaurant and hotel facilities. Kayak rentals. Float plane dock.

Inn at Port Hadlock

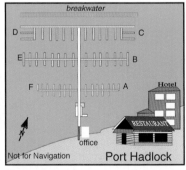

breakwater
D C
E B
F A
Hotel
RESTAURANT
office
Not for Navigation   Port Hadlock

Reserve space at parks: Go to *www.stateparks.com*

Fort Flagler Marine State Park

Marrowstone Island. Chart 18464
256' docks. vaul toilets, showers, portadump.
Launch ramp. 7 Mooring buoys. Scuba diving underwater park. Campground. Trails. Museum. Military fort historic buildings. Boat rentals. Mini store. Fishing supplies. Mind strong currents.

Mystery Bay Marine State Park (map page 283)

Kilisut Harbor, Marrowstone Island. Launch ramp. 683' of docks. Pumpout, portadump. Mooring buoys. **Chart 18464.**

47° 55.170' N   122° 40.893' W

Port Ludlow Marina

Kori Ward
1 Gull Dr, Port Ludlow WA 98365
Ph: 360-437-0513 Fax: 360-437-2428
Toll free: 1-800-308-7991
Charts 18477, 18473, 18441 VHF 68
kward@portludlowresort.com
www. portludlowresort.com
Moorage: Visitor docks, available slips.
Water. Power: 30, 50 amps.
Fuel: Gas, diesel, propane. Pumpout.

Above and bottom: Port Ludlow Marina visitor docks. Below right: A quiet garden at the marina. Opposite page: Port Hadlock Marina and the Inn overlooking the docks. The inset photo shows the view from the docks.

Laundry, showers, washrooms. Garbage disposal. gifts, clothing, walking trails, kayak rentals. **Nearby/adjacent:** Restaurants. Lounge. Golf course shuttle. Store, groceries, books, fishing tackle and supplies, bait, ice. Marine mechanic. Repairs.

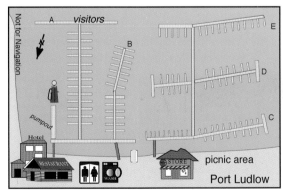

Herb Beck Marina

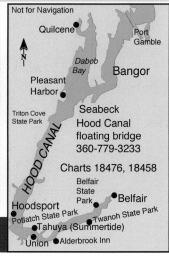

Not for Navigation

Quilcene

Port Gamble

Dabob Bay

Bangor

Pleasant Harbor

Triton Cove State Park

Seabeck

Hood Canal floating bridge 360-779-3233

Charts 18476, 18458

Belfair State Park

Belfair

Hoodsport

Potlatch State Park

Twanoh State Park

Tahuya (Summertide)

Union • Alderbrook Inn

Hood Canal

VHF 9, 16.
Chart 18476

Hood Canal *(side tab)*

Herb Beck Marina–Quilcene

Tami Rudy

1731 Linger Longer Rd, PO Box 98
Quilcene WA 98376
Ph: 360-765-3131

info@portofpt.com www.portofpt.com

Chart 18476

Guest moorage when slips available. **Fuel:** Gas, diesel. **Power:** 30 amps. **Washrooms, showers,** pumpout. **Launch Ramp.**
Adjacent: Ice, supplies. repairs, service. Camping. Barbeque. Town less than 1 mile. Shrimping popular in April and May. (Formerly Quilcene Boathaven).

Above: Herb Beck Marina, at the head of Dabob Bay, was formerly known as Quilcene Boat Haven.

Pleasant Harbor Marina

Diane Coleman   **VHF 16, 22**

308913 Highway 101, Brinnon WA 98320
Ph: 360-796-4611 Fax: 360-796-4898
Toll free: 1-800-547-3479

info@pleasantharbormarina.com
www.pleasantharbormarina.com

Fuel: Gas, diesel.
Moorage: Guest moorage 50 slips. Reservations suggested.
Power: 30, 50 amp. **Washrooms, show-ers**–free for moorage customers, **laundry,** pumpout. Internet access**.** Garbage disposal. Hot tub. Boaters lounge, swimming pool. Store, delicatessen, groceries, fishing and marine supplies. Ice, gifts, espresso. Beer and wine. Order-in or take-out pizza.
Nearby: Marine repairs. Launch ramp.

Bangor is a restricted military area.
Use charts 18473, 18476 and 18477.

Left: Pleasant Harbor is well named for its delightful surroundings. The nearby State Park is also popular.

Photo courtesy of Pleasant Harbor Marina

Pleasant Harbor

47° 47.964' N
122° 51.896' W

Pleasant Harbor Marine State Park
Ph: 360-753-5771 *www.parks.wa.gov*
Chart 18448 Guest dock 218 feet.
Portadump. Pumpout. Scuba diving.

Photo courtesy of Pleasant Harbor Marina

Pleasant Harbor Marina has space for visitors. This and Alderbrook are the marinas of choice in Hood Canal for all, including larger boats.

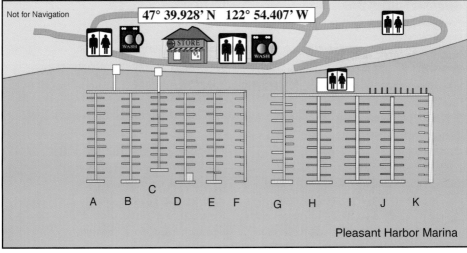

Not for Navigation

47° 39.928' N 122° 54.407' W

STORE

A B C D E F G H I J K

Pleasant Harbor Marina

47° 24.512' N   123° 08.165' W

Hoodsport Marina

24080 Highway 101
Hoodsport WA 98548
Ph: 360-877-9250
Fuel: Gas. Pumpout.
Moorage: Free use of new public dock.
Nearby: Grocery store. Sunrise Motel and Resort.

47° 20.983' N   123° 04.087' W

Alderbrook Resort and Spa

Harbormaster–Cindy Sund
10 E Alderbrook Drive, Union WA 98592
Ph: 360-898-2252 Fax: 360-898-4610
hoodcanalmarina@hctc.com
www.alderbrookresort.com
Guest moorage 1500'. **Power** 30, 50 amp.
Water, pumpout, showers. Seaplane dock.
Hotel rooms, cottages, indoor pool, 18 hole
golf course, restaurant, banquet facilities,
watercraft rentals. Boat launch nearby.

47° 21.215' N   123° 04.783' W

Hood Canal Marina

Harbormaster–Cindy Sund.
E 5101 Hwy 106
PO Box 305, Union WA 98592
Ph: 360-898-2252 Fax: 360-898-8888
hoodcanalmarina@hctc.com
Fuel: Gas, diesel.
Moorage: Limited guest moorage.
Nearby: Groceries. Mobile tech repairs, marine service. Launch ramp.

47° 22.099' N   123° 03.432' W

Summertide Resort & Marina

Bev Vos-Pepredis
1578 NE Northshore Rd
Tuhuya WA 98588 Ph: 360-275-9313
summertide_resort@msn.com
Website: www.summertideresort.com
Moorage: Seasonal, reservations suggested.
Boats to 45 feet. **Washrooms, showers.**
Adjacent: Launch ramp. RV sites. Cottage rentals.
Store–ice, propane, groceries, fishing supplies.

Twanoh State Marine Park

Near Belfair Ph: 360-902-8844
www.parks.wa.gov
7 Mooring buoys, pumpout.
200 feet of moorage for overnight use.
Launch ramp, playground, picnic areas,
campsites, toilets, swimming, tennis,
hiking trails. Fishing, crabbing, oysters.

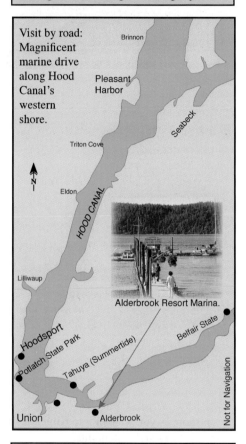

Visit by road: Magnificent marine drive along Hood Canal's western shore.

Alderbrook Resort Marina.

Not for Navigation

Triton Cove State Marine Park

Chart 18476   In Hood Canal
Seasonal dock. 100' for launching use.

Potlatch State Marine Park

Ph: 360-877-5361 Chart 18476
3 miles south of Hoodsport
Adjacent: Mooring buoys. Park, picnic
sites, hiking trails, scuba diving, launch
ramp. Washrooms, showers.

Fuel dock and visitor moorage at Kingston

Central Puget Sound

Port of Kingston | 47° 47.635' N   122° 29.958' W |

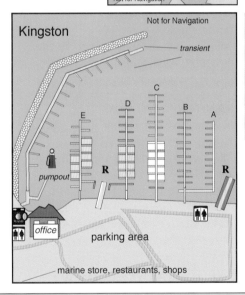

Port Townsend · Whidbey Island
Admiralty Inlet
Port Ludlow · N. Puget Sound
Hood Canal · Kingston
Edmonds
Not for Navigation

Harbormaster–Kevin Van Vliet
25864 Washington Blvd
PO Box 559 Kingston WA 98346
Ph: 360-297-3545 Fax: 360-297-2945
Charts 18446, 18473, 18441, 18445
VHF 65

ptkingston@aol.com   www.portofkingston.org

Moorage: Slips for 49 guests. Guest moorage located just inside breakwater. Limited reservation with advance notice.

Fuel: Gas, diesel. **Power:** 30 amps. **Laundry, showers, washrooms.** Pump-out. Porta-dump. **Launch ramp.** Free electric car for moorage customers. Internet access.

Nearby: Medical services. Playground. The ferry from Edmonds lands next to the marina at Kingston. Watch for the heavy motor traffic on shore as you wander into Kingston to visit the stores and restaurants.

Kingston — Not for Navigation
transient
C
D
B
A
E
R
pumpout
R
office
parking area
marine store, restaurants, shops

Central Puget Sound

Launch ramp at Kingston

Edmonds

Courtesy of Port of Edmonds - Keitth Opp photo

47° 48.5565' N   122° 23.485' W

Port of Edmonds

Bob McChesney
336 Admiral Way, Edmonds WA 98020
Ph: 425-775-4588 Fax: 425-670-0583
info@portofedmonds.org
www.portofedmonds.org   **VHF 69**
Charts 18441, 18446, 18473

Moorage: Permanent and guest moorage reservations. **Showers, restrooms.**
Fuel docks: Gas, diesel. Pumpout. Ice. Garbage disposal. **Power: 30, 50 amp.**
Water. Haulouts, sling launch, storage, workyard. 50 ton travel lift. Visit the NOAA weather center. Fishing pier.
Adjacent: Bait shop. Fishing pier. Beach.
Nearby: Downtown Edmonds. Laundry, shops. Anthony's, Arnies restaurants. Public beaches. Good scuba diving at nearby artificial reef. Courtesy van available.

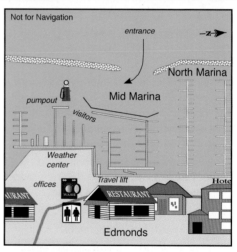

Not for Navigation

entrance

—z—

North Marina

pumpout

Mid Marina

visitors

Weather center

offices

WASH

Travel lift

RESTAURANT

Hote

URANT

Edmonds

Edmonds

Edmonds

PORT OF EDMONDS   WEATHER CENTER

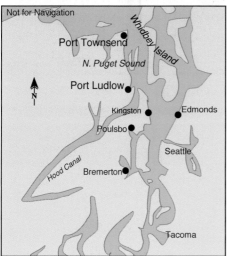

Not for Navigation

Whidbey Island

Port Townsend

N. Puget Sound

N

Port Ludlow

Kingston   Edmonds

Poulsbo

Seattle

Hood Canal

Bremerton

Tacoma

Above and opposite: Port of Edmonds Marina. Visitor dock at Edmonds. Traveling south to Seattle, convenient stops may be made at Kingston or at Edmonds. Either place is a pleasant stopover with spacious moorage, facilities and adjacent restaurants and nearby stores. Below: The fuel dock is conveniently located alongside the visitor docks near the entrance to the marina at the Port of Edmonds.

Opposite bottom left: A large restaurant overlooks the marina at Edmonds. Opposite, bottom right, a substantial NOAA mariners' weather center provides helpful, instant weather reporting and navigation information for Puget Sound, including distances to other ports.

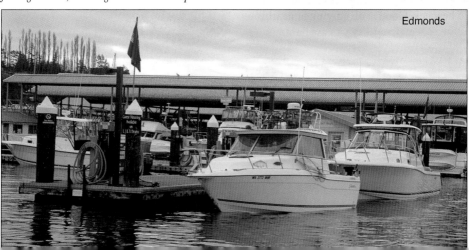

Poulsbo

47° 43.965' N   122° 38.963' W

Port of Poulsbo Guest Marina

Bainbridge Island vicinity

Central Puget Sound

Port of Poulsbo

Ken Stickels
18809 Front St
Poulsbo WA 98370
Ph: 360-779-3505 Fax: 360-779-8090
reservations@portofpoulsbo.com
www.portofpoulsbo.com
Moorage: Slips for 123 guests.
Call or go online for reservations. Internet
access. **Water. Power:** 30 amp.
Fuel: Gas, diesel. **Laundry, showers,
washrooms.** Free pump-out. Launch ramp.
Nearby: Bistros, bakery, shops and all
facilities for visitors. Playground.

Chart 18446
VHF 66A

Poulsbo is a character town. This small
town is built in traditional Viking style and
has a beautiful setting with ethnic restaurants, bakeries, gift and book stores.

Poulsbo

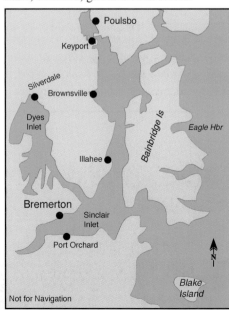

Not for Navigation

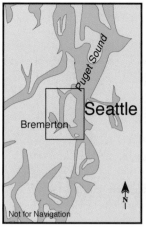

Poulsbo

Poulsbo

Opposite, top: The marina at Poulsbo. Inset: Visitor docks at Poulsbo. Left: A downtown street scene. Opposite, bottom: The fuel dock at the marina. This Norwegian village has a strong appeal to tourists.

Port of Silverdale

Teresa Heider
PO Box 310, Silverdale WA 98383
Phone: 360-698-4918
Fax: 360-698-3402   Chart 18449
www.portofsilverdale.com
Visitor moorage 1,300'. Overnight reservations available on line.
Washrooms. Launch ramp.
Nearby: Restaurants, shopping. Waterfront park picnic and play areas.

Below: The dock at Silverdale serves a park and a launch ramp. It can accommodate some larger boats.

Silverdale

47° 38.564' N   122° 41.526' W

47° 39.035' N
122° 36.811' W

Central Puget Sound

Port of Brownsville

Jerry Rowland
9790 Ogle Rd NE
Bremerton WA 98311
Ph: 360-692-5498 Fax: 360-698-8023
pob@portofbrownsville.org
www.portofbrownsville.org
Charts 18446, 18449   VHF 16, 66A
Moorage: 1,000'. 500 linear ft on breakwater plus visitor docks 20 40' and 25 24' slips available. **Water. Power:** 30 amp. **Fuel:** Gas, diesel, propane, snacks. **Laundry, showers, washrooms.** Launch ramp. Free pump-out. **Nearby:** ATM, park, deli, convenience store, meat market.

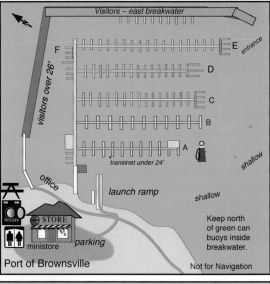

Visitors – east breakwater
F
visitors over 26'
E
entrance
D
C
B
A
transinet under 24'
shallow
office
launch ramp
shallow
WASH
STORE
ministore
parking
Keep north
of green can
buoys inside
breakwater.
Port of Brownsville
Not for Navigation

Illahee   Chart 18449

Illahee State Park
Port Orchard Bay.
Ph: 360-902-8844
Visitor dock. Up to 360 feet of dock space. Mooring buoys located beyond floating breakwater. Swimming, scuba. Picnic. **Washrooms, showers.**

47° 35.979' N   122° 35.584' W

Eagle Harbor Waterfront Park

**370 Brien Dr, Bainbridge Island
WA 98110** Harbor master Tami Allen
Ph: 206-780-3733 Fax: 206-780-8596
tallen@ci.bainbridge-isl.wa.us
www.ci.bainbridge-isl.wa.us
Chart 18449. Moorage 100 ft. **Showers,
Washrooms. Pumpout.** Playground, picnic
tables. **Nearby:** Launch ramp. 400' linear
mooring buoys. Downtown location and near
Seattle ferry. Speed limit 5 knots. Summer
concerts on Wednesdays in season. **Also
known as: Bainbridge Waterfront Park**.

47° 37.039' N 122° 31.774' W

Harbour Marina

Fred Adams   Chart 18449
**233 Parfitt Way SW, Eagle Harbor
Bainbridge Island WA 98110
Ph: 206-550-5340 Pub Fax: 206-842-5047**
dockmaster@harbourmpub.com
www.harbourpub.com
Visitors in available slips. **Showers, laundry, washrooms. Power:** 30 amp.
Pumpout. Marina is adjacent to an Eng-
lish-style pub. Close to town.

There are public boat launching ramps at Fort Ward
State Park, at Fay Bainbridge State Park and at Eagle
Harbor Waterfront Park. Overnight moorage is available on the pier at Eagle Harbor Waterfront Park and
anchorage buoys at Fay Bainbridge State Park.

47° 37.220' N 122° 30.497' W
Eagle Harbour

Winslow Wharf Marina

Winslow Wharf Marina

Dave LaFave   **Chart 18449   VHF 9**
**141 Parfitt Way SW, Bainbridge Island WA 98110
Ph: 206-842-4202 Fax: 206-842-7785**
www.winslowwharfmarina.com
Limited visitor moorage. **Power:** 30 amp.
Showers, laundry, washrooms.
Nearby: Launch ramp. Pumpout. Chandlery.
This marina is very close to town and adjacent
to the park and Seattle ferry.

Eagle Harbor Marina

Tod Hornick
**5834 Ward Ave NE, Bainbridge Island
WA 98110 Ph: 206-842-4003**
harbormaster@eagleharbormarina.com
www.eagleharbormarina.com
Chart 18449
Guest moorage, 30' to 66'.
Power: 30, 50-amp, club house, mobile
pumpout, cable, phone, wi-fi, high speed
internet, shower, laundry, exercise room,
sauna.

*Left: Eagle Harbor Marina is across the bay from
town. It is mostly permanent moorage.*

305

Trophy Lakes Golf Course 360-874-8337

Port Orchard

Photo Courtesy Port of Bremerton

47° 33.281' N 122° 38.198' W
for Port of Bremerton Marina

USS *Turner Joy*

Bremerton - Port Orchard

Bremerton Marina

Steve Slaton (also Port Orchard Marina)
120 Washington Beach
Bremerton WA 98337
Ph: 360-373-1035 Fax: 360-479-2928
Charts 18448, 18449 VHF 66A, 16, 9
guest@portofbremerton.org
www.portofbremerton.org
Moorage: Lots of guest moorage. Call.
Water. Power: 30, 50 amps. **Pumpouts.**
Laundry, showers, washrooms. Adjacent City of Bremerton, ferries, bus service, restaurants, stores, Naval museum. Fuel at Port Orchard Marina.

47° 34.748' N 122° 38.634' W
for Port Washington Marina

Port Washington Marina

Bob & Stephanie Stanberry
1805 Thompson Dr, Bremerton WA 98337
Ph/Fax: 360-479-3037   Chart 18449
portwamarina@comcast.net
www.portwashingtonmarina.com
Moorage: Limited guest moorage. Phone for reservations. Located near ferry dock.
Water. Power: 30, 50 amps. Pumpout.
Laundry, showers, washrooms.

Central Puget Sound

Photo at top shows a view of the docks at Bremerton. The USS Turner Joy is an attraction at the marina.

Not for Navigation

North entrance

visitors

pumpout

pumpout

visitors

South entrance

harbor tours

visitors

E

Public dock

Ferry terminals

Exhibit: USS Turner Joy

D boardwalk

C

office

B

A

Bremerton Marina

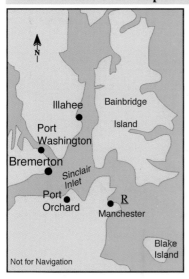

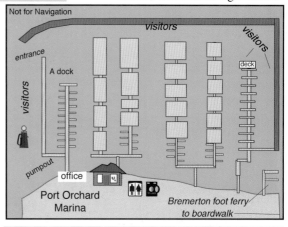

Port Orchard Marina

Steve Slaton (also Bremerton)
707 Sidney Pkwy
Port Orchard WA 98366
www.portofbremerton.org
Ph: 360-876-5535 Fax: 360-895-0291
Charts 18448, 18449 VHF 66A
Moorage: Transient and permanent–call
for reservations. **Water. Power:** 30, 50
amps. **Fuel:** Gas, diesel, ice. **Laundry,
showers, washrooms.** Garbage disposal.
Internet access.
Nearby: Boardwalk and waterfront park.
Playground. Ferry to Bremerton and Seat-
tle. Bus, bank, restaurants, shops.
Marine hardware and marine services are
located nearby off the property.

Blake Island State Marine Park

Blake Island, Yukon Harbor, Puget Sound
Ph: 360-731-8330 (near Port Orchard)
Charts 18474, 18448, 18449, 18441
Moorage, water, 1744' dock space. **Power** 30 amp.
23 mooring buoys. Camping, volleyball, wash-
rooms, trails, wildlife, scuba diving. The Tillicum
Village restaurant is a typical longhouse replica.

47° 33.328' N   122° 32.521' W

Port of Manchester

PO Box 304 Manchester WA 98353
Ph: 360-871-0500 Chart 18448
info@portofmanchester.com
www.portofmanchester.com
Day moorage only. Launch ramp.
Adjacent: Pomeroy Park and picnic tables.
Nearby: Washrooms, Restaurants, stores.
Visitor dock 400 feet. Shallow, may dry at
extreme low tides.

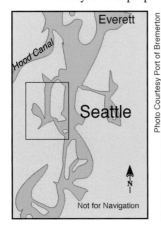

47° 32.678' N   122° 38.355' W
for Port Orchard Marina   Port Orchard

Seattle and South Puget Sound

Fuel

pumpout

Shilshole Marina

Photo courtesy Port of Seattle/Don Wilson

Seattle

Charts: 18447, 18474, 18448/9, 18441

Shilshole Bay Marina

Sharon Briggs

Fuel dock: 206-783-7555.

7001 Seaview Ave NW, Suite 100, Seattle WA 98117

Ph: 206-787-3006 Fax: 206-787-3754

Toll free 1-800-426-7817 ext 3006

sbm@portseattle.org   www.portseattle.org   **VHF 17**

Fuel. Gas, diesel. **Power:** 30, 50, 100 amp. Marine supplies. Mechanic. **Laundry, showers, washrooms.** Guest slips for over 100 boats including megayachts. 55 ton travelift. Dry moorage for 92 boats to 40 feet. Internet access. Garbage/recycling. Boat yard. Pump-out. Hazardous waste disposal. Restaurants, conference facilities, pub within walking distance. Groceries. Fishing supplies. Large grass garden and plaza area. **Nearby:** Shops. **Launch ramp.** The marina's location makes it an ideal stop for those heading into or out of Lake Washington.

Shilshole Marina
Ballard Mill Marina
Hiram M Chittenden Locks
Fishermen's Terminal (Salmon Bay)
Morrison's Fuel dock
HC Henry Marina
Chandler's
Elliot Bay Marina
No Overnight Anchoring in Seattle
Elliot Bay
Seattle
Bell Harbor Marina
Alki Point
Not for Navigation

Shilshole Marina

Ballard Mill Marina

Willy Jenkins
4733 Shilshole Ave NW   VHF 66A
Seattle WA 98107 Ph: 206-789-4777
ballardmillmarina@gmail.com
(located in ship canal, Salmon Bay). Limited
visitor moorage. **Power:** 20, 30 amp.
Washrooms. Showers. Pumpout.
Nearby: Launch ramp. Fuel dock nearby.

Fishermen's Terminal–For location
of listings on this page please see
diagram on page 310.

Fuel at Morrison's
North Star Marine. Ph: 206-284-6600

Opposite, top: Shilshole Marina.
Opposite, bottom: Canal to Lake Washington.
Above: Docks at Fishermen's Terminal.

Marina Park

25 Lakeshore Plaza Dr
123 Fifth Ave, Kirkland WA 98032
Ph: 425-587-3300 Fax: 425-828-1220
www.ci.kirkland.wa.gov
Visitor moorage 77 slips. Washrooms.
Nearby: Launch ramp. Picnic. Kirkland
city access. Ice. Liquor store, post office.
Restaurants in the area. All amenities.

Fishermen's Terminal

3919 18th Ave West,
Seattle WA 98199, Salmon Bay
Ph: 206-787-3395 Fax: 206-787-3280
ft@portseattle.org   www.portseattle.org
Moorage: 200' concrete dock. Boats to
250 ft. **Showers, laundry, washrooms.**
Power: 30, 50, 100 amp. Repairs. Ways.
Pumpout. Adjacent restaurants, shops.

Salmon Bay Marina

Leslie Campbell
2100 W Commodore Way, Seattle WA 98199
Ph: 206-282-5555 Fax: 206-282-8482
sales@salmonbaymarina.com
www.salmonbaymarina.com
Moorage: Overnight, 60' plus vacancies.
Power: 30, 50-amp. Garbage/recycling.
RV park. Boat trailer storage.

Chandler's Cove

901 Fairview Ave N Seattle WA 98901
Ph: 206-216-4199
No overnight–3 hour stops only. Pumpout.
Nearby restaurants.

Carillon Point Marina

Megan Curfman
4100 Carillon Point, Kirkland WA 98033
Ph: 425-822-1700 Fax: 425-828-3094
megan@carillonprop.com
www.carillon-point.com
Visitor moorage. Power: 30, 50 amp.
Showers, washrooms. Pump-out station.
Portadump. Adjacent to hotel and shops.

Central & South Puget Sound

Lake Washington moorage is available on a very limited basis. Stop at Parkshore Marina, the Kirkland dock or possibly at Gene Coulon Park. If you are a member of a yacht club with reciprocal privileges you will be able to stay on a first come basis at club facilities on the lake.

Lakewood Moorage

Randy Johnson
4500 Lake Washington Blvd S
PO Box 18403 Seattle WA 98118
Ph: 206-722-3887
www.seattle.gov/parks
Moorage: 50' guest dock. Power: 30 amps. Water. **Washrooms. Laundry,** snacks. Picnic area.

Parkshore Marina

9050 Seward Park Ave
Seattle WA 98118
Ph: 206-725-3330 Fax: 206-418-6734
info@parkshoremarina.net
www.parkshoremarina.net
Washrooms, showers, laundry. Pumpout station. Launch ramp.
Adjacent to Rainier Yacht Club.

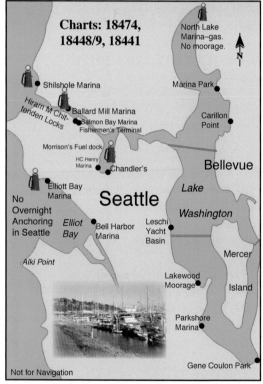

Charts: 18474, 18448/9, 18441

Top: Elliot Bay Marina can accommodate very large pleasure craft. Visitors should call ahead to arrange moorage.

Gene Coulon Memorial Beach Park
1201 Lake Washington Blvd
Renton WA 98055
Ph: 425-430-6700 Fax: 425-430-6701
Moorage for day use. Picnic, park with facilities. Showers, washrooms. Tennis, swimming, trails. Nearby: 8-lane launch ramp. Restaurant. *www.ci.rentonwa.gov*

Elliott Bay Marina

47° 37.599' N   122° 23.127' W

Elliott Bay Marina   VHF 78A

Brian Kaloper
2601 W Marina Pl, Seattle WA 98199
Ph: 206-285-4817 Fax: 206-286-3129
brian@elliottbaymarina.net
www.elliottbaymarina.net
Moorage: 20' to 300' **Fuel:** Gas, diesel,
Power: 30.50, 100, 150 amp. **Water.**
Showers, laundry, washrooms.
Slipside **pumpout.**
Garbage disposal, marine mechanic and
repairs. Hazardous waste disposal. Line
assist. Internet access.
Restaurants, convenience store.
Scenic views and walkway around the bay.

Restaurant at Elliott Bay Marina

*Top: Elliott Bay Marina looking towards downtown
Seattle. Right: One of two restaurants at Elliot Bay
Marina. It overlooks the marina with a view across
Elliott Bay towards Seattle (photo above right). Bottom
right: View from Elliott Bay Marina walkway.*

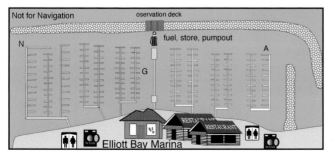

Elliott Bay Marina

47° 36.617' N   122° 21.061' W

Bell Harbor

Bell Harbor Marina   VHF 66A

Ramel Winslow, Pati Lockeman
Pier 66, 2203 Alaskan Way, Seattle WA 98121
Ph: 306-787-3952 Fax: 206-787-3965
Toll free 1-800-426-7817 ext 3952
bhm@portseattle.org
www.portseattle.org

Moorage: Marina on Seattle waterfront.
Many visitor slips. **Power:** 30, 50, enquire for
100 amps. **Washrooms, showers. Pumpout.**
Garbage/recycling.
Nearby: Restaurants, stores. Near Aquarium,
science center, Space Needle and Pike Place
Market. Downtown core free bus service.

Restaurant overlooking the dock

Vessels over 100' should inspect entrance
angle before entering.

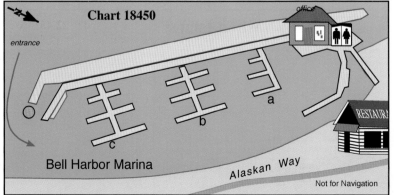

Chart 18450

entrance

office

a

b

c

Bell Harbor Marina

Alaskan Way

RESTAURA

Not for Navigation

Seattle

Tacoma

47° 24.086' N   122° 19.897 ' W

Above: Des Moines Marina. Entrance is at the north end of the marina (inset), south of the fishing jetty.

City of Des Moines Marina

Joe Dusenbury
22307 Dock Ave S
Des Moines WA 98198
Ph: 206-824-5700 Fax: 206-878-5940
Charts 18474, 18448   VHF 16/68
www.desmoineswa.gov
Moorage: Large permanent marina with section for visitors to 55'–about 65 slips. **Power:** 30, 50 amps. **Fuel:** Gas, diesel, propane, engine and outboard oils. Marine repairs. Free pumpout. **Washrooms. Showers**.
Adjacent: Boatyard, repairs and services, marine store, ice, snacks, restaurants. Playground. **Laundry** nearby. Entrance to the marina is south of the fishing jetty.

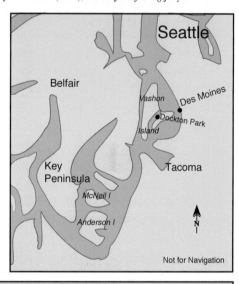

Not for Navigation

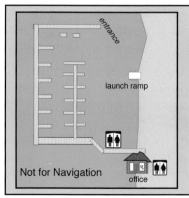

Not for Navigation

Vashon Island.

47° 22.451' N
122° 27.552' W

Dockton Park
9500 SW Dock St, Vashon WA 98070
Ph: 206-205-5275   Chart 18474
www.kingcounty.gov/reecreation/parks
Moorage. Visitors–no permanent–year round.
Water. Pumpout. Washrooms. Showers.
Garbage disposal. Park adjacent to moorage.
Launch ramp. Picnic shelter.

Dockton Park, Vashon Island

| 47° 19.601' N   122° 34.527' W | Jerisich Park dock |

Gig Harbor

Jerisich Park Dock

Gig Harbor public marina
3211 Harborview Drive,
Gig Harbor WA 98335
Ph: 253-851-6170
Fax: 253-853-7597
www.cityofgigharbor.net

Moorage: Maximum moorage 48 hours. Up to 420 feet of space for visitors' boats. Note the dinghy dock in the foreground of the photo above. Free pumpout station at outer end of dock is open in summer only.

Adjacent: Picnic tables, walkways, gardens. Stores, groceries, restaurants and services nearby. The marina is located in the centre of downtown Gig Harbor.

Use chart 18474.

The public dock at Gig Harbor is close to all facilities. A sculpture commemorates fishermen. Gig Harbor is a top-rated destination.

Arabella's Landing

Arabella's Landing

John Moist
**3323 Harborview Dr
Gig Harbor WA 98332
Ph: 253-851-1793
Fax: 253-851-3967**
arabellas@harbornet.com
www.arabellaslanding.com

Moorage: Up to 30 visitor boats. **Water. Power:** 30, 50 amps. Garbage disposal. **Pumpout. Showers. Laundry. Washrooms.**

This is a high quality marina with all amenities. Clubhouse, lounge, walkways, gardens, wheelchair access. Town center, stores and services nearby. Reservations are recommended.

Top: Arabella's Landing at Gig Harbor.
Above: Another view of Arabella's Landing Marina.
Left: Arabella's docks.

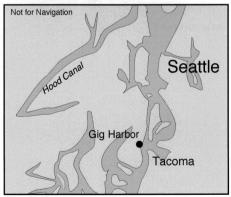

Not for Navigation

Hood Canal

Seattle

Gig Harbor

Tacoma

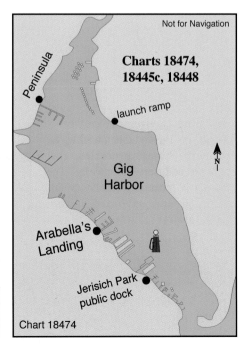

Not for Navigation

Peninsula

Charts 18474, 18445c, 18448

launch ramp

Gig Harbor

N

Arabella's Landing

Jerisich Park public dock

Chart 18474

Pick up a copy of Cleats & Eats Tacoma *for restaurant guide information.*

Foss Harbor Marina

Tacoma   Charts: 18453, 18474, 18448

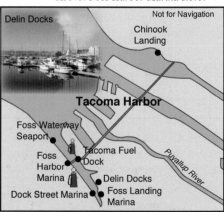

Above: Foss Harbor Marina store.

Dock Street Marina

Craig Perry
Thea Foss Waterway   VHF 78A
1817 Dock St, Tacoma WA 98402
Ph: 253-250-1906 Fax 253-572-2768
info@dockstreetmarina.com
www.dockstreetmarina.com
Moorage: 25 guest slips, boats to 125'.
Water. Power: 30, 50, 100 amps. Garbage/recycling.Cable TV. Slipside pumpout.
Showers. Laundry. Washrooms.
Nearby: Fuel, stores–groceries, restaurants, fishing supplies, post office. Tacoma city.

Foss Harbor Marina

Tracy McKendry
821 Dock St, Tacoma WA 98402
Ph: 253-272-4404 Fax 253-272-0367
susan@fossharbormarina.com
www.fossharbor.com
Moorage. Transient moorage–upgraded docks and facilities **Water. Power**: 30, 50 amps. **Showers. Laundry. Washrooms.**

Delin Docks

Not for Navigation

Chinook Landing

Tacoma Harbor

Foss Waterway Seaport

Foss Harbor Marina

Tacoma Fuel Dock

Delin Docks

Foss Landing Marina

Dock Street Marina

Puyallup River

47° 15.725' N   122° 26.335' W

Hoist. Pumpout. Marine store, groceries, fishing supplies, post office. **Nearby:** Toy Boat Museum. Dock Street Landing Bar and Grill. Glass museum. University. Theatres, restaurants. Shoreline walkway. Tacoma city. **Fuel:** Gas and diesel.

Thea Foss Waterway with Dock Street Marina in the foreground.

Foss Landing Marina

Shaun Hislop
Thea Foss Waterway
1940 East D St
Tacoma WA 98421
Ph: 253-627-4344 Fax:
253-627-4878
info@fosslanding.com
www.fosslanding.com

Foss Landing Marina .

47° 14.391' N   122° 33.671' W

Moorage. Permanent moorage. Guest moorage in winter only by reservation.
Power: 50 amp. **Pumpout. Showers, washrooms.**
Fuel nearby. Marine supplies at J&G Marine Supply, Tacoma.

Narrows Marina

Lauren Karamatic
9011 S 19th St, Tacoma WA 98466
Ph: 253-564-3032 Fax: 253-565-2136
lauren@narrowsmarina.com
www.narrowsmarina.com
Moorage. Some visitor slips.
Water. Power: 20 amps.
Fuel: Gas, diesel.
Washrooms. Marine store-charts, tackle, bait, electronics.
Adjacent: Launch ramp.

Foss Waterway Seaport

253-272-2750
www.fosswaterwayseaport.org
Large visitor dock. No services.

Chinook Landing Marina

William Dillon
3702 Marine View Dr   VHF 79
Tacoma WA 98422   Chart 18453
Ph: 253-627-7676 Fax: 253-779-0576
Moorage. 450' long side tie dock.
Pumpout. Water. Power: 30, 50 amps.
Showers, Laundry. Washrooms. Garbage disposal. Oil disposal. Marina store. Espresso. Ice. Clothing.

NOTE: *A free tram service carries passengers along Tacoma's city streets. Restaurants, museum, stores.*

Tacoma Fuel Dock on the Thea Foss Waterway and downtown Tacoma. .

Chinook Landing Marina

47° 16.811' N   122° 24.218' W

Larger vessels by arrangement

317

Point Defiance
Boathouse

Breakwater Marina

Tacoma

Charts 18453, 18474, 18448

Boathouse Marina

Point Defiance Marina & Boathouse

Supervisor: Scott Knox	**47° 18.125' N**
5912 N Waterfront Dr	**122° 30.574' W**
Tacoma WA 98407	

Ph: 253-591-5325

boathouse@tacomaparks.com
www.pointdefiancemarina.com

Moorage: 400 ft and boat launching.
Fuel: Gas. Boat rentals,
Pumpout. Washrooms. Water.
Adjacent: Public fishing pier, restaurant. Gift and tackle shop, Point Defiance Zoo.

Breakwater Marina

Michael Marchetti
5603 N. Waterfront Dr
Tacoma WA 98407
Phone: 253-752-6663 Fax: 253-752-8291
info@breakwatermarina.com
www.breakwatermarina.com

Moorage: Many slips for visitors. Check in at Fuel dock. **Power:** 15, 30 amp.
Fuel: Gas, diesel, propane, snacks.
Broadband Express. **Pumpout. Laundry.**
Washrooms. Showers. Garbage disposal.
Adjacent: Vashon Island ferry. Launch ramp. Restaurant. **Nearby**: Liquor store, Fort Nisqually historic site. Point Defiance Park, zoo, aquarium. On Tacoma bus line.

Port of Allyn Dock

Lynch Cove. Near Belfair. Ph: 360-275-2430
Brief stops at small dock: 10 slips.
Seasonal. **Power, water**, pump out.
Launch Ramp. Beware of shallows.
Case Inlet, near Allyn Ph: 360-275-2430
10 slips. Seasonal. No power. Pump out. Park, restrooms, launch ramp.

Top: The launch ramp is at the entrance to Breakwater Marina and the Tacoma Yacht Club. Above, left: A view of Boathouse Marina.

Point Defiance
Boathouse Marina

Not for Navigation

Dash Point

**Tacoma
Area**

Point Defiance

Breakwater
Marina

Brown's Point

Commencement Bay

Chinook
Landing

Thea Foss Waterway

docks

Tacoma

Foss
Waterway
Marina

Chart 18474

Foss Landing
Marina

Dock Street Marina

Narrows Marina

Puyallup River

Fair Harbor

47° 20.021' N   122° 49.801' W

Fair Harbor
Charts 18457, 18448

South Puget Sound

Fair Harbor Marina
Susan and Vern Nelson
5050 Grapeview Loop Rd
PO Box 160, Grapeview WA 98546
Ph: 360-426-4028
info@fairharbor.us www.fairharbormarina.us
Moorage: Visitors docks 350 feet. Overnight moorage guests-complimentary.
Power: 20, 30 amps. **Fuel:** Gas, alcohol, kerosene, propane. **Washrooms, showers.**
Marine store–groceries, hardware, fishing tackle and bait, charts. Gift shop. Limited repairs and service. Picnic area. Golf course–transport by arrangement.

Oakland Bay Marina VHF 16
21 W. Sanderson Way, Shelton WA. 98584
Ph: 360-426-1425 Chart 18457
www.portofshelton.com
Guest moorage: Long float with 30 amp power. Pumpout, toilet ashore. About one mile to Shelton–groceries, stores, restaurants. Marina operated by Port of Shelton.

Penrose State Marine Park
Chart 18448. Guest moorage 300 ft.
Mooring buoys. Pumpout, showers.

Joemma Beach State Marine Park
Chart 18448. Guest moorage 500 ft.
Mooring buoys. Pumpout, campsite. Ramp.

Longbranch

47° 12.588' N   122° 45.131' W

Longbranch Marina
Mark Jones   **VHF16/68**
PO Box 111, Longbranch WA 98349
Ph: 253-884-5137
Moorage: Large visitors dock. Two-thirds of marina is dedicated for visitors. **Portapottie toilets. Water. Power**: 30 amps. Garbage disposal. Mechanic, divers available. Dinghy dock.
Adjacent: anchorage nearby.

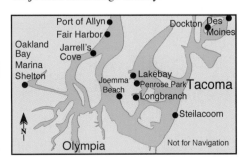

photo courtesy of Jarrell's Cove Marina

47° 17.200' N   122° 53.130' W

Jarrell's Cove

South Puget Sound

Jarrell's Cove Marina
Lorna and Gary Hink
Located on Harstine Island
220 East Wilson Rd, Shelton WA 98584
Ph: 360-426-8823 Fax: 360-432-8494
Toll Free: 1-800-362-8823 Charts 18457, 18448
Moorage: As space available.
Check in at fuel dock. Pumpout.
Water. Power: 30 amps. **Fuel:** Gas,
diesel, propane. **Laundry, showers,
washrooms.** Convenience store–Seasonal.
Hardware, fishing tackle, groceries, books,
shaved ice sno-cones, ice, beer.
Three RV sites, games area, picnic area,
beach, point of interest–historic log cabin.

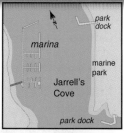

*This is one of the most
attractive settings in the
south Puget Sound area.
There is moorage at the
marina as well as at the
park on the opposite
side of the cove.*

47° 17.146' N   122° 53.211' W

Jarrell's Cove State Park
Harstine Island. Located at northwest
end of island. 650 foot guest dock.
14 mooring buoys, washrooms,
showers, pumpout, portadump. Picnic
areas. See *www.parks.wa.gov* for more.

Lake Limmerick Country Club 360-426-6290

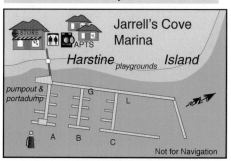

47° 08.496' N   122° 54.214' W

Boston Harbor

Boston Harbor Marina

Don McHugh and Pam McHugh
312 73rd Ave NE   Chart 18448
Olympia WA 98506   VHF 16
Ph: 360-357-5670 Fax: 360-352-2816
bhm@bostonharbormarina.com
www.bostonharbormarina.com
Moorage. 290'. Large vessels welcome.
Water. Power: 20 amps.
Fuel: Gas, diesel, CNG.
Toilets. Marine store–gifts, marine
supplies, fresh seafood, groceries, ice.
picnic area, beach, park. Kayak and
boat rentals
Adjacent: Launch ramp.

*Boston Harbor Marina is a good place to sit and
watch the sunsets. The store has a friendly staff to
welcome you to the harbor.*

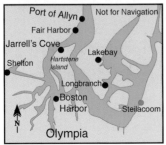

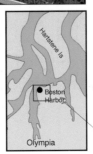

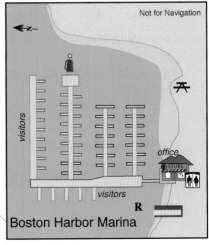

Airport Golf Center 360-786-8626

Swantown Marina

47° 02.727' N   122° 54.295' W

Olympia

Charts ...
18456, 18448

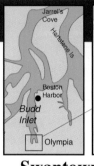

Jarrel's Cove

Harstene Is

Budd Inlet

Beston Harbor

Olympia

Olympia Harbor   Not for Navigation

West Bay Marina

Swantown Marina

Percival Landing

Olympia

N

Percival Landing

Scott River
217 Thurston Ave
Olympia WA 98501
Ph: 360-753-8380   Fax: 360-753-8334
Charts 18456, 18448
olympiaparks@ci.olympia.wa.us
www.ci.olympia.wa.

Moorage east side Port Plaza dock–public.
Water. Washrooms. Pumpout.

Nearby: Grocery store, uptown stores, restaurants and all facilities. This dock is on the west side of the Olympia Yacht Club. The marina extends down the east side of the harbor and along the south waterfront. It is a downtown feature of Olympia. Approaching vessels should observe 'No Wake' speeds.

Swantown Marina

Bruce Marshall
1022 Marine Dr NE   VHF 16/65A
Olympia WA 98501
Ph: 360-528-8049 Fax: 360-528-8094
marina@portolympia.com
www.portolympia.com

Moorage. Visitors. **Laundry. Washrooms. Showers. Pumpout. Power**: 20, 30, 50 amp. Wi-fi internet access. Restaurants, groceries, liquor store, PO, launch ramp. Chandlery, repairs, service. Market. **Fuel:** 7 miles, at Boston Harbor.

Left: Percival Landing–Port Plaza dock on the east side of the marina and west of the yacht club.

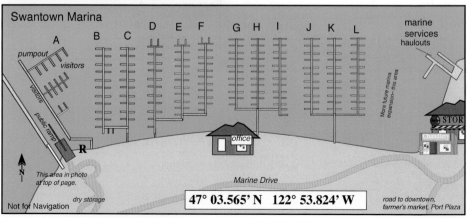

Swantown Marina

A B C D E F G H I J K L

marine services haulouts

pumpout

visitors

visitors

public ramp

R

office

More future marina expansion this area

STOR

Chandlery

N

This area in photo at top of page.

dry storage

Marine Drive

Not for Navigation

47° 03.565' N   122° 53.824' W

road to downtown, farmer's market, Port Plaza

South Puget Sound

Index

324

For comprehensive information on coastal marine parks and anchorages see the companion guide to this book– *Anchorages and Marine Parks*.

Bibliography and recommended reading

A Guide to the Western Seashore. Rick M. Harbo. Hancock House, Surrey, BC. 1988.

Anchorages and Marine Parks. Guide to anchorages and marine parks in British Columbia and the San Juan Islands. Peter Vassilopoulos. Pacific Marine Publishing. 2008.

BC Cruising Guide Series–Desolation Sound, Gulf Islands, Sunshine Coast. Bill Wolferstan. Whitecap Books.

Best Anchorages of the Inside Passage. Bill Kelly and Anne Vipond. 2006

Canadian Tide and Current Tables. Pacific Coast all volumes. Ottawa-Department of Fisheries and Oceans. Annual.

Charlies Charts North to Alaska. Charles E. Wood. Margo Wood. Polymath Energy Consultants Ltd. Surrey B.C.

Cruising Atlas Queen Charlottes to Olympia, Evergreen Pacific, 1990

Exploring the Gulf Islands and Desolation Sound to Port Hardy and Blunden Harbour. A Cruising Guide. Don Douglass. Fine Edge Productions. Anacortes WA.

Exploring the Inside Passage to Alaska. A Cruising Guide. Don Douglass. Fine Edge Productions. Anacortes WA.

Exploring the South Coast of British Columbia. A Cruising Guide. Don Douglass. Fine Edge Productions. Anacortes WA.

Exploring Vancouver Island's West Coast. A Cruising Guide. Don Douglass. Fine Edge Productions. Anacortes WA.

Local Knowledge. Kevin Monahan. Fine Edge, Anacortes, WA, 2003

Marine Parks of British Columbia. An Explorer's Guide. Peter Chettleburgh. Special Interest Publications. Vancouver. BC. 1985.

Marine Weather Hazards Manual. A guide to local forecasts and conditions. Vancouver. Environment Canada. 1990.

Mariner Series Cruising Guides to BC Coast: North of Desolation Sound. Gulf Islands Cruising Guide, Cruising to Desolation Sound. Peter Vassilopoulos Pacific Marine Publishing. Delta BC.

Oceanography of the British Columbia Coast. Richard E. Thomson. Department of Fisheries and Aquatic Sciences. 1981.

Radar Book (The), Kevin Monahan. Fine Edge, Anacortes, WA, 2003

Sailing Directions. British Columbia Coast. Ottawa. Department of Fisheries and Oceans.

Sea Kayak Series, (Around Vancouver Isl/Gulf Islands/Nootka Sound) Rocky Mountain Books, Surrey BC, 2004

Sea Kayaking Canada's West Coast. John Ince and Hedi Kottner. Raxas Books. Vancouver, BC. 1996.

The San Juan Islands. Afoot and Afloat. Marge and Ted Mueller. The Mountaineers. Seattle. 1988.

Waggoner. Robert Hale. Robert Hale Publishing. Seattle. Annual. *This is an excellent cruising publication with up-to-date information about marinas, anchorages, waterways and facilities. It includes planning and piloting information.* Ph: 800-733-5330.

Weatherly Waypoint Guides for GPS and Loran Navigation. Robert Hale. Robert Hale Publishing. Volumes 1–3: Puget Sound, San Juan Islands, Strait of Juan de Fuca. Gulf of Georgia, including Gulf Islands, Jervis Inlet. Desolation Sound to Port Hardy.

West Coast of Vancouver Island. Don Watmough. Evergreen Pacific. Shoreline WA.

My wife Carla and I have cruised the area this guide covers for more than 35 years. We have visited all areas described in the book and have stopped at and moored at most moorages included in the foregoing pages. Mariners who adventure beyond the known routes and popular areas will enjoy discovering for themselves others I may have omitted. There are numerous books on cruising the coast and these along with your charts and reference books should enable you to extend your cruising range substantially and safely. Happy boating.

By the same author

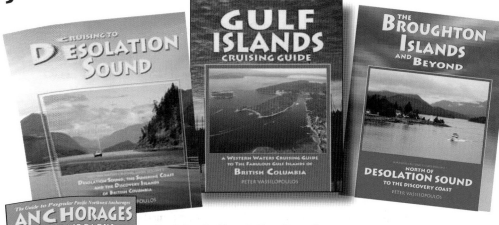

Cruising to Desolation Sound:
Guide to the Sunshine Coast and Desolation Sound. $49.95

Gulf Islands Cruising Guide:
Full colour aerial and ambient photos with directions and recommendations. $46.95

The Broughton Islands and Beyond
*Formerly North of Desolation Sound. Expanded. $46.95

Anchorages and Marine Parks:
Guide to to popular anchorages and parks. $29.95

Cruising to Desolation Sound–a coffee table styled full colour, illustrated guidebook. Two Books in One–on the Sunshine Coast and Desolation Sound.
Peter Vassilopoulos $49.95. This is a comprehensive reference book/guide to the Sunshine Coast, Princess Louisa Inlet and Desolation Sound. Filled with full colour photos, aerial pictures and diagrams. A must for serious mariners cruising to the most popular destination on the BC inland coast.

Gulf Islands Cruising Guide–a coffee table styled full colour, illustrated guidebook.
Peter Vassilopoulos $46.95. Packed with information and loaded with colourful diagrams and photographs of the area. See the most popular cruising area, the Gulf Islands, from the air and from a mariner's perspective.

*The Broughtons and Beyond–a coffee table styled full colour, illustrated guidebook. This new, expanded and revised edition is due out in summer 2011.
Peter Vassilopoulos $46.95. This is a comprehensive reference book/guide to the Broughton Islands area and routes from Stuart Island to Seymour Inlet. Filled with full colour photos, aerial pictures and diagrams. A must for serious mariners cruising the BC inland coast.

Anchorages and Marine Parks–Peter Vassilopoulos $19.95
A companion guide to Docks and Destinations providing information on places to find sheltered anchorage over-night and to facilities and features of marine parks. It covers, in a south to north progression, the San Juan Islands and all of BC coastal waters including the west coast of Vancouver Island, to Ketchikan.

These books are available at marine stores or you may order direct:
Phone 604-943-4618 Pacific Marine Publishing, 4805 7A Ave, Delta BC V4M 1R3 or PO Box 984, Point Roberts WA 98281-0984.

Docks and Destinations

Comments about this and other cruising guides by the same author

My wife and I have sailed this area for the past three summer vacations and despite the distance from England we keep coming back. We have found your guides essential reading and enormously useful and our holidays have been all the more enjoyable as a result.   *–David D. Cotterell, England.*

We often refer to our copy of **Docks and Destinations** while out on the water. We ALWAYS refer to your book when we are working in our store. What a great book!
                    –Dan and Leah Lee, Thrifty Foods, Salt Spring Island.

I have been to a number of places mentioned in your two books and found your information to be very accurate and extremely useful. I have pointed them out to boating friends and clients and gained points with them for doing so.
                    –Robert McMurray, artist, accountant, mariner.

Our best and most informative cruising guide. Always our first recommendation to our customers looking for a cruising guide on the coast. (We use it on our own boat.)
                    –Brad Mah, Ocean Yacht Equipment, Vancouver.

Mariners have commented on the clarity of your book. It is well designed—succinct yet containing enough information to enable the boater to make wise cruising decisions.   *–Ann Taylor, Greenway Sound.*

This guide is updated when reprinted. Major updates and changes will be made periodically when new editions are published. Please write to me if you have any information or suggestions for inclusion in future editions. Your comments are welcome.
                              –Peter Vassilopoulos.

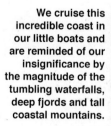

We cruise this incredible coast in our little boats and are reminded of our insignificance by the magnitude of the tumbling waterfalls, deep fjords and tall coastal mountains.

Canada: 4805 7A Ave, Delta, British Columbia, Canada V4M 1R3
USA: PO Box 984, Point Roberts, WA 98281-0984
Ph: 604-943-4618 Fax: 604-604-943-4618
boating@dccnet.com Please contact us for updating information.